FRAGMENTS OF OLD COMEDY

I

LCL 513

FRAGMENTS OF OLD COMEDY

VOLUME I

ALCAEUS TO DIOCLES

EDITED AND TRANSLATED BY

IAN C. STOREY

HARVARD UNIVERSITY PRESS
CAMBRIDGE, MASSACHUSETTS
LONDON, ENGLAND
2011

Copyright © 2011 by the President and Fellows
of Harvard College
All rights reserved

First published 2011

LOEB CLASSICAL LIBRARY® is a registered trademark
of the President and Fellows of Harvard College

Library of Congress Control Number 2010937704
CIP data available from the Library of Congress

ISBN 978-0-674-99662-5

Composed in ZephGreek and ZephText by
Technologies 'N Typography, Merrimac, Massachusetts.
Printed on acid-free paper and bound by
The Maple-Vail Book Manufacturing Group

CONTENTS

CONTENTS

PREFACE

Aristophanes (career: 427–380s BC) is the only poet of Old Comedy of whom we have complete plays. His eleven extant comedies plus nearly a thousand fragments are available in Jeffrey Henderson's five previously published volumes in the Loeb Classical Library. In my three volumes I have included the principal *testimonia* to and fragments of nearly sixty poets whom the ancient sources allow us to assign to the period of Old Comedy (roughly 485–385 BC). Nearly half of these are explicitly named as exponents of Old Comedy, another dozen appear on inscriptions that place them within the heyday of Old Comedy, and a further dozen are associated by ancient sources with the poets of the first age of comedy. For some, inclusion in a collection of Old Comedy rests on shaky ground, but I have chosen to present the evidence about them, although I have drawn the line at including Antonius Diogenes, whose unlikely self-description as "an author of Old Comedy" Photius presents at *Library* 111a.

For some (Cratinus, Eupolis, Pherecrates, Platon) fragments are numbered in the hundreds, for others (e.g., Euetes, Xenophon) we have only a name and a rough indication of date. I have provided Greek text and translation for the testimonia and the bulk of the fragments, but where the fragment is a single word or phrase, I have followed the practice of Collard and Cropp (*Euripides VII/VIII*) in omitting the Greek text and providing an English translation under "Brief fragments." I have made a special point of providing both text and translation of the fragments that deal with *kōmōidoumenoi,* since these are often the reasons that the Old Comic fragments are consulted.

For the most part I print the Greek text as given in Kassel and Austin's (K.-A.) definitive edition of the remains of Greek comedy, *Poetae Comici Graeci* (*PCG*) volumes II, IV–V, VII–VIII. Where I print or translate something other than their text, I have indicated this in the notes. I have kept their numbering of the fragments but have reordered the testimonia to take account of my additions, exclusions, expansions, and so forth. For the fragments preserved on papyrus, I have provided a Greek text and English translation only when there was enough material to provide some sort of continuity. This is especially true of the three fragmentary commentaries to Eupolis (F 172, 259, 268), where much of what we have consists of scraps. While K.-A. VIII print nearly a thousand *comica adespota,* I have restricted mine (*CA*) to just under a hundred, where on balance the fragment seemed reasonably to have come from Old Comedy.

I have provided introductions to each of the poets, as well to each of the lost comedies. Some are obviously more extensive than others. I have added notes on textual readings, where the translation is clearly affected, as well as identifications of *kōmōidoumenoi* and explanations of allusions that would otherwise mystify the reader. I suspect that for some there will be, like Mozart's music in *Amadeus,* "too many notes," and for others not nearly enough. To avoid duplicating the bibliographies in K.-A., I have for both poets and certain lost comedies provided a "recent bibliography" of major studies published since the appearance of the relevant volume of *PCG.*

The bulk of work on these volumes was done on a year of sabbatical leave (2008–9), when I was fortunate enough to be the T.B.L. Webster Fellow at the Institute of Classical Studies (autumn 2008) and subsequently an Oliver Smithies Lecturer and Visiting Fellow at Balliol College, Oxford (Hilary and Trinity terms, 2009). To thank everyone who helped with the preparation of these fragments would take a volume in its own right, but I do want to mention Mike Edwards and the ever-helpful staff at the Institute of Classical Studies; Penny Bulloch, Adrian Kelly and the Fellows (and chef) of Balliol College; James Morwood, Nigel Wilson and Chris Collard, who always seemed to be in the Sackler Library at the right time. Sarah Miles (on Strattis), Emmanuela Bakola (on Cratinus), Paul McKenna (on Platon), and Tom Phillips (on many topics) provided more help than perhaps they realise. On the other side of the Atlantic, Jeff Henderson, Toph Marshall, George Kovacs, and Donald Sells always answered my frequent queries without complaint and always with helpful thoughts on the matter at hand. Audiences at Toronto, London, Oxford, and Nottingham proved very useful sounding boards for my forays into Cratinus and Archippus.

On a personal note I would acknowledge the friendship and support of three individuals: Kevin (who long ago ceased being my student and is now a valued colleague),

Ian (whom C. S. Lewis would call my "second friend"), and Jacob (who always makes me smile). To them I dedicate these "little books," which to whom they can sort out among themselves.

ABBREVIATIONS

A&R	*Atene e Roma*
Aevum (Ant.)	*Aevum Antiquum*
AFLB	*Annali della Facoltà di Lettere e Filosofia di Bari*
AHB	*Ancient History Bulletin*
AION (fil.)	*Annali dell'Istituto Universitario Orientale di Napoli. Sezione filologico-letteraria.*
AJPh	*American Journal of Philology*
Bakola	E. Bakola, *Cratinus and the Art of Comedy* (Oxford 2010)
BICS	*Bulletin of the Institute of Classical Studies*
C&M	*Classica et Mediaevalia*
Campbell *GL*	D. A. Campbell (ed.), *Greek Lyric*, 5 vols. (1982–1993)
Capps	E. Capps, "Epigraphical Problems in the History of Comedy," *CPh* 28 (1907) 179–99
CGA	A. López Eire (ed.), *Sociedad, Política y Literatura: Comedia griega antigua* (Salamanca 1997)
CGFP	C. Austin (ed.), *Comicorum Graecorum Fragmenta in Papyris Reperta* (Berlin/New York 1973)

Companion	G. W. Dobrov (ed.), *Brill's Companion to the Study of Greek Comedy* (Leiden 2010)
CPh	*Classical Philology*
CQ	*Classical Quarterly*
CW	*Classical World*
Demianczuk	J. Demianczuk (ed.), *Supplementum Comicum* (Krakow 1912)
Dobrov (*BA*)	G. Dobrov (ed.), *Beyond Aristophanes* (Atlanta 1993)
Dobrov (*City*)	G. Dobrov, *The City as Comedy* (Chapel Hill, NC 1995)
Edmonds	J. M. Edmonds (ed./tr.), *The Fragments of Attic Comedy*, vol. I (Leiden 1957)
Euripides VII	C. Collard and M. Cropp, *Euripides Fragments:* Aegeus–Meleager (Cambridge, MA 2008)
Euripides VIII	C. Collard and M. Cropp, *Euripides Fragments:* Oedipus–Chrysippus, *other fragments* (Cambridge, MA 2008)
G&R	*Greece and Rome*
Geissler	P. Geissler, *Chronologie der altattischen Komödie*, 2nd ed. (Dublin/Zurich 1969)
GRBS	*Greek, Roman and Byzantine Studies*
GrGr	*Grammatici Graeci*, ed. G. Uhlig and others, 4 vols., in 6 (Leipzig 1867–1910)
ICS	*Illinois Classical Studies*
IG	*Inscriptiones Graecae*
JHS	*Journal of Hellenic Studies*
Kaibel	Extracts from Kaibel's unpublished writings on Old Comedy appear *ad loc.* in *PCG*

Kassel-Austin [K.-A.]	= *PCG*
Kock	T. Kock (ed.), *Comicorum Atticorum Fragmenta*, vol. I (Lepizig 1880)
Koster	W. J. W. Koster (ed.), *Scholia in Aristophanem, Pars I: fasc. IA. Prolegomena de Comoedia* (Groningen 1975)
ΚΩΜΩΙΔΟΤΡΑΓΩΙΔΙΑ	E. Medda, M. S. Mirto, and M. P. Pattoni (eds.), ΚΩΜΩΙΔΟΤΡΑΓΩΙΔΙΑ *Intersezioni del tragico e del comico nel teatro del V secolo a.C.* (Pisa 2006)
LCM	*Liverpool Classical Monthly*
MCr	*Museum Criticum*
Meineke	A. Meineke (ed.), *Fragmenta Comicorum Graecorum.* (Berlin 1839–1857)
MH	*Museum Helveticum*
Norwood	G. Norwood, *Greek Comedy* (London 1931)
Olson	S. D. Olson, *Broken Laughter* (Oxford 2007)
PAA	J. Traill (ed.), *Persons of Ancient Athens*, 20 vols. (Toronto 1994–)
PCG	R. Kassel and C. Austin (eds.), *Poetae Comici Graeci* (Berlin 1983–)
PCPhS	*Proceedings of the Cambridge Philological Society*
Pellegrino (*Utopie*)	M. Pellegrino, *Utopie e immagini gastronomiche nei frammenti dell' archaia* (Bologna 2000)
PMG	D. L. Page (ed.), *Poetae Melici Graeci* (Oxford 1962)
P. Oxy.	Oxyrhynchus Papyrus

PSI	*Pubblicazioni della Società italiana per la ricerca dei papyri greci e latini in Egitto*
QUCC	*Quaderni Urbinati di Cultura Classica*
Revermann	M. Revermann, *Comic Business* (Oxford 2006)
RFIC	*Rivista di Filologia e di Istruzione Classica*
Rivals	D. Harvey and J. Wilkins (eds.), *The Rivals of Aristophanes* (London 2000)
Rothwell	K. S. Rothwell, *Nature, Culture and the Origins of Old Comedy* (Cambridge 2007)
RPh	*Révue de Philologie*
SemRom	*Seminaria Romana*
SIFC	*Studi Italiani di Filologia Classica*
SPhV	*Studia Philologica Valentina*
Storey	I. C. Storey, *Eupolis: Poet of Old Comedy* (Oxford 2003)
TCP	A. H. Sommerstein, S. Halliwell, J. Henderson, and B. Zimmermann (eds.), *Tragedy, Comedy and the Polis* (Bari 1993)
Tessere	A. M. Belardinelli et al. (eds.). *Tessere. Frammenti della commedia greca: studi e commenti* (Bari 1998)
Thompson (*Birds*)	D.W, Thompson, *A Glossary of Greek Birds* (London 1936)
Thompson (*Fishes*)	D. W. Thompson, *A Glossary of Greek Fishes* (London 1947)

ABBREVIATIONS

TrGF	B. Snell (corrected edition by R. Kannicht), *Tragicorum Graecorum Fragmenta*, vol. I (Göttingen 1986)
Tsantsanoglou	K. Tsantsanoglou, *New Fragments of Greek Literature in the Lexicon of Photius* (Athens 1984)
ZPE	*Zeitschrift für Papyrologie und Epigraphik*

INTRODUCTION

The scholars of later antiquity divided ancient Greek comedy into three distinct subgenres: Old, Middle, and New, sometimes called "First," "Second," and "Third." But there was some dispute about what these subgenres actually were and which comic poets belonged where and when. To some "Old" was the earliest era, that of the primitive and unorganised comedy by Susarion and Magnes, to be succeeded by the more coherent and sophisticated "Second" comedy of Cratinus, Aristophanes, and Eupolis (the traditional triad), and finally by the more elegant and less offensive situation comedy of Menander, Philemon, etc. We find this distinction, for instance, in Tzetzes (*About Old Comedy* [*AOC*] 9, 11) and Diomedes (*AOC* 13). But for most others, "Old" comedy was the great age of Aristophanes and his contemporaries (late fifth century), "New" again Menander's comedy of manners of the late fourth century, and "Middle" a transitional phase, sometimes connected with the name of Platon, "not the philosopher" as we are often reminded. This is certainly the default position found in Platonius (*AOC* 3, 4) and the majority of the anonymous writers (*AOC* 5–7), and that which is commonly employed today.

In terms of chronology, the canonical date for the first official performance of Old Comedy, "eight years before the Persian Wars" (Chionides T 1), is usually taken to mean 487/86, although the evidence from the list of victors at the Dionysia (*AOC* 15) allows for a somewhat more flexible date anywhere in the 480s. The lower limit of Old Comedy is usually set as the end of Aristophanes' career. The last play (*Wealth*) by Aristophanes is dated securely to 388, and we know of two later comedies (*Cocalus* and *Aeolosicon*), produced through his son. The end of his career, if not his death, thus belongs in the mid to late 380s. A useful dating for Old Comedy, then, is the century from c. 485 to c. 385, although some poets active in Old Comedy may have continued to write after that lower date (Platon, Strattis, Theopompus).

We would not expect any genre in art or literature to remain static for a period of a hundred years, and the ancient sources themselves admit that "there are differences within Old Comedy" (*AOC* 7). One such difference is the purely chronological progression of "generations" of Old Comic poets, each with its own style of comic drama. While we are not at all well informed about the nature of earliest Old Comedy (roughly 485–455), the names Susarion, Myllus, and Magnes are found on a number of occasions. One ancient source (*AOC* 7) describes this earliest comedy as haphazard and unstructured. Aristophanes tells us something about Magnes' brand of comedy at *Knights* 518–25 (Magnes T 8), which seems (though this comes from a comic poet with his own agenda) to have featured choruses of men dressed up as animals with a primitive and simple sort of humour. Yet Magnes is known to have won more victories (eleven) than any other poet of Old Comedy.

With the debut of Cratinus c. 454 we encounter the

next generation of comic poets, coming immediately before Aristophanes and the great age of Old Comedy. Again we have no complete plays, but a reasonable number of revealing play titles, fragments, and testimonia, including much of the hypothesis to Cratinus' *Dionysalexander*, allow us to conclude that it was in this period (455–425) that Old Comedy began to develop coherent plots, aggressive personal and political themes, and an engagement with both the stories of myth and their treatment in tragedy. One anonymous source (*AOC* 7) attributes to Cratinus (career: 454–423) the use of three actors, bringing order to a previously chaotic art form, and attacks on prominent people in Athenian society. It was also in this period, probably around 440, that dramatic competitions, for both tragedy and comedy, became part of a second festival at Athens, the Lenaea held in late January or early February. In the case of comedy this doubled the number of plays produced each year, from five to ten. Rusten (*ZPE* 157 [2006] 22–26) dates this a little earlier, i.e., 445–441, and considers the comedy at the Lenaea to have been more politically directed than that at the Dionysia. Cratinus is the leading name from this period, but we know of others, such as Hermippus, Callias, Telelclides, Pherecrates, and Crates. They dominated the comic stage during the 430s, and between 435 and 426 no new poet won a victory at the Dionysia.

But in the 420s four new and significant comic poets burst on the scene with a vengeance. The best known of these is Aristophanes (career: 427–c. 385), of whose forty plays eleven have survived complete along with nearly one thousand fragments. He would become synonymous with Old Comedy, and one benefit of examining the fragments of the other poets of Old Comedy is to realise that Aristophanes' work may not necessarily be typical of all the comic drama that was written and performed between 427 and 385. His earliest extant play, *Acharnians,* the first-prize winner in 425, shows that he was immediately successful and that his comedy, heavy on political content, personal jokes, and parody of tragedy, began at the very outset of his career. Also from the 420s comes Eupolis (career: 429–411), victorious with half of the comedies he produced, comedies very much in the same style as Aristophanes, but without the engagement (some would say "obsession") with Euripidean tragedy. His comedy *Demes,* in which four dead leaders of Athens are raised from the Underworld to put things right at Athens, was probably the best attested and most read comedy apart from those by Aristophanes. In 1911 three pages from *Demes* were published from the Cairo Papyrus (F 99), showing that this comedy was still being read and copied in the fourth or fifth century AD but not answering many of the great questions we had about the play. Other important poets from the 420s are Phrynichus (career: 429 to at least 405) and Platon (career: 424–380s). Platon, like Aristophanes, had a long career and was still active when comedy began to change drastically in the early fourth century. He seems to have written not only the politically charged comedy we associate with Aristophanes, including three plays with demagogues of the day as the central character (their names not hidden under a *Spitzname*), but also burlesques of myth, a type of comedy very popular in the first part of the fourth century. That Platon's topical plays belong to the fifth century and the burlesques of myth to the fourth is an appealing but unproven conclusion.

From the end of the War to the death of Aristophanes (403 to the late 380s), we find a number of poets, but none with any staying power or with any great influence on the genre. Platon and Aristophanes may have had more to do with the change that came over comedy in the fourth century than these "small-fry, empty words, a swallows' chorale, who bring their art down, who once they are granted one chorus, are gone" (*Frogs* 92–95). Granted that Aristophanes is applying this description to the tragic poets of 405, but it also describes well the last generation of Old Comic poets. Three of these are worthy of note: Strattis (career: 410–380), who like Aristophanes makes comedy out of tragedy of the late fifth century (especially Euripides), Theopompus (career: 410–380), who also mixes political comedy with travesties of myth, and Archippus (career: 415–390), whose best-known comedy, *Fishes,* seems to have done for fishes what Aristophanes' *Birds* did for birds. The papyrus fragment known as the "Comoedia Dukiana" (*PCG* VIII.1146) *may* contain fifty lines from this comedy.

As Aristophanes is the only comic poet for whom we have complete comedies, he is often taken as the archetype for all Old Comedy, but a brief look at the fragments shows that there is much more to Old Comedy than what Aristophanes chose as his subjects. One theme that we have only hints of in Aristophanes is the Golden Age or the Utopia, where life is ideal and pleasures, especially those of food and drink, are realised without labour. This motif goes back as far as the Islands of the Blest in *Odyssey* 4 or the Golden Race of Hesiod (*Works and Days* 109–20) and is a staple of Old Comedy in the generation before Aristophanes. Utopias can be in the past (paradise lost), in the future (paradise regained), and somewhere out there (paradise found). Athenaeus (267e–70a) presents several examples from comedy, the connecting theme being usually that good things are provided on their own (*automata*), especially culinary delights. These include the good times of the past (Cratinus' *Wealth-Gods*), those promised for the future (Crates' *Beasts*), and those to be found somewhere else (e.g., below the earth as in Pherecrates' *Miners,* or in Thurii as in Metagenes' *Thurio-Persians*). In the 410s we find a number of comedies with the theme of escape from the "real" world to an imagined better place, Aristophanes' *Birds* (414), Pherecrates' *Wild Men* (420), Phrynichus' *Hermit* (414).

Except in his last two comedies, Aristophanes did not write burlesques of myth, preferring instead to write parodies of tragedy, especially the controversial plays of Euripides. But again the fragments show that making fun of the traditional stories of myth was a strong part of comedy before the debut of Aristophanes, and again the early part of the fourth century. Thus the rash of mythological burlesques that we find in the later Old Comic poets such as Theopompus, Philyllius, Platon (if indeed these plays of his are late), are not the rise of a new type of comedy, but a resurgence of a type that Cratinus and Hermippus, in particular, put on, and perhaps going as far back as the comedy of Epicharmus of Sicily in the early fifth century. In fact one-third of the comedies of Cratinus are parodies of myth, and not of a particular literary model—this is especially true of *Dionysalexander,* where we cannot immediately identify an obvious source other than the general story known from the epic cycle. Hermippus wrote a "birth comedy" (*Birth of Athena*) at least thirty years before the run of birth comedies popular in the early fourth century—of the five titles that we know for the minor comedian Polyzelus, three are "birth plays." Here the major influence may be the *Homeric Hymn to Hermes,* which told the story of Hermes' birth and his mischievous behaviour on his first day of life.

Dionysus and Heracles are the most popular divine figures to appear in comedy, and in satyr drama also for that matter. There are comedies which make fun of the traditional myths about these two or which exploit their presence in a mythical setting, e.g., *Dionysalexander* by Cratinus, in which Dionysus replaces Paris for the infamous Judgement. But more common is the insertion of Heracles or Dionysus into a modern contemporary setting, such as Heracles' appearance in *Birds* or *Frogs* or that of Dionysus in *Frogs,* who is so concerned with the state of tragedy at Athens in 405 that he takes it upon himself to bring Euripides back from the Underworld. In the lost comedies we know that Dionysus goes to learn the "rules of war" from the Athenian admiral Phormion in Eupolis' *Officers,* while the titles *Dionysus in Training* by Aristomenes and Nicochares' *Heracles the Producer* strongly suggest that the divine figure is entering a contemporary situation. Comedy has created a recurring figure of "Dionysus as antihero," the point being to put the bumbling comic god into the most unlikely situations, where he will fail to rise to the occasion. At Phrynichus F 61 Hermes finds himself drawn into the paranoia following the scandals of 415, while at Platon F 46 Heracles is being entertained by a hetaera with a cottabus game before dinner. Again the setting is modern, not mythical.

It would be fair to say that Aristophanes' comedy is

more concerned with the *polis* (city) than with the *oikos* (household), although in both *Wasps* and *Knights* the two are combined metaphorically—in the latter the state becomes a household, with Demos (the People) as the master, and the political leaders as household slaves. But there is not a great deal of domestic humour in Aristophanes; perhaps the closest we get are the household scenes at the end of *Assembly-Women* and *Wealth*. In the fragments we certainly have the domestic situation in Cratinus' *Wine-Flask*, where Cratinus makes himself his own chief character and casts Comedy as his own abandoned wife, or Eupolis' *Spongers*, set in the house of Callias and very probably the source for Plato's *Protagoras*. Athenaeus insists that many comedies were named after hetaerae, and the fragments show us more than a few scenes with women entertaining or drinking, most notably Pherecrates' *Korianno*. This seems to have been the mainstay of Pherecrates' comedy, since we find little of his that is political or personally aggressive, and only one comedy that makes fun of a story from myth (*Ant-Men*). Aristophanes is known for his three extant "women's plays" (*Lysistrata, Thesmophoriazusae, Assembly-Women*), but in his comedy women cross the line between home and city and intrude into the affairs of state. Other comic poets found their humour within the house itself, especially in the fourth century as comedy made its way toward the domestic comedy of manners and errors of Menander and his contemporaries.

The last half of the fifth century was a critical time politically for Athens. It saw the development of the Delian League from a defensive alliance into an Athenian *archē,* the revolt of Samos in 440 from that *archē,* continuing hostilities with Sparta and her allies that would culminate in what we call the "Peloponnesian War" (431–404), the effects of the plague in the early 420s, the death of Pericles and rise of the popular politicians known as the demagogues, the scandals of 415, the military disaster in Sicily (413), the right-wing political coup of 411, final defeat at the hands of the Spartans, and the oligarchy which would become known as the "Thirty Tyrants." Platonius (*AOC* 3) is certainly correct to connect the free spirit of Old Comedy with the democracy at Athens, and as the fifth century unfolded, the issues and personalities of the day become more and more the stuff of comedy. It was probably Cratinus who first wove the political and personally abusive strands, but it was Eupolis and Aristophanes who raised political comedy to its height, the latter pioneering the demagogue comedy with his *Knights* in 424. Here an entire comedy is devoted to a hostile caricature of a new politician (Cleon), who is depicted as being crude, dishonest, and illiterate, coming from a menial background, having suspect citizenship, perverse personal habits, and a vulgar and aggressive political style, and being motivated by greedy self-interest. In this Aristophanes was followed by Eupolis in *Maricas* (421—against Hyperbolus), and by Platon with comedies about *Peisandros* (421?), *Hyperbolus* (418), and *Cleophon* (405). Archippus' *Rhinon,* and *Teisamenus* by Theopompus *may* also be examples of this comic subgenre.

Even before Aristophanes and Eupolis became the dominant and most influential poets of Old Comedy, we can see politics at work in the comedy of the 430s. Cratinus' *Dionysalexander* might seem at first glance to be an excellent example of the comic burlesque of the myth of the Judgement of Paris, the humour being the substitution of the comic Dionysus for the Trojan prince. But at the end of the hypothesis comes the arresting sentence, "In the drama Pericles is very convincingly made fun of by innuendo for bringing the war on the Athenians." Elsewhere Pericles is described as "Zeus" on a number of occasions, and Hermippus F 46 is a choral song attacking Pericles for his policy of *Sitzkrieg* in the early years of the War. But there is no evidence that any of these plays is a sustained political "allegory." Many have seen in *Dionysalexander* a play-length political comedy in which Dionysus is meant always to stand for Pericles, whereas all we can say for certain is that at some point in that comedy an analogy was developed between the Trojan War and "the War," which may be either the Peloponnesian War or the Samian War. The connection may not lie with Pericles and Dionysus at all, but with Pericles and Alexander (Paris), and may have come from a choral song at the end of the comedy, or perhaps through some visual clue.

Critics have often detected in the poets of Old Comedy a deliberate and consistent right-wing agenda, that there is more than just exploitative humour in the attacks on Pericles or Aristophanes' plays opposing the War and championing Peace. Sommerstein (1996) shows that in terms of the *kōmōidoumenoi* (those made fun of in comedy), political figures on what we would call "the left" are considerably more likely to be caricatured than the traditional aristocrats or what we would call "the right." But two factors need to be considered. First the demagogues were something new in the political landscape of the 420s, and, simply put, were better comic material than the traditional conservatives. Comic poets will be attracted by what makes good material, what spectators will laugh at. Once

Pericles, with his distinctive cranium, controversial mistress, and lingering hints of tyranny, had died, Cleon and the vulgar and flamboyant populists were a godsend. Aristotle describes Cleon's behaviour before the assembly (*Athenian Constitution* 28.3):

> Cleon, who seems to have been the first to bellow up there on the rostrum, to engage in slanging matches, and to speak in public with his robe girt up around him, when everyone else would speak in an orderly fashion.

Much Old Comic humour depends on exaggeration for its effect, and any spectator, whatever his political allegiance might be, could laugh at the vulgar and overdrawn caricature. It has often been observed that Aristophanes could be awarded first prize for this hatchet job on Cleon, and then six weeks or so later witness Cleon's election as general.

Also to be considered is Rosen's discussion of Aristophanes and his fellow comic poets within the tradition of "blame poetry," such as the iambics of Archilochus and Hipponax. Here the poet creates a target figure (his "enemy"), Lycambes for Archilochus, and Bupalus for Hipponax, and weaves an entire comic fabric of alleged bad behaviour around that figure. If Cratinus was responsible for the topical and personal element in Old Comedy and saw himself as operating in a literary continuum, then it follows that he too would need his personal adversary, i.e., Pericles, and that the caricature is thus less personally than artistically motivated. Aristophanes would then have his Cleon, and Eupolis his Hyperbolus, and so on.

As early as the late fourth century Aristotle (*Ethics*

1128a23 = *AOC* 1) would outline the difference between older comic poets and modern ones, in that the former poets relied on *aischrologia* as the basis of their humour, and the latter on *hyponoia*. *Hyponoia* is usually translated as "innuendo," while *aischrologia* denotes a combination of personal humour, obscenity, and the use of vigorous and aggressive language. But it is personal humour (*to onomasti kōmōidein,* to make fun of by name) that attracted the attention of most ancient commentators. Horace (*Art of Poetry* 281–84) refers not only to the acclaim that Old Comedy enjoyed but also to a "freedom that descended into a licence that had to be controlled by law." Earlier (*Satires* 1.4.1–7) he claims Old Comedy as the literary ancestor of Roman satire, since "the poets made fun of people who deserved to be pointed out." This would be the redeeming social value for comedy, that it made fun of people who deserved to be made fun of, and for the serious-minded Romans and the sometimes humourless scholars of later antiquity, something as offensive as Old Comedy needed a redeeming value. These later commentators almost exclusively regard personal humour as the quintessence of Old Comedy and explain both the rise and the demise of the genre in terms of permitting and restricting the poets' freedom to say whatever they wanted about whomever they wanted. A brief example is that of the twelfth-century Byzantine poet and scholar John Tzetzes:

> Consider comedy as three-fold: first, middle, and then last. Open insult is characteristic of first ‹comedy›, of which the inventor and founder was Susarion. Concealed insult was characteristic of second ‹comedy›, of which there were Cratinus, Eu-

polis, Pherecrates, Aristophanes, Hermippus, and Platon. Of third ‹comedy› insult was also concealed except for slaves and foreigners and barbarians, of which Menander was a practitioner, also Philemon.

(*On the Distinction between Poets* 78–87 = *AOC* 11)

Here the sole distinction between the three ages of comedy is personal abuse and whether it is open and direct or concealed.

Ancient writers were constantly on the lookout for legal actions and restrictions on comedy, such as Horace's law, or the story that Alcibiades took revenge for his caricature in Eupolis' *Dyers* not only by drowning (or perhaps just submerging) Eupolis in the sea but also by passing a law against personal humour in comedy (Platonius, Tzetzes). There is no evidence of any external restrictions upon comedy, either allowing the poets the freedom to make fun of their targets or preventing them from doing so, apart from one decree passed in 440/39 ("not to make fun of by name") and repealed three years later (Σ *Acharnians* 67). It has been suggested that Cratinus' *Odysseus and Company*, which Platonius 1 (*AOC* 3) insists had no personal jokes—and there are none in the fragments that remain—belongs to this three-year moratorium, and perhaps also his *Dionysalexander*, which made fun of Pericles "through innuendo"—because open attack had been banned?

Certainly the plays of Aristophanes and the fragments of the other poets are full of jokes against real persons, usually identified by name or patronymic. These jokes range from brief one-liners (e.g., Eupolis F 2, "I once ate sprats at Phaeax' house"), to sequences of jokes (as at

Pherecrates F 155, where four dithyrambic poets have successively been abusing Music, or at Eupolis F 99.1–22, where the chorus lists a number of men who should be "screwed"), to witty choral songs directed at one target (e.g., Hermippus F 47, at Pericles), to whole scenes aimed at one person (Cratinus F 171, against Hagnon as one "unjustly rich"), to entire plays centred on a single prominent person (the demagogue comedies mentioned above, or Eupolis' *Spongers* set in the house of Callias).

Through all of this it is important to avoid the modern assumption that making a joke at someone means that you are out "to get" that person, that personal animus operates behind the joke. Modern social attitudes frown on exploitative joking, merely to raise a laugh, while Plutarch anticipates this with his comment that "Aristophanes seems to have written his slanderous and bitter passages for the envious and malicious" (*Moralia* 854d). Much more perceptive is Philosophy's response in Lucian's *Fisherman* (14) to the morally outraged philosophers:

> So then you are upset at being called names? And yet you knew, did you not, that in spite of the bad way that Comedy treats me at the Dionysia, I still consider her my friend? I have never taken her to court or ever gone up to her and complained; I just let her have the fun that is appropriate and proper for the festival. For I know that no harm could come from a joke.

But the fragments show that not all poets indulged in personal humour to the same extent. The minor poets of the early fourth century, who wrote domestic comedy or burlesques of myth, are almost completely lacking in such jokes, although their remains are meagre and not nearly as extensive as earlier poets. Aristotle (*Poetics* 1449b5) claims that "Crates was the first to abandon the iambic mode and write whole stories and plots" (Crates T 12), while one of the anonymous writers on comedy (Koster III = *AOC* 5) states that "Pherecrates emulated Crates and also refrained from personal abuse." The fragments confirm this, since in the sixty fragments of Crates there is not one example of personal humour, and of the three hundred fragments of Pherecrates there are perhaps ten which make fun of anyone. Thus while Norwood may exaggerate when he talks of "The School of Crates," we have evidence for a less political and personally abusive sort of Old Comedy, the sort that would ultimately prevail by the end of the fourth century. One can argue that for Aristotle, working with the benefit of hindsight, the comedy of Aristophanes and his contemporaries was something of a detour on the road toward the end point of comedy. Or in other words, Old Comedy died without issue.

Aristotle (*Poetics* 1449b1 = *AOC* 2d) further maintains that Old Comedy developed out of less formal productions performed by "volunteers," which in the 480s became part of the official state-sponsored dramatic competitions at the Dionysia. But what happens at the other end, in the early fourth century? There is no evidence for a law such as that postulated by Horace (*Art of Poetry* 281–84), and, in fact, apart from the decree mentioned above, in effect from 440/9 to 437/6, none of the various laws on comedy mentioned variously in the ancient sources has any basis in fact. We are probably dealing with a number of factors in the early fourth century: (1) the decline of the chorus, already noticeable in tragedy, on which the vigorous comedy of Aristophanes depended, (2) the atmosphere of the times in an Athens that had sustained catastrophic losses in war and two coups and restorations—making fun of the *dēmos* or its leaders was not the same (or as funny) in the 390s as it was in the 420s, (3) the resurgence of the mythological burlesque, found in comedy in the 430s and also in satyr drama, a genre which itself would decline in the fourth century, (4) the influence of Euripidean "Romantic Tragedy," whose happy endings and themes of recognitions and reunions would become the heart and soul of Menander's comedy, and (5) the simple fact that tastes change, both those of the spectators and those of the poets. An early casualty of fourth-century comedy is the politically charged drama, and while personal jokes can be found as late as Menander (*Samian Woman* 602), large-scale caricature of and jokes about political leaders vanish soon after the turn of the century. The most frequent *kōmōidoumenos* of the fourth century is in fact Plato.

Why was Aristophanes the only poet of Old Comedy whose plays survived, and the plays of Eupolis and Cratinus, the other members of the comic triad, did not? Certainly the papyrus fragments show that there were commentaries to Eupolis' plays being written in the Roman period and that Eupolis' *Demes* was still read and copied in the fourth or fifth century AD, while Tzetzes in the twelfth century records Cratinus, Eupolis, Platon, and Pherecrates as "still being studied." Other ancient sources record that the works of some poets had already disappeared (Susarion, Magnes) or that some of these early plays were revised at a later date. Cratinus' *Satyrs* and *Tempest-Tossed*, Eupolis' *New Moons*, and Platon's *Security* are known from sources that were using the official re-

bring together the scattered elements of comedy by making it into an art form. In terms of time, he lived around the 73rd Olympiad [488/7–485/4]; in terms of style he was fond of maxims, and was creative and ingenious. Forty plays of his are preserved, of which four are in dispute.

MAGNES: of Athens, competed at Athens and won eleven victories. None of his plays has survived, but there are nine attributed to him.

CRATINUS: of Athens, won a victory after the 85th Olympiad [440/39–437/6]. He died when the Spartans invaded for the first time [431] as Aristophanes says [*Peace* 702–3]:

> He just fainted away, because he could not bear to
> watch a full jar of wine being smashed.

He was a very creative poet, composing in the style of Aeschylus. Twenty-one plays of his are preserved.

CRATES: of Athens: they say that he was at first an actor who overlapped with Cratinus, very funny and ridiculous, the first to bring drunken characters on stage. His plays are seven in number.

PHERECRATES: of Athens. He won a victory in the archonship of Theodorus[1] [438/7]. He had been an actor and emulated Crates, and also refrained from personal jokes. His success lay in introducing new themes and in inventing plots.

PHRYNICHUS: the son of Phradmon died in Sicily.[2]

---

1 ἐπὶ Θεοδώρου is Dobree's correction of ἐπὶ θεάτρου.
2 Material has clearly been lost in this entry. Polyphradmon was the father of the tragic poet Phrynichus. It is not clear which poet is supposed to have died in Sicily.

Εὔπολις Ἀθηναῖος. ἐδίδαξεν ἐπὶ ἄρχοντος Ἀπολ-
λοδώρου, ἐφ᾽ οὗ καὶ Φρύνιχος, γεγονὼς δυνατὸς τῇ
λέξει καὶ ζηλῶν Κρατῖνον· πολὺ γοῦν λοίδορον καὶ
σκαιὸν ἐπιφαίνει. γέγραπται δὲ αὐτῷ δράματα ιδ´.

Ἀριστοφάνης Φιλίππου Ἀθηναῖος. μακρῷ λογιώ-
τατος Ἀθηναίων καὶ εὐφυΐᾳ πάντας ὑπεραίρων, ζήλῳ
δὲ Εὐριπίδου ††, τοῖς δὲ μέλεσι λεπτότερος. ἐδίδαξε δὲ
πρῶτος ἐπὶ ἄρχοντος Διοτίμου διὰ Καλλιστράτου. τὰς
μὲν γὰρ πολιτικὰς τούτῳ φασὶν αὐτὸν διδόναι, τὰ δὲ
κατ᾽ Εὐριπίδου καὶ Σωκράτους Φιλωνίδῃ. διὰ δὲ τού-
των νομισθεὶς ἀγαθὸς ποιητὴς τὰ λοιπὰ ἐπιγραφό-
μενος ἐνίκα. ἔπειτα τῷ υἱῷ ἐδίδου. τὰ δράματα ὄντα
τὸν ἀριθμὸν νδ´, ὧν νόθα δ´.

6 Anonymous *On Comedy* (Koster IV)

τὸ παλαιὸν οἱ ἐν ταῖς κώμαις ἀδικούμενοι παρὰ τῶν
πολιτῶν νυκτὸς ἀπήρχοντο παρὰ τὸν δῆμον ἐκεῖνον,
ἔνθα ὁ ἀδικήσας ἦν, καὶ ἔλεγον, ὅτι ἔστι τις ἐνταῦθα
ποιῶν εἰς τὸν γεωργὸν τάδε. καὶ τοῦτο ποιοῦντες
ὑπεχώρουν μὴ ἐπιλέγοντες καὶ τοὔνομα· ὀνομαστὶ
γὰρ κωμῳδεῖν ὁ νόμος οὐ δίδωσιν. μεθ᾽ ἡμέραν δὲ ὁ
δράσας ἐξητάζετο, καὶ οὕτως αἰσχυνόμενος ἀνεστέλ-
λετο τοῦ ἀδικεῖν. ὁρῶντες οὖν οἱ πολῖται τοῦτο χρήσι-
μον τῇ πόλει καὶ ἀδικίας ἀποτρεπτικὸν ἐκέλευσαν
τοὺς ἀδικουμένους ἐπὶ μέσης ἀγορᾶς τοὺς ἀδικήσαν-

EUPOLIS: he produced in the archonship of Apollo-
dorus [430/29], the same year as Phrynichus, a powerful
poet in his language and an emulator of Cratinus. He dis-
plays much that is abusive and clumsy [unseemly?].[3] Four-
teen plays are written by him.

ARISTOPHANES: son of Philippus, of Athens, by far
the most eloquent of the Athenians and exceeding them
all in ability, and emulating Euripides . . . but more delicate
in his songs. He put on a play for the first time in the
archonship of Diotimus [428/7] through Callistratus. They
say that he gave his political comedies to this man, but his
plays against Euripides and Socrates to Philonides. When
he gained a reputation as a good poet through these plays,
he was successful by producing the rest of his plays in his
own name. He also gave some plays to his son. ⟨His plays⟩
are forty-four in number, of which four are spurious.

[3] Geel and Kaibel propose αἰσχρὸν (unseemly) for σκαιὸν
(clumsy).

6 Once upon a time some people in the villages [kōmai]
were wronged by men of the city and went by night to
the community [dēmos] where the offender lived and said
that here lived the man who had done these things to the
farmer. Having done this they went away, never mention-
ing the person's name, for the law did not allow them to
make fun of by name. When day came, the guilty person
came under close scrutiny and being ashamed gave up
doing wrong. When the people of the city saw that this was
beneficial to the city and a deterrent to wrongdoing, they
commanded those who had been wronged to make fun of
the offenders in the middle of the agora. As they were

τας κωμῳδεῖν. οἱ δὲ δεδιότες αὐτοὺς ὡς πλουσίους πηλὸν χρίοντες καὶ τρύγα ἐπὶ μέσης ἀγορᾶς τοὺς ἀδικοῦντας ἐκωμῴδουν. ἐπεὶ δὲ μεγάλως ἡ πόλις ὠφελεῖτο ἐκ τούτου, ποιητὰς ἔταξαν ἐπὶ τούτῳ κωμῳδεῖν, ὃν ἂν βούλωνται, ἀκωλύτως. ἐπεὶ δὲ ἡ κακία προέκοπτεν, οἱ πλούσιοι καὶ οἱ ἄρχοντες μὴ βουλόμενοι κωμῳδεῖσθαι τὸ μὲν φανερῶς κωμῳδεῖν ἐκώλυσαν, ἐκέλευσαν δὲ αἰνιγματωδῶς. εἶτα δὴ καὶ τοῦτο ἐκώλυσαν, καὶ εἰς ξένους μὲν καὶ πτωχοὺς ἔσκωπτον, εἰς δὲ πλουσίους καὶ ἐνδόξους οὐκέτι.

γέγονε δὲ τῆς μὲν πρώτης κωμῳδίας ἄριστος τεχνίτης οὗτος ὁ Ἀριστοφάνης καὶ Εὔπολις, τῆς δὲ δευτέρας Πλάτων, τῆς δὲ τρίτης Μένανδρος. κωμῳδία οὖν ἢ ὅτι ἀπὸ κωμῶν συναγόμενοι ᾖδον ταῦτα ἢ ὅτι ἐν καιρῷ κώματος ᾖδον· ἔστι δὲ ταύτην εἰπεῖν καὶ τραγῳδίαν, οἱονεὶ τρυγῳδίαν τινὰ οὖσαν, ὅτι τρύγα χριόμενοι ἐκωμῴδουν. καὶ τῆς μὲν τραγῳδίας σκοπὸς τὸ εἰς θρῆνον κινῆσαι τοὺς ἀκροατάς, τῆς δὲ κωμῳδίας τὸ εἰς γέλωτα. διό φασιν· ἡ μὲν τραγῳδία λύει τὸν βίον, ἡ δὲ κωμῳδία συνίστησιν.

7 Anonymous *On Comedy* (Koster V)

τῆς κωμῳδίας τὸ μέν ἐστιν ἀρχαῖον, τὸ δὲ νέον, τὸ δὲ μέσον. τῆς δὲ νέας διαφέρει ἡ παλαιὰ κωμῳδία χρόνῳ, διαλέκτῳ, ὕλῃ, μέτρῳ, διασκευῇ. χρόνῳ μὲν καθὸ ἡ μὲν νέα ἐπὶ Ἀλεξάνδρου, ἡ δὲ παλαιὰ ἐπὶ τῶν

afraid because these were rich men, they smeared mud and wine-lees on themselves and made fun of the wrong-doers in the middle of the agora.[1] Since the city was bene-fiting greatly from this, they appointed poets for this pur-pose, to make fun of whomever they wanted, without interference. But since wickedness was on the rise, the rich men and those in power, not wanting to be made fun of, prevented them from openly making fun, but told them to do it indirectly. Then they prevented even this, and the poets started poking fun of foreigners and beggars, and no longer at rich and important people.

The best practitioner of First Comedy was this Aris-tophanes and Eupolis, of Second Comedy Platon, and of Third Menander. Comedy, then, <is so called> either be-cause they would sing these songs after gathering in the villages [*kōmai*] or because they would do their singing at the time of deep sleep [*kōma*]. One can also call this and tragedy as being a sort of *trygōidia,* because they would have their fun with the faces smeared with wine-lees [*tryx*]. The aim of tragedy is to move its hearers to lamenta-tion, that of comedy toward laughter. As they say, tragedy breaks up life, but comedy restores it.

[1] The story of the wronged farmers and the city folk became a standard feature of the history of comedy and is found also in the Anonymous Cramer I (= Koster XIb) and the scholiast to Dionysius Thrax (= Koster XVIII).

7 There is Old Comedy, New Comedy, and Middle Com-edy. Old Comedy differs from New Comedy in time, lan-guage, subject matter, metre, and structure. Time, insofar as New belongs to the age of Alexander, while Old reached

23

Πελοποννησιακῶν εἶχε τὴν ἀκμήν. διαλέκτῳ δέ, καθὸ ἡ μὲν νέα τὸ σαφέστερον ἔσχε τῇ νέᾳ κεχρημένη Ἀτθίδι, ἡ δὲ παλαιὰ τὸ δεινὸν καὶ ὑψηλὸν τοῦ λόγου· ἐνίοτε δὲ καὶ ἐπιτηδεύουσι λέξεις τινάς. ὕλη δέ, καθὸ ἡ μὲν νέα †† κατὰ τὸ πλεῖστον στρέφεται περὶ τὸ ἰαμβικόν, σπανίως δὲ μέτρον ἕτερον, ἐν δὲ τῇ παλαιᾷ πολυμετρία τὸ σπουδαζόμενον. διασκευῇ δέ, ὅτι ἐν μὲν τῇ νέᾳ χοροῦ οὐκ ἔδει, ἐν ἐκείνῃ δὲ δεῖ.

καὶ αὐτὴ δὲ ἡ παλαιὰ ἑαυτῆς διαφέρει. καὶ γὰρ οἱ ἐν Ἀττικῇ πρῶτον συστησάμενοι τὸ ἐπιτήδευμα τῆς κωμῳδίας—ἦσαν δὲ οἱ περὶ Σαννυρίωνα—καὶ τὰ πρόσωπα εἰσῆγον ἀτάκτως, καὶ μόνος ἦν γέλως τὸ κατασκευαζόμενον. ἐπιγενόμενος δὲ ὁ Κρατῖνος κατέστησε μὲν πρῶτον τὰ ἐν τῇ κωμῳδίᾳ πρόσωπα μέχρι τριῶν στήσας τὴν ἀταξίαν καὶ τῷ χαρίεντι τῆς κωμῳδίας τὸ ὠφέλιμον προσέθηκε τοὺς κακῶς πράττοντας διαβάλλων καὶ ὥσπερ δημοσίᾳ μάστιγι τῇ κωμῳδίᾳ κολάζων. ἀλλ᾽ ἔτι μὲν καὶ οὗτος τῆς ἀρχαιότητος μετεῖχε καὶ ἠρέμα πως τῆς ἀταξίας. ὁ μέντοι γε Ἀριστοφάνης μεθοδεύσας τεχνικώτερον τῶν μεθ᾽ ἑαυτοῦ τὴν κωμῳδίαν ἐνέλαμψεν ἐν ἅπασιν ἐπίσημος ὀφθεὶς οὕτως καὶ οὕτως πᾶσαν κωμῳδίαν ἐμελέτησε. καὶ γὰρ τὸ τούτου δρᾶμα ὁ Πλοῦτος νεωτερίζει κατὰ τὸ πλάσμα· τήν τε γὰρ ὑπόθεσιν ὡς ἀληθῆ ἔχει καὶ χορῶν ἐστέρηται, ὅπερ τῆς νεωτέρας ὑπῆρχε κωμῳδίας.

its high point during the Peloponnesian War. Language, insofar as New Comedy used new Attic and was much easier to understand, while Old possessed a strange and elevated manner of speaking, and at times they even invent certain expressions. In subject matter, insofar as New . . . relies principally on the iambic <trimeter> and occasionally on other metres, but in Old Comedy a wide variety of metres is practised. Structure, because there was no need for the chorus in New Comedy, but in the other there was.

Old Comedy has differences within itself. For those at Athens who first put together the business of comedy— these were Sannyrion[1] and his people—would bring characters on haphazardly and the humour lay in the performance. But when Cratinus followed these, he first fixed the number of characters at three, thereby stopping the disorder, and to the fun of comedy he added a usefulness by attacking those who behaved badly and punishing them by using comedy as a sort of public whip. But he too did share partly in the old style and in some degree of its lack of order. Now Aristophanes was more technically adept than his contemporaries in creating comedy, and being recognized as such shone forth among them all. He devoted considerable care to each of his comedies. His play, *Wealth,* is innovative in style, for it possesses a plotline that is realistic, and lacks choral parts as was the nature of later comedy.

[1] An error for "Susarion," who is the traditional inventor of Comedy.

ABOUT OLD COMEDY

8 *Names and Plays of the Poets of Old Comedy* (Koster VIII)

Θεοπόμπου δράματα ιζ'.
Στράττιδος δράματα ις'.
Φερεκράτους δράματα ιη'.
Κράτητος δράματα η'.
Πλάτωνος δράματα κη'.
Τηλεκλείδου δράματα ς'.
Φρυνίχου δράματα ι'.

9 Tzetzes *Prolegomena on Comedy* (Koster XIa 69–104)

αὕτη ἡ κωμῳδία τριττή ἐστι· πρώτη, μέση καὶ ὑστέρα,
ὧν τῆς μὲν πρώτης ἦν γνώρισμα λοιδορία συμφανὴς
καὶ ἀπαρακάλυπτος· τῆς μέσης δὲ καὶ δευτέρας ἦν
γνώρισμα τὸ συμβολικωτέρως, μὴ καταδήλως λέγειν
τὰ σκώμματα, οἷον τὸν ῥίψασπιν στρατηγὸν ἀετὸν
ὄφιν ἀσπίδα κρατήσαντα καὶ δηχθέντα ὑπ' αὐτῆς
αὐτὴν ἀπορρίψαι. ἐχρᾶτο δὲ αὕτη ἡ μέση τοῖς συμ-
βολικοῖς τούτοις σκώμμασιν ὁμοίως ἐπί τε ξένων καὶ
πολιτῶν. καὶ ἡ τρίτη δὲ καὶ ὑστέρα συμβολικῶς
ὁμοίως ἐχρᾶτο τοῖς σκώμμασιν, ἀλλὰ κατὰ δούλων
καὶ ξένων, οὐ μέντοιγε κατὰ πολιτῶν· ἤδη γὰρ οἱ
πολῖται ἀδικεῖν ἀναιδέστερον ἤρξαντο καὶ οὐκ ἤθελον
παρὰ ποιητῶν, τῶν καὶ διδασκάλων καλουμένων,
ἐλέγχεσθαι.
τῆς οὖν κωμῳδίας τῆς καλουμένης πρώτης πρῶτος
καὶ εὑρετὴς γέγονεν ὁ Μεγαρεὺς Σουσαρίων ὁ Τρι-

8 Theopompus: 17 plays
   Strattis: 16 plays
   Pherecrates: 18 plays
   Crates: 8 plays
   Platon: 28 plays
   Teleclides: 6 plays
   Phrynichus: 10 plays.

9 Comedy itself exists in three forms: First, Middle, and Later, of which the First is distinguished by open and unrestricted personal humour; Middle or Second by more allusive ‹personal humour›, not making the jokes openly, for example the general who threw his shield [*rhipsaspis*] away becomes an eagle holding a snake or *aspis* and being bitten by it letting go [*rhiptein*] of his shield. Middle Comedy also used these allusive jokes, but at foreigners and slaves, The Third and Later also relied on ‹personal› jokes, but only at foreigners and slaves, and not at all against citizens. For at this time the citizens had begun to commit crimes without fear and did not want to be accused by the poets, who were also called "teachers."

The man who invented what is called First Comedy was a Megarian, Susarion of Tripodisce, the son of Philinnus.

ποδίσκιος, υἱὸς ὢν Φιλίννου, ὃς φαύλῃ γυναικὶ συν-
οικῶν ἀπολιπούσῃ αὐτὸν Διονυσίων ἠγμένων εἰσ-
ελθὼν εἰς τὸ θέατρον τὰ τέσσαρα ἰαμβεῖα ταυτὶ
ἀνεφθέγξατο, ἃ μόνα τῶν ἐκείνου συγγραμμάτων
ἐφεύρηνται τῶν ἄλλων ἁπάντων ἠφανισμένων·

ἀκούετε λεῴ· Σουσαρίων λέγει τάδε,
υἱὸς Φιλίννου, Μεγαρόθεν Τριποδίσκιος·
κακὸν γυναῖκες, ἀλλ' ὅμως, ὦ δημόται,
οὐκ ἔστιν εὑρεῖν οἰκίαν ἄνευ κακοῦ.

οὕτως ἡ πρώτη κωμῳδία τὸ σκῶμμα εἶχεν ἀπαρα-
κάλυπτον· ἐξήρκεσε δὲ τὸ ἀπαρακαλύπτως οὑτωσὶ
κωμῳδεῖν μέχρις Εὐπόλιδος. ἐπεὶ δ' οὗτος εἰς Ἀλκι-
βιάδην τὸν στρατηγὸν ἀπέρριψε σκῶμμα καὶ φανε-
ρῶς τὴν τραυλότητα τούτου διελοιδόρησεν—ἔτυχον δὲ
τότε καὶ ταῖς τριήρεσιν ὄντες ὡς ναυμαχίας προσ-
δοκωμένης—κελεύει τοῖς στρατιώταις, καὶ ἢ ἅπαξ
ἐκβράττουσιν αὐτὸν εἰς τὴν θάλατταν καὶ ἀπώλετο, ἢ
σχοίνῳ δεδεμένον ἀνάγοντες καὶ κατάγοντες ἦσαν εἰς
θάλατταν καὶ τέλος περιέσωσαν τοῦτον τοῦ Ἀλκι-
βιάδου εἰπόντος αὐτῷ· "βάπτε με σὺ θυμέλαις, ἐγὼ δέ
σε κατακλύσω ὕδασιν ἁλμυρωτάτοις". καὶ ἢ οὕτως ἢ
παντελῶς διεφθαρμένος τοῖς κύμασι τῆς τε φανερᾶς
καὶ τῆς συμβολικῆς κωμῳδίας ἐπαύθη, ἢ τοῦ τοιούτου
θανάτου περισωθεὶς οὐκέτι κωμῳδίαν μετῆλθεν
ἀπαρακάλυπτον.

ἀλλὰ ψήφισμα θέντος Ἀλκιβιάδου κωμῳδεῖν
ἐσχηματισμένως καὶ μὴ προδήλως αὐτός τε ὁ Εὔ-

He was living with a worthless woman who had left him, so at the time that the Dionysia was being held he went into the theatre and uttered these four iambic verses, which are the only extant lines of his, all the rest having disappeared:

> Listen, people, Susarion has this to say, the son of Philinnus, from Tripodisce in Megara: women are a bad thing, but nevertheless, my townsfolk, you cannot have a home without a bad thing.   [F 1.1–4]

In this way First Comedy had unrestricted humour, and this sort of unrestricted humour prevailed until the time of Eupolis. But when Eupolis launched a joke against the general Alcibiades and openly made fun of his speech defect—they happened at that time to be on board ship with a sea battle imminent—Alcibiades gave an order to his men. Either they pitched him once into the sea and he died, or tying a rope around him they raised and lowered him into the sea, finally sparing his life when Alcibiades said to him: "So, dye me in the theatre, but I will soak you in very bitter waters." Either he perished in this way beneath the waves and so ceased his usual open jokes, or his life was spared but no longer practised unrestricted comedy.

Then when Alcibiades passed a law to make fun of people indirectly and not openly, Eupolis himself and Cratinus

πόλις Κρατῖνός τε καὶ Φερεκράτης καὶ Πλάτων, οὐχ ὁ
φιλόσοφος, Ἀριστοφάνης τε σὺν ἑτέροις τὰ συμ-
βολικὰ μετεχειρίσαντο σκώμματα, καὶ ἡ δευτέρα
κωμῳδία τῇ Ἀττικῇ ἀνεσκίρτησεν. ὡς δ' ἐπὶ πλέον
ἐπεχείρουν οἱ Ἀττικοὶ ἀδικεῖν καὶ οὐδὲ συμβόλοις
ἐλέγχεσθαι ἤθελον, ἐψηφίσαντο συμβολικῶς μὲν
γίνεσθαι κωμῳδίας, πλὴν κατὰ μόνων δούλων καὶ
ξένων· κἀντεῦθεν καὶ ἡ τρίτη κωμῳδία ἐφάνη, ἧς ἦν
Φιλήμων καὶ Μένανδρος.

10 *Etymologicum Magnum* 764.13–24 (Koster XVI 10–
17)

ἡ δὲ κωμῳδία ὠνομάσθη, ἐπειδὴ πρότερον κατὰ κώ-
μας ἔλεγον αὐτὰ ἐν ταῖς ἑορταῖς τοῦ Διονύσου καὶ τῆς
Δήμητρος· ἢ παρὰ τὸ κωμάζειν, ⟨ἢ⟩ ἡ ἐπὶ τῷ κώματι
ᾠδή· ἐπειδὴ ἐπὶ τὸν καιρὸν τοῦ ὕπνου τὴν ἀρχὴν
ἐφευρέθη· ἢ ἡ τῶν κωμητῶν ᾠδή· κῶμαι γὰρ λέγονται
οἱ μείζονες ἀγροί. βλαπτόμενοι γάρ τινες γεωργοὶ
παρὰ τῶν ἐν Ἀθήνῃσι πολιτῶν, κατῄεσαν περὶ τὸν
καιρὸν τοῦ ὕπνου· καὶ περιϊόντες τὰς ἀγυιάς, ἔλεγον
ἀνωνυμὶ τὰς βλάβας ἃς ἔπασχον ὑπ' αὐτῶν· οἷον,
"ἐνταῦθα μένει τὶς τὰ καὶ τὰ ποιῶν"· καὶ ἐκ τούτου
ἀνοχὴ τῶν ἀδικιῶν ἐγίνετο.

11 Tzetzes *On the Distinctions between Poets* (Koster
XXIa 78–87)

τριττὴν νόει πρῶτον δὲ τὴν κωμῳδίαν·

and Pherecrates and Platon (not the philosopher) and Aristophanes with the rest fashioned their jokes allusively and so second comedy sprung into being. But when the Athenians undertook to behave even more unjustly and did not want to be chastised even in allusions, they voted that comedy should become totally allusive, except only for slaves and foreigners. Thence appeared third comedy, to which Philemon and Menander belonged.

10 Comedy got its name since in the past this is what they sang in the villages (*kōmai*) at the feasts of Dionysus and Demeter. Or from "to revel" (*kōmazein*). Or from "song in sleep" (*kōma*) because it was originally discovered at the time of sleep. Or from "song of the villagers" (*kōmētai*), since larger rural communities are called *kōmai*. Some farmers wronged by city folk from Athens went down to the city at the hour of sleep and going through the streets anonymously told of their wrongs they were suffering, such as "here lives so-and-so doing such-and-such." And this brought about a respite from wrongdoing.

11 Consider comedy as threefold: first, middle, and then

ABOUT OLD COMEDY

πρώτην, μέσην, ἔπειτα καὶ τὴν ὑστέραν.
πρώτης μὲν ἦν ἴδιον ἐμφανὴς ψόγος,
ἧς ἦν κατάρξας εὑρετὴς Σουσαρίων.
τῆς δευτέρας ἦν ὁ ψόγος κεκρυμμένος,
ἧς ἦν Κρατῖνος, Εὔπολις, Φερεκράτης,
Ἀριστοφάνης, Ἕρμιππός τε καὶ Πλάτων·
καὶ τῆς τρίτης ἦν ὁ ψόγος κεκρυμμένος,
πλὴν κατὰ δούλων καὶ ξένων καὶ βαρβάρων,
ἧς ἦν Μένανδρος ἐργάτης καὶ Φιλήμων.

12 Tzetzes *Prolegomena to Lycophron* (Koster XXIIb
21–40)

τραγικῶν, σατυρικῶν καὶ κωμικῶν ποιητῶν κοινὸν μὲν
τὸ τετραγώνως ἔχειν ἱστάμενον τὸν χορὸν καὶ τὸ
λαμβάνειν τράγον ἢ τρύγα, τουτέστιν οἶνον νέον, καὶ
μιμητικῶς ἐν τῇ θυμέλῃ τὰ τούτων δράματα λέγεσθαί
τε καὶ δρᾶσθαι, διάφορον δὲ αὐτοῖς τὸ τὴν κωμῳδίαν
γέλωτα ἔχειν καὶ σκώμματα καὶ κδ΄ χορευτάς, τὴν δὲ
τραγῳδίαν καὶ τοὺς σατύρους ἐπίσης μὲν ἔχειν χορευ-
τὰς ις΄ . . . διαφέρει δὲ καὶ κατὰ τοῦτο καὶ κωμῳδία καὶ
τραγῳδία, ὅτι ἡ τραγῳδία λύει τὸν βίον, ἡ δὲ κωμῳδία
συνίστησι. καὶ κωμῳδία δὲ ἐκλήθη ἢ ὅτι κατὰ τὸν
καιρὸν τοῦ κώματος ἤτοι τοῦ ὕπνου εὑρέθη, ἢ ὅτι ἐν
ταῖς κώμαις, τουτέστιν τοῖς μεγίστοις χωρίοις, ἢ ὅτι
ἐν τοῖς κώμοις καὶ πότοις τοῦ Διονύσου εὑρέθη . . .
κωμῳδοὶ πραττόμενοί εἰσιν οὗτοι, οἷοι Ἀριστοφάνης,
Κρατῖνος, Πλάτων, Εὔπολις, Φερεκράτης καὶ ἕτεροι.

last. Open insult is characteristic of first ‹comedy›, of which the inventor and founder was Susarion. Concealed insult was characteristic of second ‹comedy›, of which there were Cratinus, Eupolis, Pherecrates, Aristophanes, Hermippus, and Platon. Of third ‹comedy› insult was also concealed except for slaves and foreigners and barbarians, of which Menander was a practitioner, also Philemon.

12

(a) Tragedy, satyr play, and comedy have this in common: a chorus drawn up in a rectangular form, winning the prize of a goat (*tragos*) or of *tryx*, that is "new wine," and their performances (*dramata*) spoken and acted as representations in the theatre. But they differ in that comedy possesses humour and jokes and twenty-four choristers, while tragedy and satyr play each have sixteen . . . Comedy and tragedy differ on this point also, that tragedy breaks up life, while comedy restores it. Comedy is so called either because it was invented at the hour of *kōma* or sleep, or because it was invented in the *kōmai,* that is the larger communities, or because it was developed at the drunken revelries of Dionysus . . . These are the comic poets still being studied: Cratinus, Platon, Eupolis, Pherecrates and the rest.

ABOUT OLD COMEDY

Tzetzes *Scholia to Hesiod* (Koster XXIIc 13–14)

κωμικῶν δὲ ὁ γέλως μετὰ χορευτῶν καὶ προσώπων,
οἷος Ἀριστοφάνης, Εὔπολις, Φερεκράτης.

13 Diomedes *Art of Grammar* (Koster XXIV.46–59)

poëtae primi comici fuerunt Susarion, Mullus et Magnes.
hi veteris disciplinae iocularia quaedam minus scite ac
venuste pronuntiabant, in quibus hi versus fuerunt:

Σουσαρίων ταῦτα λέγει
κακὸν γυναῖκες, ἀλλ' ὅμως, ὦ δημόται,
οὐκ ἔστιν εὑρεῖν οἰκίαν ἄνευ κακοῦ.

secunda aetate fuerunt Aristophanes, Eupolis et Cratinus,
qui et principum vitia sectati acerbissimas comoedias
composuerunt. tertia aetas fuit Menandri, Diphili et Phi-
lemonis, qui omnem acerbitatem comoediae mitigaverunt
atque argumenta multiplicia †graecis† erroribus secuti
sunt. ab his Romani fabulas transtulerunt, et constat apud
illos primum latino sermone comoediam Livium Andro-
nicum scripsisse.

14 *Glossary of Ansileubus* (Koster XVII.3)

comoediae: cantica agresti[c]a graece.
comoedia: est, quae res privatorum et humilium per-
sonarum comprehendit, non tam alto ut tragoedia stilo,
sed mediocri et dulce.

(b) Comic poets, such as Aristophanes and Eupolis and Pherecrates, create humour with choristers and characters.

13 The first comic poets were Susarion, Myllus, and Magnes. They were of the old style and delivered their jokes rather less skilfully and elegantly, among whom we find these verses [F 1.1, 3–4]:

> Listen, people, Susarion has this to say: women are a bad thing, but nevertheless, my townsfolk, you cannot have a home without a bad thing.

To the second age belonged Aristophanes, Eupolis, and Cratinus, who wrote very fierce comedies attacking the vices of the leading men. The third age was that of Menander, Diphilus, and Philemon, who softened all the fierceness of comedy and followed multiple plotlines depending on errors. The Romans took their plays over from these poets and it is agreed that among the Romans the first to write a comedy in Latin was Livius Andronicus.

14

Comedies: rustic songs in Greek.
Comedy: its subject is the doings of lower-class individuals, not in the high style of tragedy, but in one that was commonplace and pleasing.

comoedia: est, quae privatorum hominum acta continet. comoediarum autem invenisse Thaliam, unam ex Musis, poetae finxerunt. dicta autem comoedia sive a loco, quia circum pagos agebatur, quos Graeci "comas" vocant, sive a comissatione; solebant enim post cibum homines ad eos audiendos venire. sed prior ac vetus comoedia ridicularis extitit; postea civiles vel privatas adgressa materias in dictis atque gestu universorum delicta corripiens in scaenam proferebat, nec vetabatur poetae pessimum quemque describere vel cui⟨us⟩libet peccata moresque reprehendere. auctor eius ⟨Sus⟩a[o]rion traditur; sed in fabulas primi eam contulerunt Magnes † † ita, ut non excederent in singulis versus trecenos.

15 *Anecdoton Estense* II.5

τῆς κωμῳδίας ἡ μὲν πρώτη, ἥτις ἐμφανῶς πάντας ἔψεγε· κατῆρξε δὲ αὐτῆς Σουσαρίων· ἡ δὲ δευτέρα, ἧς ἦν ὁ ψόγος κατὰ πάντων, ἀλλὰ κεκρυμμένος. ἄριστοι δὲ ἐν αὐτῇ Κρατῖνος, Εὔπολις, Ἀριστοφάνης, Πλάτων. τῆς δὲ τρίτης ὁ ψόγος καὶ κερυμμένος ἦν καὶ κατὰ δούλων καὶ ξένων, ἀλλ' οὐκέτι πολιτῶν· διέπρεψαν ἐν αὐτῇ Μένανδρος καὶ Φιλήμων.

16 *IG* ii² 2325.39–66, 116–38

(a) *IG* ii² 2325.39–66—the List of Victors at the Dionysia.

Comedy: it deals with the doings of individual people. The poets have conjectured that Thalia, one of the Muses, invented comedy. Comedy is so called either from the place, because it was performed among the villages which in Greek are called *comae,* or from "eating together" [*comissatio*], since people would gather after dinner to hear them. Old Comedy began as something silly, but later moved on to public and private themes, and seizing upon the shortcomings of everybody in word and deed would bring them on stage. A poet was not forbidden to portray anyone in a very bad light or to find fault with the misdeeds or character of anybody he wanted. The founder of this is said to be Susarion, but Magnes ‹and . . . › were the first ‹to put it› into dramatic form, such that they did not exceed three hundred lines at a time.

15 First comedy was that which abused everyone openly. Its inventor was Susarion. Second ‹comedy› was that in which everyone was abused, but covertly. The best at this were Cratinus, Eupolis, Aristophanes, Platon. In third comedy abuse was both covert and against slaves and foreigners only, and no longer at citizens. The leading lights here were Menander and Philemon.

16 The List of Victors at the Dionysia and at the Lenaea.

Most of the fragments of these lists of dramatic victors were found on the southern side of the Acropolis and in the area of the Theatre. They record the names of poets and actors with the number of victories, first for the Dionysia and then for the Lenaea. Poets are entered on the list on the occasion of their first victory at that festival. As we have spe-

[ΑΣΤΙΚΑΙ ΠΟΗΤΩΝ]	[ΤΗΛΕΚΛΙ]ΔΗΣ ΙΙΙ	ΝΙΚΟΦΩ[Ν
[ΚΩΜΙΚΩΝ]	.........Σ Ι	ΘΕΟΠΟΜΠ[ΟΣ
[ΧΙΩΝΙΔΗΣ]	———	Κ[Η]ΦΙΣΟ[ΔΩΡΟΣ
———	———	[ΑΡΧ]Ι[ΠΠΟΣ
———Ι	ΦΕΡ[ΕΚΡΑΤΗΣ]	
.........Σ Ι	ΕΡΜ[ΙΠΠΟΣ	
———	ΑΡΙ[ΣΤΟΦΑΝΗΣ	
[ΜΑΓΝΗ]Σ ΔΙ	ΕΥ[ΠΟΛΙΣ	
.......Σ Ι	ΚΑ[ΝΘΑΡΟΣ	
[ΑΛΚΙΜΕ]ΝΗ[Σ] Ι	ΦΡΥ[ΝΙΧΟΣ	
.......Σ Ι	ΑΜ[ΕΙΨΙΑΣ	
[ΕΥΦΡΟΝ]ΙΟΣ Ι	ΠΛΑ[ΤΩΝ	
[ΕΚΦΑΝ]ΤΙΔΗΣ ΙΙΙΙ	ΦΙΛ[ΩΝΙΔΗΣ	
[ΚΡΑΤΙ]ΝΟΣ ΙΙΙ	ΛΥΚ[ΙΣ	
[ΔΙΟΠ]ΕΙΘΗΣ ΙΙ	ΛΕΥ[ΚΩΝ	
[ΚΡΑ]ΤΗΣ ΙΙΙ	———	
[ΚΑΛΛΙΑ]Σ ΙΙ	———	

(b) *IG* ii² 2325.116–38—the List of Victors at the Lenaea.

[ΛΗΝΑΙΚ]Α[Ι ΠΟΗ]ΤΩΝ	ΠΟ[ΛΙΟΧΟΣ] Ι
[ΚΩΜΙΚΩΝ]	ΜΕ[ΤΑΓΕΝΗ]Σ ΙΙ
[Ξ]ΕΝΟΦΙΛΟΣ Ι	ΘΕΟ[ΠΟΜΠ]ΟΣ ΙΙ
[Τ]ΗΛΕΚΛΕΙΔΗΣ ΙΙ	ΠΟΛ[ΥΖΗΛΟΣ] ΙΙΙΙ
ΑΡΙΣΤΟΜΕΝΗΣ ΙΙ	ΝΙΚΟΦ[ΩΝ]

38

*cific dates for some of the poets from other sources (IG ii²
2318, the hypotheses to the plays of Aristophanes), we can
come to some reasonable conclusions about the relative
chronology of the lists.*

I	II	III
[Poets at the Dionysia]	[Telecli]des 3	Nicopho[n]
[Comic Poets]	[.........]s 1	Theopomp[us]
[Chionides]	———	C[e]phiso[dorus]
———	———	[Arch]i[ppus]
——— 1	Pher[ecrates]	
[.........]s 1	Herm[ippus]	
———	Ari[stophanes]	
[Magne]s 11	Eu[polis]	
[......]s 1	Ca[ntharus]	
[Alcime]ne[s] 1	Phry[nichus]	
[.....]s 1	Am[eipsias]	
[Euphron]ius 1	Pla[ton	
[Ecphan]tides 4	Phil[onides]	
[Crati]nus 3	Lyc[is]	
[Diop]eithes 2	Leu[con]	
[Cra]tes 3		
[Callia]s 2		

I	II
[Poets at the Lenaea]	Po[liochus] 1
[Comic poets]	Me[tagene]s 2
[X]enophilus 1	Theo[pomp]us 2
[T]eleclides 2	Pol[yzelus] 4
Aristomenes 2	Nicoph[on]

ABOUT OLD COMEDY

ΚΡΑΤΙΝΟΣ III   ΑΠΟ[ΛΛΟΦΑΝΗΣ] I
ΦΕΡΕΚΡΑΤΗΣ II   ΑΜ[ΕΙΨΙΑΣ]
ΕΡΜΙΠΠΟΣ IIII   Ν[ΙΚΟΧΑΡΗΣ]
ΦΡΥΝΙΧΟΣ II   ΧΕΝΟ[Φ]ΩΝ I
ΜΥΡΤΙΛΟΣ I   ΦΙΛΥΛΛΙΟΣ I
[ΕΥ]ΠΟΛΙΣ III   ΦΙΛΟΝΙΚΟΣ I
————   ....Σ I
————
————
————
————

40

ABOUT OLD COMEDY

Cratinus 3

Pherecrates 2

Hermippus 4

Phrynichus 2

Myrtilus 1

[Eu]polis 3

Apo[llophane]s 1

Am[eipsias]

N[icochares]

Xeno[ph]on 1

Philyllius 1

Philonicus 1

[.......]s 1

ΑΛΚΑΙΟΣ

Testimonia

i *Suda* α 1274

Ἀλκαῖος, Μιτυληναῖος, εἶτα Ἀθηναῖος, κωμικὸς τῆς ἀρχαίας κωμῳδίας πέμπτος, υἱὸς δὲ Μίκκου. ἔγραψε δράματα δέκα.

ii Hypothesis III Aristophanes *Wealth*

ἐδιδάχθη ἐπὶ ἄρχοντος Ἀντιπάτρου, ἀνταγωνιζομένου αὐτῷ Νικοχάρους μὲν Λάκωσιν, Ἀριστομένους δὲ

ALCAEUS

Alcaeus clearly belongs to the last phase of Old Comedy. His one attested date (T 2) is the production of his Pasiphae *which competed against Aristophanes'* Wealth *in 388. The* Suda *(T 1) assigns him ten plays—we have eight titles, of which over half seem to be burlesques of myth, of the sort which became increasingly popular in the first half of the fourth century. The titles suggest also plays with women as heroines, or as with* Endymion *and* Ganymede, *males on the receiving end of erotic advances by gods. None of the plays appears to have a title reflecting the chorus of that comedy.*

Testimonia

i Alcaeus, of Mytilene, later of Athens, a poet of Old Comedy, fifth, and son of Miccus. He wrote ten plays.[1]

[1] Or "then ⟨there is one⟩ of Athens." "Fifth" may refer to an encyclopaedic list of men named "Alcaeus." Miccus is not a known Athenian name until the 2nd c., but Micus is documented for the late 5th c., and Micon is quite common. "Of Mytilene" is a clear allusion to the lyric poet.

ii It [*Wealth*] was produced in the archonship of Antipatros. Competing poets were Nicochares with *Laconians,*

43

Ἀδμήτῳ, Νικοφῶντος δὲ Ἀδώνιδι, Ἀλκαίου δὲ Πασιφάῃ.

Fragments

ΑΔΕΛΦΑΙ ΜΟΙΧΕΥΟΜΕΝΑΙ

1 Athenaeus 316b

ἠλίθιον εἶναι νοῦν τε πουλύποδος ἔχειν

ΓΑΝΥΜΗΔΗΣ

The abduction of the beautiful Trojan prince Ganymede by Zeus, to become his cupbearer and bedmate, was a well-established myth by the late fifth century, especially common on vases. Both fifth-century poetry (Theognis and Pindar) and tragedy (Trojan Women 820–39) make it clear that Ganymede's beauty had attracted the erotic attention of Zeus. It would have been a natural story for a comic burlesque of myth, and indeed Lucian's brilliant sketch (Dia-

Aristomenes with *Admetus,* Nicophon with *Adonis,* and Alcaeus with *Pasiphae.*

Fragments

SISTERS IN ADULTERY

Choral titles often indicate the chorus of a comedy, but in this instance, like Plautus' Bacchides, *it more likely refers to characters in the play. The "stupid male" of F 1 suggests that the women were in control and the perpetrators of adulterous behaviour. Ameipsias wrote a* Moichoi *(Adulterers).*

1 For him to be stupid and have the wits of an octopus.

GANYMEDE

logue of the Gods *10) in which an attractive, but not-too-bright, Ganymede meets his would-be lover may well be based on comic originals. We know of two later versions by poets of Middle Comedy. F 3 is part of a conversation between Zeus and Hephaestus. Did Zeus have to take along the clumsy-footed Hephaestus rather than his usual accomplice, Hermes?*

2 Pollux 7.23, Athenaeus 110a

{A.} διπύρους τε θερμούς. {B.} οἱ δίπυροι δ᾽ εἰσὶν
τίνες;
{A.} ἄρτοι τρυφῶντες.

3 The Antiatticist p. 102.29

κατάχωλε, θᾶττον, ἢ κεραυνοπλὴξ ἔσῃ.

4 Photius (b, z) α 509

ἔοικεν αἰγίθαλλος
διακωλύειν τὸ πρᾶγμα

5 Choeroboscus *On the Canons of Theodosius, GrGr*
IV.2, p. 143.7–10

κατέχεσον τῆς Νηρηίδος

ΕΝΔΥΜΙΩΝ

2 (A) And hot double loaves.
  (B) Double loaves? What are they?
  (A) Luxury bread.

3 [to Hephaestus] (ZEUS): Lame one, hurry up, or you will be struck by lightning.

4 The tomtit seems to be discouraging the matter.

5 And I [they?] shat all over the daughter of Nereus.

Brief fragments: (F 6) "queen," (F 7) "malpractice," (F 8) "I shall hang," (F 9) "fond of drinking."

ENDYMION

Three early stories about Endymion were known: one (attested in Hesiod Catalogue F 198) made him part of a romantic triangle, involving himself, Zeus, and Hera, as a result of which Zeus expelled him from Olympus to Hades; in the second (Hesiod Catalogue F 10.58–62) Zeus allowed Endymion to select the manner of his own demise—he chose an endless sleep; and the more familiar story (known to Sappho, F 199, and Apollonius of Rhodes, 4.57–8) about the passion of the Moon (Selene) for the sleeping Endymion. Lucian (Dialogue of the Gods 19) creates the witty scene where Selene confesses her passion to Aphrodite. F 10 reveals that someone has been watching over Endymion. F 11 and 12 suggest a doctor as a character in the comedy—was a doctor fetched to wake up Endymion (cf. the healing of Wealth in that comedy or the comic doctor Lexiphanes in Lucian's sketch of that name)? Dramatic purposes require that someone wake up Sleeping Beauty.

10 Priscian *Grammatical Foundations* 18.180

ὁτιὴ σχεδόν τι μῆνας ἐγγὺς τρεῖς ὅλους
φρουρῶ τὸν Ἐνδυμίωνα.

11 Σ Aristophanes *Birds* 1701

ἔστι δὲ καὶ ἕτερος, ἰατρός, οὗ μνημονεύει Ἀλκαῖος ἐν
Ἐνδυμίωνι.

12 Pollux 9.53

νοσημάτων ταλαντιαίων

ΙΕΡΟΣ ΓΑΜΟΣ

14 Photius p. 479.4–5

ἀνδράποδα πέντε, πωλικὸν ζεῦγος βοῶν

15 Athenaeus 424e

κεραννύουσιν ἀφανίζουσί τε

ΚΑΛΛΙΣΤΩ

ALCAEUS

10 Because for nearly three whole months now I have been keeping watch on Endymion.[1]

[1] From a prologue? But who has "been keeping watch on Endymion"? Perhaps Sleep, or Hermes who "kept an eye" on the young Ganymede for Zeus (Lucian *Judgement* 6).

11 There is another [Gorgias], a doctor, whom Alcaeus mentions in *Endymion*.

12 A talent's worth (weight?) of diseases.

Brief fragment: (F 13) *"I was/they were in service."*

SACRED MARRIAGE

Meineke thought that the poet was making fun of the marriage of Zeus and Hera, celebrated in some communities as an annual festival. Just about any divine union might do: Dionysus and Ariadne, Heracles and Hebe. The fragments do suggest some sort of formal occasion.

14 Five slaves, a brace of young oxen.

15 They mix the wine and make it disappear.

Brief fragment: (F 16) *"water for the hands."*

CALLISTO

Two possible identifications have been proposed for the title character: (i) the mythical daughter of Lycaon, the lover of Zeus, who was eventually transformed into the constellation of the Great Bear, and (ii) a well-known pros-

17 Athenaeus 399ef

{A.} κορίαννον ἵνα τί λεπτόν;   {B.} ἵνα τοὺς
  δασύποδας
οὓς ἂν λάβωμεν ἁλσὶ διαπάττειν ἔχῃς.

ΚΩΜΩΙΔΟΤΡΑΓΩΙΔΙΑ

*titute at Athens, best-known from a story by Aelian (His-
torical Miscellany 13.32) about her encounter with Socra-
tes. Comedies named after prostitutes are well documented
(Athenaeus 567c). But Artemis has a role in some versions
of the myth (see Amphis F 46), and F 17 does sound as if
a hunt is being prepared. Aeschylus wrote a Callisto, of
which only the title and one fragment are known (a satyr
play?).*

17 (A) Powdered coriander? What for?
    (B) So that you can sprinkle any hares we catch with
salt.

Brief fragment: (F 18) "cause to mount."

TRAGICOMEDY

*The great divide between tragedy and comedy is well-
known. Tragedy always preserves the dramatic illusion,
comedy does all it can to remind the spectators that they
are spectators. No poet is known to have written both com-
edy and tragedy, although Plato has Socrates maintain at
the end of Symposium that this should be possible. Plautus
called his Amphitruo a tragicomoedia (59), a play very
probably based on a Middle Comic original. Given the par-
allels of comic characters such as Comedy in Cratinus'
Wine-Flask or Music and Justice in Pherecrates' Chiron, I
wonder if we had a title character dressed partly in tragic
fashion and partly in comic fashion (cf. the contrast of
characters on the Choregos vase or the gender confusion in
the dress of Dionysus in Frogs, Eupolis' Officers, Bacchae
or Aeschylus' Edonians).*

THE POETS OF OLD COMEDY

19 Macrobius *Satires* 5.20.11

ἐτύγχανον μὲν ἀγρόθεν †πλείστους† φέρων
εἰς τὴν ἑορτὴν †ὅσσον οἷον† εἴκοσι,
ὁρῶ δ᾽ ἄνωθεν γάργαρ᾽ ἀνθρώπων κύκλῳ.

πλείστους codd., ναστοὺς Hermann, πλεκτοὺς van Herwerden.

ΩCCΟΝΟΙΟΝ N, ΩCCΟΝ ΩΙΟΝ P, ὡς ἄν, οἶομ᾽ Schneidewin.

20 Photius ε 1794

ηὔλει δ᾽ ἐπίχαλκον τὸ στόμα λήκυθόν ⟨τ᾽⟩ ἔχων.

ΠΑΛΑΙΣΤΡΑ

22 Athenaeus 396c

ὁδὶ γὰρ αὐτός ἐστιν· εἴ τι γρύξομαι
ὧν σοι λέγω πλέον τι γαλαθηνοῦ μυός

23 Athenaeus 691b

μυρίσασα συγκατέκλεισεν ἀνθ᾽ αὑτῆς λάθρᾳ.

24 Athenaeus 370f

ἤδη δ᾽ ἧψε χύτραν ῥαφάνων.

19 I happened to be bringing cakes (?) from the farm to the feast, around twenty or so, I think, when I saw from above heaps of men in a circle.

20 He played the *aulos* with a mouthpiece of bronze and a throat . . .

Brief Fragment: (F 21) "gluttonous" (of a lamp).

PALAESTRA

The title could also mean "Wrestling-ground," and plays with places as titles are known, e.g., Kitchen *by Pherecrates or* Bath-house *by Timocles. But Palaestra is also the name of a prostitute in Plautus'* Rudens, *an appropriate enough name in fact. F 23 suggests that a female character anointed someone with scent and put him or her to bed, presumably with a male—a prostitute's client or the master of F 22?*

22 Here's master now. If I let slip anything of what I have been telling you, even as much as the squeak of a suckling mouse,

23 After anointing him/her with scent she put him/her to bed in her place.

24 Just now heated up a pot of cabbage.

Brief fragment: (F 25) "a little bit of liver."

ΠΑΣΙΦΑΗ

26 Bachmann's *Lexicon* p. 154.3.

νῦν οὖν γένοιτ᾽ ἀστεῖος οἰκῶν ἐν πόλει.

27 Pollux 10.11

καὶ ναὶ μὰ Δί᾽ ἄλλα σκευάρι᾽ οἰκητήρια

28 Orus *Orthography* fol. 280ᵛ 1

Μίνωαν; ἀλλ᾽ οἴμωζε σαυτὸν περιθέων.

PASIPHAE

This comedy competed with Aristophanes' Wealth in 388 (T 2) with unknown result. Pasiphae was the wife of Minos of Crete and mother of Ariadne and Phaedra. Her love for a bull required the inventor Daedalus to construct an artificial cow, so that she might assuage her passion. This resulted in the birth of the Minotaur, the monster imprisoned in the Labyrinth. Bacchylides 26 (early fifth century) tells the story, while Pasiphae was a character in Euripides' Cretans (438)—she gives an eloquent defence at F 472e. It seems odd that this story, with all sorts of potential for the comic poets, was rarely treated by them.

26 Now may he become refined by living in a city.

27 Yes, by Zeus, and other household vessels.

28 . . . Minoa? But run around and weep for yourself.[1]

[1] The citation mentions Minoa as an island, in which case the reference is likely to the port of Megara, but there were two cities on Crete called Minoa.

Brief fragment: (F 29) "sardis stone."

ΑΔΗΛΩΝ ΔΡΑΜΑΤΩΝ

30 Athenaeus 316c

ἔδω δ' ἐμαυτὸν † ὡς πουλύπους.

31 The Antiatticist p.86.1

ἐβίασέ μου τὴν γυναῖκα.

UNASSIGNED FRAGMENTS

30 I shall eat myself like an octopus.

31 He raped my wife.

Brief fragments: (F 32) "wife!," (F 33) "puppy dog."

DOUBTFUL FRAGMENTS

*The bare name "Alcaeus" is more likely than not to desig-
nate the lyric poet, but K.-A. list seven fragments (F 34–40)
as "dubia." I include four as possibly by the comic poet:*

*(F 34) "is deceiving you [sing.]," (F 35) "not to go around a
large teasel in one circle," (F 37) "wanderer," (F 38) "apple-
faced."*

ΑΛΚΙΜΕΝΗΣ

Testimonia

i *Suda* α 1284

Ἀλκιμένης· Μεγαρεύς, τραγικός. ἔστι δὲ καὶ ἕτερος Ἀλκιμένης, Ἀθηναῖος, κωμικός.

ii *IG* ii² 2325.46

Ἀλκιμε]νη[ς] I

ALCIMENES

This figure depends for his inclusion on identifying the comic poet known from the Suda *(T 1) with a restored name on the comic victors' list for the City Dionysia (T 2) as Alcimenes. The latter is found on that list between those of Magnes (victor in 472) and Euphronius (victor in 458). If this is Alcimenes, then he was active in the 460s.*

Testimonia

i Alcimenes, of Megara, a tragic poet [*TrGF* I.201]. There is another Alcimenes, of Athens, a comic poet.

ii [on the list of victors at the City Dionysia]

......]ne[s] 1

ΑΜΕΙΨΙΑΣ

Testimonia

i Suda α 1572

Ἀμειψίας· Ἀθηναῖος, κωμικός

ii P. Oxy. 2659 F 1 col. i.1

    Μοιχοί
    Σ]απφώ

AMEIPSIAS

Ameipsias belongs to the last quarter of the fifth century, his career probably extending into the early fourth century. Fixed dates are: D-423 (a second-place finish for his Connus *[T 5]) and D-414 (a first-place finish for* Revellers *[T 6]). His mention by Aristophanes in the opening scene of* Frogs *[T 7] shows that he was still active in the last decade of the fifth century, and his victory at the Lenaea [T 4] seems to have been rather later, since we find him in the company of poets from the last years of Old Comedy. We have here a poet of the second rank with a reasonably long career, but for whom not many play titles are known (probably six). The three choral titles (*Cottabus-players, Adulterers, Revellers*) suggest a robust and vigorous sort of comedy, very much in the traditional fashion of Old Comedy.*

Recent bibliography: P. Totaro, in Tessere *133–94.*

Testimonia

i Amepsias: of Athens, a comic poet.

ii [from a list of comic poets and their plays—the poet's name is lost]

   Adulterers/S]appho

iii *IG* ii² 2325.62

Ἀμ[ειψίας

iv *IG* ii² 2325.133

Ἀμ[ειψίας

v Hypothesis V *Clouds*

αἱ πρῶται Νεφέλαι ἐδιδάχθησαν ἐν ἄστει ἐπὶ
ἄρχοντος Ἰσάρχου, ὅτε Κρατῖνος μὲν ἐνίκα Πυτίνῃ,
Ἀμειψίας Κόννῳ.

vi Hypothesis I *Birds*

ἐδιδάχθη ἐπὶ Χαρίου ἄρχοντος διὰ Καλλιστράτου
ἐν ἄστει, ὃς ἦν δεύτερος τοῖς Ὄρνισι· πρῶτος Ἀμει-
ψίας Κωμασταῖς, τρίτος Φρύνιχος Μονοτρόπῳ.

vii Aristophanes *Frogs* 12–15

{ΞΑΝΘΙΑΣ.} τί δῆτ᾽ ἔδει με ταῦτα τὰ σκεύη φέρειν,
εἴπερ ποήσω μηδὲν ὧνπερ Φρύνιχος
εἴωθε ποιεῖν καὶ Λύκις κἀμειψίας
σκεύη φέρουσ᾽ ἑκαστότ᾽ ἐν κωμῳδίᾳ;

viii Com. adespot. K.-A. VIII F 244

οὐδ᾽ Ἀμειψίαν ὁρᾶτε πτωχὸν ὄντ᾽ ἐφ᾽ ὑμῖν;[1]

---

[1] ὑμῖν A, ἡμῖν DIH, ὑμῶν Σ.

iii [from the list of victors at the Dionysia—from the early 410s, quite likely the victory with *Revellers* in 414].

Am[eipsias

iv [from the list of victors at the Lenaea—from the late 400s or 390s]

Am[eipsias]

v The first version of *Clouds* was produced at the City Dionysia in the archonship of Isarchus [424/3], when Cratinus won with *Wine-Flask,* then Ameipsias with *Konnos.*

vi [*Birds*] was performed at the Dionysia in the archonship of Charias [415/4] through Callistratus. Aristophanes was second with *Birds.* Ameipsias was victorious with his *Revellers,* Phrynichus third with his *Hermit.*

vii (XANTHIAS) So why did I have to carry this baggage if I won't be doing any of the jokes that Phrynichus is used to doing, and Lycis and Ameipsias, people carrying baggage in every comedy?

viii And you people don't even notice a beggar Ameipsias among you?[1]

[1] Meineke, followed by K.-A., read the name as "Amynias," the *pseudoploutos* at *Wasps* 1267–74. The MS tradition is divided between "you" and "us."

ix

(a) *Clouds* 521–25

ὡς ὑμᾶς ἡγούμενος εἶναι θεατὰς δεξιοὺς
καὶ ταύτην σοφώτατ᾽ ἔχειν τῶν ἐμῶν κωμῳδιῶν
πρώτους ἠξίωσ᾽ ἀναγεῦσ᾽ ὑμᾶς, ἣ παρέσχε μοι
ἔργον πλεῖστον· εἶτ᾽ ἀνεχώρουν ὑπ᾽ ἀνδρῶν
    φορτικῶν
ἡττηθεὶς οὐκ ἄξιος ὤν. ταῦτ᾽ οὖν ὑμῖν μέμφομαι
τοῖς σοφοῖς, ὧν οὔνεκ᾽ ἐγὼ ταῦτ᾽ ἐπραγματευόμην.

(b) Σ *Clouds* 525

"ταῦτ᾽ οὖν ὑμῖν μέμφομαι", ἐπεὶ οὐ Κρατίνου, ἀλλ᾽
Ἀμειψίου δεύτερος ὤφθη.

ΑΠΟΚΟΤΤΑΒΙΖΟΝΤΕΣ

Cottabus *was a game played at drinking parties, and existed in two forms (see Rosen [CQ] 1989, 355–59). In one drinkers would flick the wine-lees at the bottom of their drinking cups at a plate suspended on a pole, the winner being the first to dislodge the plate. In the other form drinkers would flick the lees at saucers floating in a large pan, the aim being to sink the saucers with the wine-lees. Much of the evidence for this game and its variations is collected at Athenaeus 665d–68c. At* Acharnians *523–24 we have a stereotypical picture of an evening's carousal by*

ix

(a) And I thinking you were clever spectators and that this was the best of my comedies, deemed it right that you get first taste of the play, over which I took so much trouble. Then I went away defeated by inferior men, all very undeservedly. So I blame this on you clever people, for whom I spent all this effort.

(b) "And so I blame this on you": because he finished not just behind Cratinus, but also Ameipsias.

COTTABUS-PLAYERS

"drunken young cottabus players." This may give us a hint of the nature of the chorus in this play. It has also been suggested that Ameipsias' play dramatised the incident mentioned in Acharnians: *the theft of a Megarian prostitute as a drunken lark. F 4 has been taken to indicate that Dionysus was a character in the play. Athenaeus (666a) knows another meaning associated with* apocottabus *(drunken vomiting), but insists this is not a classical usage "unless you assume that the people in Ameipsias are vomiting." Speaker A of F 1 would seem to be a* kolax *figure, following B around in search of a free meal.*

Fragments

1 Athenaeus 307de

{A.} ἐγὼ δ᾽ ἰὼν πειράσομαι
εἰς τὴν ἀγορὰν ἔργον λαβεῖν. {B.} ἧττόν γ᾽ ἂν οὖν
νῆστις καθάπερ κεστρεὺς ἀκολουθήσαις ἐμοί.

2 Athenaeus 667e

ἡ Μανία, φέρ᾽ ὀξύβαφα καὶ κανθάρους
καὶ τὸν ποδανιπτῆρ᾽, ἐγχέασα θύδατος.

3 Photius ε 100

δυοῖν ὀβολοῖν ἔγχουσα καὶ ψιμύθιον

4 Athenaeus 426ef

ἐγὼ δὲ Διόνυσος πᾶσιν ὑμῖν εἰμι πέντε καὶ δύο.

ΚΑΤΕΣΘΙΩΝ

Fragment

6 Athenaeus 316b

Ἀμειψίας Κατεσθίοντι· δεῖ μέν, ὡς ἔοικε, πολλῶν που-
λύπων

---

1 Or as Ameipsias: "For a gobbler, it seems, we need a lot of oc-
topus."

Fragments

1 (A) I'm off to the marketplace now to try and get a job.

(B) Then you won't be hanging around me so much, as hungry as a grey mullet.[1]

---

[1] The *kestreus* (grey-mullet) was called *nestis* (hungry) as it was often caught with an empty stomach.

2 Mania, bring the vinegar saucers and the drinking cups and the water basin, and pour in some water.

3 Rouge and white lead at two obols.[1]

---

[1] Rouge on top of a white-lead base was a regular feature of women's makeup, to give the impression of robust health (Xenophon *Oeconomicus* 10.2).

4 For all of you I am Dionysus, five and two.

Brief fragment: (F 5) "pan-baked bread."

GOBBLER (?)

This play is known from this one fragment only, and it is possible to construe the citation with the word "gobbler" as part of the quotation. It might be safer to include F 6 among the unassigned fragments.

Fragment

6 Ameipsias in *Gobbler*:

It seems we need a lot of octopus.[1]

ΚΟΝΝΟΣ

This play finished ahead of Clouds *at the Dionysia of 423, and, like* Clouds, *seems to have had a theme of culture and teaching. Connus (PAA 581470), a musician associated with the lyre, is known as Socrates' teacher of music (Plato* Euthydemus 272c, Menexenus 236a). *A teacher of music and dance was a central character in Eupolis'* Goats *(424?), while Damon, music teacher of Pericles, seems to have been a character in a comedy by Platon (F 207). Could* Clouds' *poor showing partly be due to having two plays with similar themes at the same festival? Did one comic playwright get wind of what a rival was working on, and if allotted an earlier slot, take advantage of being first? A Connus is also mentioned at* Wasps 675, *where the phrase, "Connus vote," applied to the people of Athens, is explained by the scholiast as a play on "Connus brain," Connus not being terribly bright.*

It would seem from T 2 (below) that the chorus was composed of intellectuals (phrontistai) *and did not include Protagoras. This has led some to wonder whether all twenty-four choristers were individually named—but were there that many well-known sophists? As the title character was a musician and as F 7 implies the presence of a priest and F 10 the oracle-monger Diopeithes,* phrontistai *may have included experts of every field, not just*

CONNUS

sophists. If F 9 belongs to this play, it suggests that Socrates was a character, rather than a member of the chorus. His conspicuous behaviour at the battle of Delion in late 424 (Plato Symposium 221a) may have made him a good target for comedy at this time.

A Connus is attributed also to the comic poet Phrynichus, of which three fragments survive. As both Ameipsias and Phrynichus wrote a Revellers, some have concluded that these two poets collaborated or that Ameipsias produced plays by Phrynichus, but Connus may be an error in citation for Phrynichus' Cronus, while Revellers would have been a common enough comic title.

Is this Connus the same as the Connas mentioned in a number of passages in comedy, most notably Knights 534 and Cratinus F 349? The context in both places is that of a celebration, and Connas appears as an honoured victor in reduced circumstances and dying of thirst. There is much going on metatheatrically since it is the thirsty Cratinus who in Knights is compared to Connas and who also made fun of him.

Recent bibliography: A. H. Sommerstein, CQ 33 (1983) 480–81, R. P. Winnington-Ingram, in Gentili and Pretagostini, La Musica in Grecia (1988) 246–63; C. Carey, in Rivals 420–23.

THE POETS OF OLD COMEDY

Testimonia

i See T 5 (above).

ii Athenaeus 218c

ἐν οὖν τούτῳ τῷ δράματι Εὔπολις τὸν Πρωταγόραν ὡς
ἐπιδημοῦντα εἰσάγει, Ἀμειψίας δ' ἐν τῷ Κόννῳ δύο
πρότερον ἔτεσιν διδαχθέντι οὐ καταριθμεῖ αὐτὸν ἐν τῷ
τῶν φροντιστῶν χορῷ. δῆλον οὖν ὡς μεταξὺ τούτων
τῶν χρόνων παραγέγονεν.

Fragments

7 Athenaeus 368e

ἐντευθενὶ δίδοται μάλισθ' ἱερώσυνα,
κωλῆ, τὸ πλευρόν, ἡμίκραιρ' ἀριστερά.

8 Athenaeus 327d

ὀρφῷσι σελαχίοις τε καὶ φάγροις βορά.

9 Diogenes Laertius 2.27–28

Σώκρατες ἀνδρῶν βέλτιστ' ὀλίγων, πολλῶν δὲ
    ματαιόταθ', ἥκεις
καὶ σὺ πρὸς ἡμᾶς; καρτερικός γ' εἶ. πόθεν ἄν σοι
    χλαῖνα γένοιτο;
τουτὶ τὸ κακὸν τῶν σκυτοτόμων κατ' ἐπήρειαν
    γεγένηται.

AMEIPSIAS

Testimonia

i See T 5 (above).

ii In this play [*Spongers*] Eupolis brings Protagoras on as
a visitor, but Ameipsias in *Connus*, which was produced
two years earlier, does not include him among the chorus
of intellectuals. It is clear that he arrived between these
two occasions.

Fragments

7 And from this beast the priest's portion is offered:
haunch, ribs, left half of the head.

8 As food for sea perch, rays, and sea bream.

9 Socrates, best of men when the company is few, but
when many the most foolish, have you also come to us?
You *are* adventurous. But where would you get a cloak?

Your poor condition is an insult to shoemakers every-
where.

οὗτος μέντοι πεινῶν οὕτως οὐπώποτ' ἔτλη
κολακεῦσαι.

10 Σ Aristophanes *Birds* 988

ὥστε ποιοῦντες χρησμοὺς αὐτοὶ
διδόασ' ᾄδειν
Διοπείθει τῷ παραμαινομένῳ.

ΚΩΜΑΣΤΑΙ

ΜΟΙΧΟΙ

This man, however, for all his hunger has never stooped to sponging a meal.[1]

[1] Diogenes Laertius attributes this fragment only to Ameipsias, and it has been assigned by many to this play. It could just as easily have come from *Revellers*. Jokes at Socrates seem to turn on an antithesis: praise, followed by derision for his unworldly way of life (cf. Eupolis F 386, 395).

10 And so they make these oracles up themselves, then give them to that madman Diopeithes to sing.[1]

[1] Comedy has several references to an inspired (over-inspired?) prophet named Diopeithes (*PAA* 363105), who in the 430s proposed a law against atheistic beliefs (Plutarch *Pericles* 32).

Brief fragment: (F 11) "ladder."

REVELLERS

This play is known only from the hypothesis to Birds *(T 6), and as Phrynichus also wrote a* Revellers *(with attested fragments), it has been suggested that Ameipsias produced this play for him or that the authorship became confused in antiquity.*

ADULTERERS

Two plays of this title are known from later Middle Comedy, as well as Alcaeus' Sisters *in Adultery. If the title refers to the chorus, we might compare the chorus in Eupolis'* Spongers, *who in F 172 outline their way of life.*

Fragment

12 *Suda* α 2142

καὶ σὺ μὲν < > ἦλθες καββαλὼν τριώβολον,
καί τι που κἀμαρτύρησας ψεῦδος, ὥστ᾽ ἀνεψύχης.

ΣΑΠΦΩ

ΣΦΕΝΔΟΝΗ

Fragment

12 And you went away, putting down three obols and giv-
ing some false statement, and just chilled out.[1]

[1] A professional *moichos* in action? Compare the similar in-
structions at *Clouds* 1079–82.

*Brief fragments: (F 13) "I/they opened," (F 14) "red-ochre
mine."*

SAPPHO

Cratinus wrote a comedy called Archilochuses, *Teleclides
one called* Hesiods, *and Platon a play named* Cinesias, *af-
ter the contemporary dithyrambic poet and familiar target
of Old Comedy. In view of the gender theme that does de-
velop in late fifth-century comedy, we would like to know
whether* Sappho *was essentially a literary comedy or a
"women's play."*

Brief fragment: (F 15) "more sluggish."

SLING

The meaning of the title is not immediately obvious.
Sphendone *is used of the sling used by light-armed troops,
and also of the sling bolts that they fired. It describes
also anything that encircles, such as "hoop," bandage," or
"headband." Could it also be a hetaera name, "she who en-
circles"? F 16 shows that the play was produced after the
siege of Plataea (431–427).*

Fragments

16 Pollux 10.144

τὸ μὲν δόρυ
μετὰ τῆς ἐπιχάλκου πρὸς Πλαταιαῖς ἀπέβαλεν.

17 Athenaeus 446d

λαγὸν ταράξας πῖθι τὸν θαλάσσιον.

18 Athenaeus 270f

κοὐδείς σοὐστὶν τῶν πλουτούντων, μὰ τὸν
  Ἥφαιστον, προσόμοιος,
καλλιτράπεζος καὶ βουλόμενος λιπαρὸν ψωμὸν
  καταπίνειν

ΑΔΗΛΩΝ ΔΡΑΜΑΤΩΝ

21 Athenaeus 783e

            {Α.} αὔλει μοι μέλος,
σὺ δ᾽ ᾆδε πρὸς τήνδ᾽· ἐκπίομαι δ᾽ ἐγὼ τέως.
{Β.} αὔλει σύ, καὶ <σὺ> τὴν ἄμυστιν λάμβανε.
"οὐ χρὴ πόλλ᾽ ἔχειν θνητὸν ἄνθρωπον,
ἀλλ᾽ ἐρᾶν καὶ κατεσθίειν· σὺ δὲ κάρτα φείδῃ."

Fragments

16 At Plataea he threw his spear away along his bronze ‹shield›.[1]

[1] The most famous man in comedy to abandon his shield is Cleonymus. Was he one of the eighty Athenians left at Plataea on garrison duty in 430 (Thucydides 2.78.3), and did he flee with the two hundred or so Plataeans who escaped to Athens in 427, perhaps abandoning his weapons en route? The words "threw away" (*apoballein*) and "bronze" (*epichalkon*) are used of Cleonymus at *Wasps* 18–19.

17 Stir in some sea slug and drink.[1]

[1] As sea slug (lit. "sea hare") was a known poison, this may just be a comic way of saying "drop dead!" Compare Heracles' instructions on how to get to Hades at *Frogs* 120–34.

18 Of all rich men there is not one like you, no by Hephaestus, keeping a clean table and ready to gulp down a gleaming morsel of bread.

Brief fragments: (F 19) "the stake at dice," (F 20) water for the hands."

UNASSIGNED FRAGMENTS

21 (A) ‹*Aulos*-girl›, play me a tune, and you [sing.] sing along with her while I drink up.
  (B) Play then, and you take up the goblet:

"A mortal man does not need many things, to make love and to eat, but you are really stingy."

22 Σ Aristophanes *Wasps* 1169

εἰ μὴ θανοῦσιν ἔστι τις τιμὴ ‹κάτω›,
καταβῶμεν.

μὲν codd., μὴ Meineke.

23 Athenaeus 8e

ἔρρ’ ἐς κόρακας, μονοφάγε καὶ τοιχωρύχε.

24 Athenaeus 62ef

οὐ σχῖνος οὐδ’ ἀσφάραγος, οὐ δάφνης κλάδοι

25 Pollux 2.200

ἐπ’ αὐτὸν ἥκεις τὸν βατῆρα τῆς θύρας.

26 Σ Aristophanes *Wealth* 883

δακτύλιον δὲ τὸν λεγόμενον φαρμακίτην. Εὔπολις
Βάπταις μέμνηται. ὁ δ’ Εὔδαμος φαρμακοπώλης, καὶ
Ἀμειψίας, ἢ χρυσοπώλης, τετελεσμένους δακτυλίους
πωλῶν.

27 *Life of Aristophanes* (Koster XXVIII.7–10)

εὐλαβὴς δὲ σφόδρα γενόμενος τὴν ἀρχὴν ἄλλως τε
καὶ εὐφυὴς τὰ μὲν πρῶτα διὰ Καλλιστράτου καὶ
Φιλωνίδου καθίει δράματα· διὸ καὶ ἔσκωπτον αὐτὸν

22 If there is some respect ‹below› for those who are not dead, then let us go down.[1]

[1] The text is uncertain, and the passage is quoted to explain a reference to a man named Lycon.

23 Go to hell, you selfish crook.

24 No mastic or asparagus, no branches of laurel

25 You are come to the very threshold of the door.[1]

[1] A proverb for arriving at the truth of the matter ("hit the nail on the head").

26 ‹He means› a ring with magical properties. Eupolis mentions him [Eudamus] in *Dyers* [F 96]. Eudamus was a seller of drugs and potions, and Ameipsias, or a gold merchant who sold rings with magical powers.

27 At the start of his career being especially cautious as well as especially talented, he [Aristophanes] produced his first plays through Callistratus and Philonides. That is

Ἀριστώνυμος καὶ Ἀμειψίας "τετράδι" λέγοντες "γεγο-
νέναι" κατὰ τὴν παροιμίαν ⟨ὡς⟩ ἄλλοις πονοῦντα.

28 Photius (b, z) α 796

ἄκοπος ἀνήρ

why Aristonymus [F 3] and Ameipsias would make fun of him, saying that he was "born on the fourth," proverbial of those who laboured for others.

28 A trouble-free man.

Brief fragments: (F 29) "I will bring up," (F 30) "I have come up," (F 31) "you, stand up," (F 32) "to be witless," (F 33) "he has had his figs plucked," (F 34) "Baucus dance," (F 35) "newly married," (F 36) "marjoram," (F 37) "nod one's eyebrows," (F 38) "darkness," (F 39) "bag for bedclothes."

ΑΠΟΛΛΟΦΑΝΗΣ

Testimonia

i *Suda* α 3409

Ἀπολλοφάνης, Ἀθηναῖος, κωμικὸς ἀρχαῖος. δράματα αὐτοῦ Δάλις, Ἰφιγέρων, Κρῆτες, Δανάη, Κένταυροι.

ii P. Oxy. 2659 F 1 col. i.5 [list of comic poets and their plays]

Ἀπολ]λοφάνους/Δά]λις/Κρ]ῆτες

iii *IG* ii² 2325.132

Ἀπο[λλοφάνη]ς I

iv Lysias F 195 Carey

οὐ μετὰ τούτου ποτὲ Ἀπολλοφάνης καὶ Μυσταλίδης καὶ Λυσίθεος συνειστιῶντο, μίαν ἡμέραν ταξάμενοι τῶν ἀποφράδων, ἀντὶ δὲ νουμηνιαστῶν κακοδαιμονιστὰς σφίσιν αὐτοῖς τοὔνομα θέμενοι;

---

1 Athenaeus (551f–52b) is quoting a lost speech of Lysias for this attack on Cinesias. Neither identifies this Apollophanes with

APOLLOPHANES

*Apollophanes appears on the Lenaean victors' list (T 3)
with other poets of the last generation (Theopompus, Nico-
phon, etc.). If he is the man mentioned by Lysias (T 4), this
would also suggest a date around 400 or in the 390s.*

Testimonia

i Apollophanes, of Athens, poet of Old Comedy. His plays
are *Dalis, Mighty Old Man, Cretans, Danae, Centaurs.*

ii [on a second-century AD papyrus listing comic poets
and their plays]

Apol]lophanes'/*Da*]*lis*/*Cr*]*etans*

iii [from the list of victors at the Lenaea]

Apo[llophane]s 1

iv Was it not with him [Cinesias] that Apollophanes and
Mystalides and Lysitheus often had dinner together, se-
lecting a day from those forbidden, and instead of "New-
Mooners" [*noumeniastai*] giving themselves the name of
"Evil-Spiriters" [*kakodaimonistai*]?[1]

the comic poet, but the name is not common at this time, and in
the previous line Lysias equates their behaviour with what comic
poets get away with saying every year in their plays.

83

THE POETS OF OLD COMEDY

Fragments

ΔΑΛΙΣ

1 Athenaeus 467f

{A.} οὑτοσὶ δῖνος. {B.} τί δῖνος; {A.} καὶ καλαθίσκος
οὑτοσί.

2 Athenaeus 114f

κρίνον καλούμενον καὶ σχῆμά τι χορικῆς ὀρχήσεως
παρ᾽ Ἀπολλοφάνει ἐν Δαλίδι.

ΔΑΝΑΗ

ΙΦΙΓΕΡΩΝ

APOLLOPHANES

Fragments

DALIS

Hesychius records that dalidas *means "betrothed women" —cf. the rare word* talis *with that meaning at Sophocles* Antigone *629. Diodorus of Sicily mentions Dalis as a city in far-distant Pancheatis, while Meineke thought it the proper name of a woman (a hetaera?).*

1 (A) This is a *dinos*? (B) A *dinos*? How so?
   (A) And this is a basket.[1]

   [1] Athenaeus cites this fragment to illustrate that *dinos* (whirl, eddy) is also the name of a dance. Elsewhere at 630a Athenaeus refers to the basket dance (*kalathiskos*). The joke on two meanings of *dinos* reminds one of a running gag in *Clouds*, and perhaps also the dancing lesson in Eupolis' *Goats* (F 18).

2 There is also a form of choral dance called "the lily," so Apollophanes in *Dalis*.

DANAE

Sannyrion and Eubulus also wrote comedies called Danae. *The lament of Danae was the subject of a famous poem by Simonides, and she with her infant son Perseus were characters in Aeschylus' satyr drama* Net-Haulers.

MIGHTY OLD MAN

A comedy of this name is also attributed to Strattis. The Aristophanic scholiast, citing F 3, assigns it to Apolloph-

3 Σ Aristophanes *Peace* 542

κύαθον λάβοιμι τοῖς ὑπωπίοις.

4 Harpocration 9.9

ἀδελφίζειν

ΚΕΝΤΑΥΡΟΙ

ΚΡΗΤΕΣ

APOLLOPHANES

anes. Harpocration (on F 4) identifies the play as Mighty
Old Man *by Strattis or Apollophanes, while the Antiatticist
assigns the play to Strattis. Do we have only one comedy
whose authorship is in question or two plays with the same
unusual title?*

3 I would get a ladle for my black eyes.[1]

   [1] Heated bronze implements such as ladles were used to treat
bruises and swellings.

4 To keep calling him "brother."

CENTAURS

Aristophanes wrote an early play called Dramas *or the*
Centaur, *Cratinus a comedy called* Chirons, *while the
Chiron vase reflects an Old Comedy with that character as
a central figure. Of Old Comic poets Nicochares also wrote
a* Centaurs.

CRETANS

*Plays with Cretan themes and Cretan characters are com-
mon in tragedy (Euripides'* Hippolytus *plays,* Cretan
Women, Theseus, *and* Cretans; *Sophocles'* Phaedra; *an*
Aerope *by Agathon and one by Carcinus). In comedy Aris-
tophanes wrote a* Daedalus, *and Nicochares a* Cretans.
*The speaker of F 5 is perhaps Minos the ruler of Crete or a
figure representing the People as in* Knights *and Eupolis'*
Maricas, *or possibly an anthropomorphised animal—cf.
Eupolis* Goats *F 13.*

5 Athenaeus 75c

πρώτιστα δὲ
τῶν μυρρινῶν ἐπὶ τὴν τράπεζαν βούλομαι,
ἃς διαμασῶμ᾽ ὅταν τι βουλεύειν δέῃ,
†τὰς δὲ φιβάλεως† τὰς πάνυ καλὰς στεφανωτρίδας.

6 Photius (Sᶻ) α 3404

Ἀσκληπιός, Κύννειος, Ἀφρόδιτος, Τύχων

7 Athenaeus 485e

καὶ λεπαστά μ᾽ ἀδύοινος εὐφρανεῖ δι᾽ ἁμέρας.

ΑΔΗΛΩΝ ΔΡΑΜΑΤΩΝ

9 Aelian *Nature of Animals* 6.51

δεῖ δὲ καὶ μῦθον τῷδε τῷ ζῴῳ ἐπᾷσαί με ὅνπερ οὖν
ἀκούσας οἶδα, ὡς ἂν μὴ δοκοίην ἀμαθῶς ἔχειν αὐτοῦ.
τὸν Προμηθέα κλέψαι τὸ πῦρ ἡ φήμη φησί, καὶ τὸν
Δία ἀγανακτῆσαι ὁ μῦθος λέγει καὶ τοῖς καταμηνύ-
σασι τὴν κλοπὴν δοῦναι φάρμακον γήρως ἀμυντή-
ριον. τοῦτο οὖν ἐπὶ ὄνῳ θεῖναι τοὺς λαβόντας πέπυ-
σμαι. καὶ τὸν μὲν προϊέναι τὸ ἄχθος φέροντα, εἶναι δὲ
ὥραν θέρειον, καὶ διψῶντα τὸν ὄνον ἐπί τινα κρήνην
κατὰ τὴν τοῦ ποτοῦ χρείαν ἐλθεῖν. τὸν οὖν ὄφιν τὸν
φυλάττοντα ἀναστέλλειν αὐτὸν καὶ ἀπελαύνειν, καὶ

APOLLOPHANES

5 And very first of all I want on the table some of those myrtle shoots which I may chew on whenever we must consider some matter in council, and some Phibalean . . . which makes such good garlands.

6 Asclepius, Cynneius, Aphroditus, Tychon.[1]

[1] Photius quotes this and other comic passages for the foreign gods found in Old Comedy. We may cite also the Triballian in the last scene of *Birds,* the new deities in Aristophanes *Heroes,* and Cotyto in Eupolis' *Dyers.*

7 And sweet wine in a limpet cup will cheer me all day long.[1]

[1] The dialect of this fragment is Doric, the speaker likely one of the Cretans of the title.

Brief fragment: (F 8) "Mysicarphes."

UNASSIGNED FRAGMENTS

9 I must recite the story about this creature [the snake called the *dipsas*] which I know from hearing it told, so that it might not seem that I am ignorant of it. The story goes that Prometheus stole fire, and it is said that Zeus was annoyed and rewarded those who had given information about the theft with a drug that acted as an antidote to old age. I am told that those who received it put it upon an ass and that the ass went on its way carrying this load on its back. It was summertime and the ass, being thirsty, came to a spring in need of a drink. The snake that was guarding the spring tried to force it back and drive it away, and

ἐκεῖνον στρεβλούμενον μισθόν οἱ τῆς φιλοτησίας δοῦναι ὅπερ οὖν ἔτυχε φέρων φάρμακον. οὐκοῦν ἀντί-δοσις γίνεται, καὶ ὃ μὲν πίνει, ὃ δὲ τὸ γῆρας ἀπο-δύεται, προσεπιλαβὼν ὡς λόγος τὸ τοῦ ὄνου δίψος. τί οὖν; ἐγὼ τοῦ μύθου ποιητής; ἀλλ' οὐκ ἂν εἴποιμι, ἐπεὶ καὶ πρὸ ἐμοῦ Σοφοκλῆς ὁ τῆς τραγῳδίας ποιητὴς καὶ Δεινόλοχος ὁ ἀνταγωνιστὴς Ἐπιχάρμου καὶ Ἴβυκος ὁ Ῥηγῖνος καὶ Ἀριστίας καὶ Ἀπολλοφάνης ποιηταὶ κωμῳδίας ᾄδουσιν αὐτόν.

the ass in its misery gave it as the price of a long draught the drug that it happened to be carrying. And so they made a deal—the ass got its drink, and the snake sloughed off its old age, receiving as well (so the story goes) the thirst of the ass. Well then, am I the author of that story? I would deny it, since before me Sophocles the tragic poet, and Dinolochus the rival of Epicharmus, and Ibycus of Rhegium, and Aristias and Apollophanes the comic poets have all related it.[1]

[1] Aristophanes wrote a comedy called *Geras* (Old Age), and if "Apollophanes" is an error for "Aristophanes," then this story might have formed part of the plot for *Old Age*.

Brief fragment: (F 10) "singed."

ΑΡΚΕΣΙΛΑΟΣ

Testimonium

i Diogenes Laertius 4.45

γεγόνασι δὲ καὶ τρεῖς Ἀρκεσίλαοι· ποιητὴς ἀρχαίας
κωμῳδίας, ἄλλος ἐλεγείας, ἕτερος ἀγλαματοποιός.

Fragment

1 Clement of Alexandria *Miscellanies* 7.24.5

τί δὲ καὶ θαυμαστὸν, εἰ ὁ μῦς, φησὶν ὁ Βίων, τὸν
θύλακον διέτραγεν, οὐχ εὑρὼν ὅ τι φάγῃ; τοῦτο γὰρ
ἦν θαυμαστόν, εἰ, ὥσπερ Ἀρκεσίλαος παίζων ἐνεχεί-
ρει, τὸν μῦν ὁ θύλαξ κατέφαγεν.

ARCESILAUS

Testimonium

i There have been three other men named Arcesilaus: one a poet of Old Comedy, another of elegiac poetry, and another a sculptor.

Fragment

1 Bion said [F 31], "Why is it surprising if a mouse not finding anything to eat, chewed up a sack? Now, as Arcesilaus ventured in jest, if the sack ate the mouse, that would be surprising."[1]

[1] A mouse chewing through a sack was considered a portent of ill omen. The Arcesilaus to whom Clement attributes this bon mot, is usually identified with the 3rd-c. BC philosopher.

ΑΡΧΙΠΠΟΣ

One of the lesser lights of the very late fifth century and early fourth, Archippus is credited with a victory (T 1) in the 91st Olympiad (415–412), but the play titles and fragments that we possess suggest a career closer to 400 and into the next century. Fishes *(F 27) refers to "Euclides the former archon." As he was archon in 403/2,* Fishes *at the earliest must date from 401. The comedy* Rhinon *was focussed on a political player in the transition from oligarchy to democracy in late 403. Again the earliest date lies around 400. His comedies,* Heracles' Marriage *and* Amphitryon, *seem to be burlesques of myth, a comic subgenre that was at its height in the early fourth century.*

It seems odd that Archippus would win a victory, perhaps his only victory, around 415 and then vanish for ten years or so. Much could be explained by MacDowell's theory that Archippus, along with two other comic poets (Aristomenes and Cephisodorus), were among those who fled Athens after being implicated in the profanation of the Mysteries in 415 (T 6). They would have returned to Athens either at the end of the War (405/4) or after the fall of the Thirty (404/3). If he is also the man known from Lysias (T 7–10), he was an active combatant in the law courts in the 390s.

ARCHIPPUS

*Of interest also is his connection with Aristophanes.
The* Life of Aristophanes *(T 4) records that four of Aris-
tophanes' plays were attributed to Archippus. We know
that Aristophanes (and other poets of Old Comedy) would
produce their plays through others—*Frogs *(405), for in-
stance, was produced through Philonides, himself known
as a comic poet. Did Aristophanes in the later part of his
career entrust four of his plays to Archippus and thus con-
fuse the scholars of Alexandria?*

*As far as we can gather from six play titles and sixty-one
fragments, he seems to have been a comic poet of the Old
style. F 14 and 16 bring the Athenian political system into
the comedy.* Rhinon *is a comedy based around a real politi-
cal figure—cf. Platon's* Cleophon *or* Hyperbolos*. We find
jokes against real people of the day (Hermaeus the fish
seller at F 23, Anytus at F 31, Alcibiades the younger at
F 48), and a scene from* Fishes *featured the gourmand
Melanthius brought on stage, trussed up to become food
for the fishes. T 5 tells us that Archippus was made fun of
himself for his comic wordplay, a judgement confirmed in*
Fishes *by his use of names that fit both the marine and the
human world (F 15–19, 25, 27).*

*In 1993 a papyrus known as the "Comoedia Dukiana"
(PCG VIII 1146) presented fifty lines of what was identi-*

Testimonia

i *Suda* α 4115

Ἄρχιππος, Ἀθηναῖος, κωμικὸς ἀρχαῖος, ἐνίκησεν ἅπαξ ἐπὶ τῆς ϙα´ Ὀλυμπιάδος.

ii *IG* ii² 2325.70

Ἄρχ]ι[ππος Ι

iii P. Oxy. 2659 F 1 col. ii.1

Ἀρχίπ[που
  Ἀμφι[τρύων
  Ἡρακλ[ῆς γαμῶν
  Ῥείνω[ν

iv *Life of Aristophanes* (Koster XXVIII 66–67)

ἔγραψε δὲ δράματα μδ´, ὧν ἀντιλέγεται δ´ ὡς οὐκ ὄντα αὐτοῦ· ἔστι δὲ ταῦτα Ποίησις, Ναυαγός, Νῆσοι, Νίοβος, ἅ τινες ἔφασαν εἶναι τοῦ Ἀρχίππου.

fied by Csapo as a scene from Archippus' Fishes. *Here two men are engaged first in a praise of the* silouros *(sheat fish) and then a lesson on how properly to cook the creature. If this is a fragment of Archippus' play, this would raise our knowledge of the comedy to about eighty lines and make it one of the best preserved of the lost plays of Old Comedy. See Comic Papyri.*

Recent bibliography: M. Fariola, Aevum (ant.) 12 (1999) 17–59; J. Wilkins, in Rivals 345–47; Storey & Allan 207–8; Rothwell 126–28, 188–91.

Testimonia

i Archippus, of Athens, poet of Old Comedy. He won a single victory in the 91st Olympiad [415–412].

ii [In a list of comic victors at the Dionysia, following the names of Nicophon, Theopompus, and Cephisodorus]

Arch]i[ppus[1]

[1] Lys]i[ppus is also possible here.

iii [on a second-century AD papyrus listing comic poets and their plays]

Archip[pus/*Amphitryon*/*Heracles' Marriage*/*Rhinon*.

iv He [Aristophanes] wrote forty-four plays, of which four are rejected as not being his. These are *Poetry*, [*Dionysus*] *Shipwrecked*, *Islands*, and *Niobus*, which some say are by Archippus.

v Σ Aristophanes *Wasps* 481a

τῶν τριχοινίκων ἐπῶν· ἀντὶ τοῦ τῶν εὐτελῶν. τὰ τοι-
αῦτα παρὰ τὰς φωνὰς παίζει, φορτικοῦ ὄντος ἀγοραί-
οις, ἐφ᾽ οἷς μάλιστα τῶν ποιητῶν σκώπτουσιν Ἄρ-
χιππον.

vi Andocides 1.13

τούσδε Ἀνδρόμαχος ἐμήνυσεν· Ἀλκιβιάδην, Νικίδην,
Ἀρχεβιάδην, Ἄρχιππον, Διογένην, Πολύστρατον,
Ἀριστομένη, Οἰωνίαν, Παναίτιον.

vii [Lysias] 6.11–12

καὶ ἔλαχεν Ἀνδοκίδης ⟨ὢν⟩ καὶ πεποιηκὼς ἃ οὗτος
πεποίηκε περὶ τοὺς θεοὺς καὶ (ἵνα μᾶλλον προσέχητε
τὸν νοῦν) φάσκων τὸν Ἄρχιππον ἀσεβεῖν περὶ τὸν
Ἑρμῆν τὸν αὐτοῦ πατρῷον. ὁ δὲ Ἄρχιππος ἠντεδίκει
ἦ μὴν τὸν Ἑρμῆν ὑγιᾶ τε καὶ ὅλον εἶναι, καὶ μηδὲν
παθεῖν ὧνπερ οἱ ἄλλοι Ἑρμαῖ· ὅμως μέντοι ἵνα μὴ
ὑπὸ τούτου τοιούτου ὄντος πράγματ᾽ ἔχοι, δοὺς ἀργύ-
ριον ἀπηλλάγη.

viii Lysias fr. 278 (Carey), *Against Tisis*

ἂν δὲ ὑπὲρ ἑτέρου λέγῃς, καὶ τοῦτο ἐπισημαίνεσθαι
δεῖ, ὥσπερ πεποίηκε Λυσίας λέγων· "ἐπιτήδειός μοί
ἐστιν Ἄρχιππος οὑτοσί, ὦ ⟨ἄνδρες⟩ δικασταί".

v "Our three-bushel words": instead of "down-to-earth." This is the sort of wordplays he makes, putting vulgar words with commonplace things, for which they especially attack Archippus.

vi Andromachus named the following men [for participation in the "celebration" of the Mysteries]: Alcibiades, Nicides, Meletus, Archebiades, Archippus, Diogenes, Polystratus, Aristomenes, Oionias, Panaitius.

A second list of participants at 1.15 includes Cephisodorus. Comic poets named Archippus, Aristomenes, and Cephisodorus are all known to have been active in the late fifth century, and it is an attractive supposition that a comic poet would have been the sort likely to have been involved in the parody of a solemn ceremony.

vii Even though he was Andocides and had committed the actions that he had against the gods, he lodged his formal complaint and claimed—please pay attention here— that Archippus was guilty of sacrilege against his own household Herm. Archippus made a formal counterclaim that his Herm had been whole and intact and had suffered none of the indignities that the other Herms had. However, so that he might have no further problems from a man such as this, he got rid of him by paying him off.

viii If you are speaking on behalf of someone else, you should indicate this, as Lysias has done in his speech: "This Archippus here is a friend of mine, men of the jury."

ix Dionysius of Halicarnassus *Demosthenes* 11 = Lysias fr. 279 (Carey), *Against Tisis*

Ἄρχιππος γὰρ οὑτοσί, ὦ Ἀθηναῖοι, ἀπεδύσατο εἰς τὴν αὐτὴν παλαίστραν, οὗπερ καὶ Τεῖσις ὁ φεύγων τὴν δίκην. ὀργῆς δὲ γενομένης ἐς σκώμματά τε αὐτοῖς καὶ ἀντιλογίαν καὶ ἔχθραν καὶ λοιδορίαν κατέστησαν
. . .

x P. Oxy. 2537, Verso 28–30 = Lysias fr. 308 (Carey)

παρακατα]θήκης
. . . . παρακαταθή]κην [. . . .] Ἀρχίππου ἀπαιτοῦ-
ντος . . . .] κότα [. . . .]

ΑΜΦΙΤΡΥΩΝ

Fragments

1 Athenaeus 95e

καὶ ταῦτ' ἔχων τὸ ῥύγχος οὑτωσὶ μακρόν.

ix This Archippus here, men of Athens, was a member of the same wrestling ground as Tisis, the defendant in this case. A quarrel broke out between them and they descended to jokes at one another, to argument, genuine hostility, and open insults.

The rest of the fragment tells how Tisis, a hotheaded young man, pretended to reconcile with Archippus, but after inviting him for drinks, had him bound and flogged until cooler heads prevailed. Archippus' brothers rescued him and displayed him publicly in the agora, to the great indignation of onlookers.

x [from a papyrus containing summaries of the speeches of Lysias]

deposit . . . . Archippus asking for his deposit back

AMPHITRYON

The most famous comic version of this story is in Plautus' Roman comedy of the same name (early second century). It is often thought that Platon's Long Night *was an early fourth-century comedy on the same theme. F 1, 2, and 4 refer to a "second Amphitryon," perhaps the only version that survived into the Alexandrian period.*

Recent bibliography: C. Pace, SemRom *1 (1998) 89–109.*

Fragments

1 And he, with a snout this long.

2 Athenaeus 426b

τίς ἐκέρασε σφῶν, ὦ κακόδαιμον, ἴσον ἴσῳ;

ΗΡΑΚΛΗΣ ΓΑΜΩΝ

Fragments

8 Pollux 9.70

ἀνδρῶν ἄριστος καὶ μάλιστ᾽ ἐμοὶ ξένος
ἀτὰρ παρ᾽ ἐμοί γ᾽ ὢν εἶχεν οὐδὲ σύμβολον

9 Photius (b, z) α 851

τὸ πῦρ πολὺ λίαν· ὕπαγε τὰς ἀκροβελίδας

10 Athenaeus 656b

     ταδὶ δ᾽ ἅμα χοι-
ρων ἀκροκώλια μικρῶν,
ταύρου τ᾽ αὐξίκερω φλογίδες,
αἱ δολιχαί τε κάπρου φλογίδες

11 Athenaeus 640f

ἰτρίοις ἐπιφορήμασι τ᾽ ἄλλοις γέμουσα

2 Which of them, you poor fellow, mixed it half and half?[1]

[1] "Half and half" refers to mixing water and wine in equal parts; this would be quite a strong drink.

Brief fragments: (F 3) "pick up," (F 4) "leather bag," (F 5) "attacked from behind," (F 6) "O dog," (F 7) "vessel."

HERACLES' MARRIAGE

The best-known marriage of Heracles is that with Hebe, daughter of Zeus, after his deification and entry into Olympus. Epicharmus wrote a comedy with this title. Mythological burlesques about divine births and marriages are not uncommon in Old and Middle Comedy (see Alcaeus' Sacred Marriage), *nor is Heracles a rare figure in comedy (e.g., Nicochares'* Marriage of Heracles, Heracles as choregos; Man-Heracles *by Pherecrates;* Heracles *by Philyllius, as well as appearing in* Birds *and* Frogs).

Fragments

8 Best of men and my special guest-friend—yet when he stayed with me he didn't even have a cent.

9 The fire is much too hot; take away the spit-points.

10 Here all together are trotters of young pigs, steaks from a bull calf, and long steaks of boar.

11 ⟨A table⟩ groaning with cakes and other desserts.

12 Athenaeus 307d

νήστεις κεστρέας, κεφάλους

ΙΧΘΥΕΣ

Fragments

14 Harpocration p. 231.13

αἱρουμένους τε πραγμάτων ἐπιστάτας
ἀποδοκιμάζειν, ⟨εἶτα δοκιμάζειν⟩ πάλιν.
ἦν οὖν ποιῶμεν ταῦτα, κίνδυνος λαθεῖν
ἀπαξάπαντας γενομένους παλιναιρέτους.

12 Starving mullets, grey mullets.

Brief fragment: (F 13) "a saltcellar made of boxwood."

FISHES

The best-known comedy by Archippus, it seems to have re-
sembled Birds *(414) by Aristophanes—the verbal plays in*
F 27 on fish names and human names recall a similar play
at Birds *1290ff., the cursing of Hermaeus (F 23) fulfils the*
threat at Philocrates made by the chorus at Birds *1084–87,*
and F 27 reveals both a conflict and a formal treaty be-
tween humans and fishes. The reference in F 27 to "Eu-
cleides the former archon" implies a date after 402. Anytus
(F 31) was one of the accusers of Socrates in 399. F 28 sug-
gests that in one scene the gluttonous tragic poet Melan-
thius (PAA 638275, TrGF 23) was trussed up and handed
over to the fishes to be consumed by them. If actually
staged, this scene will have resembled the packing of the in-
former Nicarchus as a pot at Acharnians *908–28.*

Fragments

14 When electing our political leaders to reject them
first, ⟨then approve⟩ them afterwards. So if we keep on
doing this, there is a real danger that without realizing it
they all become "second catch."

15 Stephanus of Byzantium p. 196.21

{A.} τί λέγεις συ; μάντεις εἰσί γὰρ θαλάττιοι;
{B.} γαλεοί γε, πάντων μάντεων φοφώτατοι.

16 Athenaeus 322a

ἐκήρυξεν βόαξ
σάλπης δ' ἐσάλπιγξ' ἔπτ' ὀβόλους μισθὸν φέρων

17 Athenaeus 315bc

ἱερεὺς γὰρ ἦλθ' αὐτοῖσιν ὀρφώς του θεῶν.

18 Athenaeus 328a

ἱερεὺς Ἀφροδίτης χρύσοφρυς Κυθηρίας

19 Athenaeus 301a

καὶ τὴν μὲν ἀφύην καταπέπωκε † ἑψητὸς ἐντυχών

20 Athenaeus 277f

ὅτε δ' ἦσθες ἀμίας παχείας

21 Athenaeus 424ab

κύαθον ἐπριάμην παρὰ Δαισίου

22 Pollux 10.29

τὴν ἀγορὰν μυληκόρῳ

15 (A) What are you saying? That there are soothsayers in the sea?

(B) Yes, sturgeons, the best of all soothsayers.[1]

[1] This joke depends on a pun: the Galeotai were a clan of Sicilian soothsayers, while *galeoi* are sturgeons.

16 The grunt fish made a proclamation, the saupe sounded, making a salary of seven obols.[1]

[1] Another Archippan play on words: *boax* (grunt fish) is meant to recall *boan* (to shout) and *salpēs* (saupe) to recall *salpinx* (trumpet). Both herald and trumpeter were part of a formal Athenian proclamation.

17 A priest of one of their gods arrived, a sea perch.

18 The priest of Aphrodite of Cythera was a gilt-head.[1]

[1] Aphrodite is often called the "golden" (*chrysē*) and thus the appropriate fish would be the "gilt-head" (*chrysophrys*).

19 A small-fry encountered and swallowed a minnow.[1]

[1] "Small-fry" (*hepsētos*) may hide the name of an actual Athenian, and Aphye (minnow) the name of an Athenian hetaera.

20 When you ate a fat bonito.

21 I bought a wine ladle at Daisias'.

22 ⟨I sweep⟩ the marketplace with a mill broom.

23 Athenaeus 227a

Αἰγύπτιος μιαρώτατος τῶν ἰχθύων κάπηλος,
Ἕρμαιος, ὃς βίᾳ δέρων ῥίνας γαλεούς τε πωλεῖ
καὶ τοὺς λάβρακας ἐντερεύων, ὡς λέγουσιν ἡμῖν

24 Athenaeus 86c

λεπάσιν, ἐχίνοις, ἐσχάραις, βαλάνοις τε τοῖς κτεσίν
τε

25 Athenaeus 86c

κῆρυξ θαλάσσης τρόφιμος, υἱὸς πορφύρας

26 Athenaeus 312a

τοὺς μαιώτας καὶ σαπέρδας καί γλάνιδας

27 Athenaeus 329b

κατὰ τὰς συγγραφὰς γὰρ τῶν ἰχθύων καὶ Ἀθηναίων
ταυτὶ πεποίηκεν·

ἀποδοῦναι δ᾽ ὅσα ἔχομεν ἀλλήλων, ἡμᾶς μὲν τὰς
Θρᾴττας καὶ Ἀθερίνην τὴν αὐλητρίδα καὶ Σηπίαν τὴν
Θύρσου καὶ τοὺς Τριγλίας καὶ Εὐκλείδην τὸν ἄρξαντα
καὶ Ἀναγυρουντόθεν τοὺς Κορακίωνας καὶ Κωβιοῦ
τοῦ Σαλαμινίου τόκον καὶ Βάτραχον τὸν πάρεδρον τὸν
ἐξ Ὠρεοῦ

23 Hermaeus the Egyptian, that most disgusting dealer in fish, who so they tell us, forcefully skins monkfish, guts and sells sea bass and sturgeons.

24 With limpets, sea urchins, flatfish, pipefish, and clams.

25 Whelk, nurseling of the Sea, and son of Murex.[1]

[1] "Sea" (Thalassa) and "Murex" (Porphyra or Purple) are probably the names of Athenian prostitutes.

26 Maeots and Nile perch and catfish.

27 In accordance with the treaty made between the fishes and the Athenians he [Archippus] has written this:

to give back what we have of each other's: in our case [the fishes] the Thracian women and Atherine the *aulos*-girl and Sepia the wife of Thyrsus and the Red Mullets and Euclides the former archon and the Tilapians from Anagyrus and the son of Goby from Salamis and Batrachus the inspector from Oreos.[1]

[1] The passage turns on finding names that are common to creatures of the sea and contemporary Athenians: *thratta* (Thracian women, herrings), *atherinē* (smelt), *sēpia* (cuttlefish), *triglē* (red mullet), *kōbios* (goby), *batrachos* (frog). In not all cases do we understand the human side of the reference, but in the last case, Batrachus, was the name of a known supporter of the Thirty (Lysias 6.45—*PAA* 264110/12).

28

(a) Athenaeus 343c

κωμῳδοῦσι δ' αὐτὸν ἐπὶ ὀψοφαγίᾳ . . . ἐν δὲ τοῖς
Ἰχθύσιν Ἄρχιππος τῷ δράματι ὡς ὀψοφάγον δήσας
παραδίδωσι τοῖς ἰχθύσιν ἀντιβρωθησόμενον.

(b) Eustathius On the Iliad p. 1201.3

ἰστέον δὲ ὅτι παίζων ὁ ποιητὴς Ἄρχιππος εἰς τὸν
κατὰ τὴν Ἡσιόνην μῦθον, ὃς αὐτὴν βορὰν τῷ κήτει
ἐκτίθεται, πλάττει Μελάνθιον τὸν τραγῳδὸν ἔν τινι
αὐτοῦ δράματι δεθῆναι, καὶ οὕτω παραδίδωσι αὐτὸν
τοῖς ἰχθύσιν ἀντιβρωθησόμενον. ἦν γὰρ ὁ ἀνὴρ ὀψο-
φάγος, κατὰ ἰχθυοφαγίαν δηλαδή.

29 Proverb of the Paris MS 676

ἀγροῦ πυγή

30 Athenaeus 331c

ἄνδρες ἰχθύες

31 Σ (Arethas) Plato *Apology* 18b

καὶ Ἄρχιππος Ἰχθύσιν εἰς σκυτέα αὐτὸν σκώπτει

28

(a) They make fun of him [Melanthius] for gluttony . . .
and in his play *Fishes* Archippus ties him up as a glutton
and hands him over to the fishes to be eaten in his turn.

(b) One needs to understand that the poet Archippus is
parodying the myth of Hesione which presents her as food
set out for the sea monster. In a play of his he has Melan-
thius the tragic poet tied up, and so hands him over to the
fishes to be eaten in turn. The fellow was a connoisseur of
food, clearly a lover of fish.

29 Rump of the land.

30 Men of the fishes.

31 Archippos also makes fun of him [Anytus] in his *Fishes*
as a shoemaker.

*Brief fragments: (F 32) "elbows flying," (F 33) "wool pluck-
ing," (F 34) "general store."*

ΟΝΟΥ ΣΚΙΑ

Testimonia

i Zenobius 6.28

καὶ Ἀρχίππῳ γέγονεν Ὄνου σκιά

ii *Suda* ο 400

Ἀριστοτελης δὲ ἐν Διδασκαλίαις καὶ δράματός τινος
φέρει ἐπιγραφὴν, Ὄνου σκιάν

Fragment

35 Harpocration p. 290.5

τροχιλίαισι ταῦτα καὶ τοπείοις
ἱστᾶσιν οὐκ ἄνευ πόνου

ΠΛΟΥΤΟΣ

ARCHIPPUS

DONKEY'S SHADOW

"To fight over a donkey's shadow" was an ancient Greek proverb, meaning "to fight over nothing." See Aristophanes' Wasps 191 plus the scholia thereto.

Testimonia

i There was a comedy by Archippos, *Donkey's Shadow*.

ii Aristotle in *Production Lists* [F 625] records the title of a play, *Donkey's Shadow*.

Fragment

35 They set these up with ropes and pulleys, not without effort.

Brief fragment: (F 36) "I have sworn."

WEALTH

Aristophanes wrote two comedies about the god of Wealth (Plutus); in the latter (388) the blind god regains his sight and changes the moral order of the world, so that the virtuous, rather than the wicked, will prosper. Cratinus wrote a Wealth-Gods (Plutoi) *about the return of the Titans, and Nicophon another comedy called* Wealth. *One wonders if Archippus' comedy had anything in common with Aristophanes' play, since F 37–38 suggest a theme about moral decline and the prevalence of wickedness.*

Fragments

37 Σ Aristophanes *Wasps* 418

{A.} οἴμοι. {B.} τί ἐστι; < > μῶν ἔδακέν τι σε;
{A.} ἔδακεν; κατὰ μὲν οὖν ἔφαγε κἀπέβρυξε. <{B.}
τίς;>
{A.} τίς; ἡ πανουργία τε καὶ θεοισεχθρία.

38 Σ Aristophanes *Birds* 1648

ἔστι δέ μοι πρόφασις καλῶς ηὑρημένη
τὸν γάρ γέροντα διαβαλοῦμαι τήμερον.

39 Porphyry *Homeric Questions* (*Iliad*) p. 283.7

νῦν δ᾽ ὡς ἐγενόμην χρημάτων ἐπήβολος

40 Pollux 10.136

ῥαφίδα καὶ λίνον λαβὼν τὰ ῥήγματα
σύρραψον

PINΩN

Fragment

42 Athenaeus 678e

ἀθῷος ἀποδοὺς θοἰμάτιον ἀπέρχεται,
στέφανον ἔχων τῶν ἐκκυλίστων, οἴκαδε

ARCHIPPUS

Fragments

37 (A) Oh no! (B) What's wrong? Did something bite you?

(A) Bite me? Gobbled me up and swallowed me.

(B) Who? (A) Who? Wickedness and the enmity of the gods.

38 I have found a fine excuse: today I shall deceive the old man.

39 Now that I have come into some money.

40 Take a needle and thread and mend these tears.

Brief fragment: (F 41) "cloaks with a wide purple border."

RHINON

Aristotle (Ath. Pol. 38.4) records how Rhinon (PAA 800615) and others were responsible for the successful transition from the oligarchic regime of the Thirty to the restored democracy. This took place in the autumn of 403. It is not immediately obvious how such a respected man would have been good material for comedy. Aeschines the Socratic named one of his philosophical dialogues after a Rhinon.

Fragment

42 After giving back the cloak, he goes home scot-free, wearing one of those rolled-up garlands.

ΑΔΗΛΩΝ ΔΡΑΜΑΤΩΝ

45 Stobaeus 4.17.8

ὡς ἡδὺ τὴν θάλατταν ἀπὸ \<τῆς\> γῆς ὁρᾶν
ὦ μῆτερ ἐστι, μὴ πλέοντα μηδαμοῦ

46 Pollux 7.48

σκαφεῦσι κηπουροῖσι τοῖς τ' ὀνηλάταις,
καὶ ταῖς γυναιξὶ προσέτι ταῖς ποαστρίαις

47 Photius α 1744

Πειθοῦς γὰρ οὐκ ἦν οὔτε βωμὸς οὔτε πῦρ,
οὔτ' ἐν γυναιξὶν οὔτ' ἐν ἀνδρείᾳ φύσει

48 Plutarch *Alcibiades* 1.7

      βαδίζει \< \>
† διακεχλιδώς, θοἰμάτιον ἕλκων, ὅπως
ἐμφερὴς μάλιστα τῷ πατρὶ δόξειεν εἶναι, †
κλαυσαυχενεύεταί τε καὶ τραυλίζεται

49 Zonaras p. 1168

φέρε καθίζωμ' ἐνθαδί

Brief fragments: (F 43) "butt cheeks," (F 44) "razor."

UNATTRIBUTED FRAGMENTS

45 Mother, it is so pleasant to watch the sea from land, especially when one no longer has to go to sea.

46 For garden diggers and donkey drivers, and for good measure, for the women who cut herbs.

47 Persuasion has no altar nor sacred fire, neither among women nor among the male race.

48 He [the son of Alcibiades] walks with affectation, trailing his cloak, to seem so very like his father. He even twists his neck and talks with a lisp.[1]

[1] The "lisp" of the elder Alcibiades was not a lisp as we understand it, but a case of lambdacism (pronouncing "l" as "r"). See *Wasps* 42–46.

49 Just let me sit down here.

50 Photius (S^z) α 3998

ὦ μάκαρ, ὃς ἐπὶ χλανιδοφόροις
κόραισι τὸν ἀφροδίσιον
κῆπον ἀποδρέπεις

51 Bachmann's *Lexicon* p. 29.28

ἀμαθὴς σοφός, δίκαιος ἄδικος

50 Lucky man, you pluck the garden of Love with cloak-clad maidens.

51 Stupid is smart, and just unjust.

Brief fragments: (F 52) "wax taper," (F 53) "blood drinking," (F 54) "I shall set up," (F 55) "accustomed to," (F 56) "worth its weight in gold," (F 57) "scraper," (F 58) "professional training," (F 59) "avert the eyes," (F 60) "Shadow feet," (F 61) "fellow soldiers, compatriots."

ΑΡΙΦΡΑΔΗΣ

Testimonium

i Aristotle *Poetics* 1458b31–59a3

ἔτι δὲ Ἀριφράδης τοὺς τραγῳδοὺς ἐκωμῴδει ὅτι ἃ οὐδεὶς ἂν εἴπειεν ἐν τῇ διαλέκτῳ τούτοις χρῶνται, οἷον τὸ "δωμάτων ἄπο" ἀλλὰ μὴ "ἀπὸ δωμάτων", καὶ τὸ "σέθεν" καὶ τὸ "ἐγὼ δέ νιν" καὶ τὸ "Ἀχιλλέως πέρι" ἀλλὰ μὴ "περὶ Ἀχιλλέως", καὶ ὅσα ἄλλα τοιαῦτα. διὰ γὰρ τὸ μὴ εἶναι ἐν τοῖς κυρίοις ποιεῖ τὸ μὴ ἰδιωτικὸν ἐν τῇ λέξει ἅπαντα τὰ τοιαῦτα· ἐκεῖνος δὲ τοῦτο ἠγνόει.

ARIPHRADES

Ariphrades may claim a place here on the basis of Aristotle's discussion of the critics of tragedy at Poetics *1458b31 (T 1). The name is rare at Athens, at this or at any other period, and is known principally for one of Aristophanes' targets at* Knights *1280–89,* Wasps *1280–83, and* Peace *883–85, the son of Automenes made fun of for his preference for cunnilingual sexual practices (PAA 202305). Aristophanes' jokes acquire a pointed edge then, if his target is also a rival comic poet. We should note also that Automenes would thus have three sons all engaged in artistic performance: Arignotus the lyre player, the actor, and Ariphrades the comic poet. While the verb used by Aristotle (ἐκωμῴδει) does not necessarily have to refer to the activity of a comic poet, it almost always carries the connotations of personal attack in a public setting.*

Testimonium

i Ariphrades would make fun of the tragic poets because they employed the sort of language that no one would ever use in conversation, such as "the halls from out" (instead of "from the halls") and "of thee" and "and I him" and "Achilles concerning" (instead of "concerning Achilles") and other such expressions. Because they are not present in ordinary conversation, these sorts of things produce an unusual effect in speech, but Ariphrades did not realise this.

ΑΡΙΣΤΑΓΟΡΑΣ

ΜΑΜΜΑΚΥΘΟΣ

ARISTAGORAS

This poet is known only for his play Blockhead, *about which there is some confusion. Three ancient sources attribute a play of this title to Platon, though with no fragments extant. Athenaeus 355a quotes a line from "Blockhead or* Breezes" *by Metagenes, but at 571b the choice is between Metagenes'* Breezes *(four other fragments known) and* Blockhead *by Aristagoras. Of the five fragments of Aristagoras in PCG, two (F 1–2) are assigned to his* Blockhead, *two just to him (F 3–4), and one (F 5) to a* Blockhead *with no poet identified. Did Aristagoras perhaps act as the producer for Platon's* Blockhead, *with confusion the result?*

BLOCKHEAD

Brief fragments: (F 1) "of flowers," (F 2) "king," (F 3) "sheets" [of sails], (F 4) "scrotum," (F 5) "aggregation."

See also Metagenes' *Breezes* and Platon's *Blockhead.*

ΑΡΙΣΤΟΜΕΝΗΣ

The evidence from the victors' list at the Lenaea (T 3) and from the hypothesis to Aristophanes' Wealth (T 5) shows that Aristomenes' career lasted from the early 430s until the 380s. It has been suggested, without much likelihood, that there were perhaps two poets of that name, or that Aristonymus' name should be read for that of Aristomenes in the hypothesis to Wealth, *or that Aristomenes competed against Aristophanes' first comedy, called* Wealth, *in 408. For this comic poet with a career of at least fifty years, very few play titles and fragments are known. Possible confusion of name with his better-known contemporary Aristophanes may have misdirected some ascriptions and citations, but on the whole it would seem that his was a long but not very productive career. We know of two victories at the Lenaea, the first of which came early in the history of that contest (c. 440), and if Capps' painstaking reconstruction of the Roman inscription is correct, he won at the Dionysia in 394 with* Dionysus (in Training).*

He is involved in two controversies of the chronology of Old Comedy. The first is whether his name, or more probably that of Aristophanes, is to be read on the victors' list for the Dionysia as Ari[—, *after Pher[ecrates and Herm[ip-*

ARISTOMENES

pus and before Eu[polis (IG ii² 2325.58). The second is whether the unnamed poet on IG Urb. Rom. 216.10–14 is to be identified with Aristomenes. There are strong grounds for accepting this latter identification. The inscription reveals a comic poet active from the archonship of Morychides (440/39) until that of Nicoteles (391/0), who produced a comedy in 395/4, whose name began with "Dion–"—Aristomenes is known to have written a Dionysus in Training (F 11–13)—and who, in a year whose archon's name ended in –es, produced a play called Koleophoroi (Sheath-Bearers). T 4 tells us that Aristomenes in the archonship of Stratocles produced a comedy called Hylophoroi (the MS tradition gives also Olophoroi).

If the suggestion by MacDowell is correct, that the Aristomenes named in Andocides 1.13 as a participant in the sacrilegious treatment of the Mysteries is the same as the comic poet, this may in part explain his long career with fewer productions than we might expect, if he had had to remove himself from Athens for over a dozen years. The name is well documented at Athens (over seventy instances), but very few for the late fifth century; in fact the only two known from the literary tradition are the comic poet and the man named by Andocides.

THE POETS OF OLD COMEDY

Testimonia

i *Suda* α 3922

Ἀριστομένης Ἀθηναῖος, κωμικὸς τῶν ἐπιδευτέρων τῆς ἀρχαίας κωμῳδίας, οἳ ἦσαν ἐπὶ τῶν Πελοποννησιακῶν, Ὀλυμπιάδι πζ΄. ἐπεκλήθη Θυροποιός.

ii Hesychius θ 949

Θυροποιός· οὕτως ἐκαλεῖτο Ἀριστομένης, ὁ κωμικὸς ποιητής, σκωπτικῶς.

iii *IG* ii² 2325.120

Ἀριστομένης ΙΙ

iv Hypothesis II Aristophanes *Knights*

ἐδιδάχθη τὸ δρᾶμα ἐπὶ Στρατοκλέους ἄρχοντος δημοσίᾳ εἰς Λήναια δι᾽ αὐτοῦ τοῦ Ἀριστοφάνους. πρῶτος ἦν· ἐνίκα δεύτερος Κρατῖνος Σατύροις, τρίτος Ἀριστομένης Ὑλοφόροις.

v Hypothesis III Aristophanes *Wealth*

ἐδιδάχθη ἐπὶ ἄρχοντος Ἀντιπάτρου, ἀνταγωνιζομένου αὐτῷ Νικοχάρους μὲν Λάκωσιν, Ἀριστομένους δὲ Ἀδμήτῳ, Νικοφῶντος δὲ Ἀδώνιδι, Ἀλκαίου δὲ Πασιφάῃ.

vi P. Oxy. 2659 F 2 col. i 23

Ἀριστομε]νους/Βοηθο]ί/Γόητε]ς

ARISTOMENES

Testimonia

i Aristomenes, of Athens, one of the second poets of Old Comedy,[1] those who were active at the time of the Peloponnesian War, in the 87th Olympiad [432–428]. He was nicknamed "Door-Maker."

[1] "Second" might also mean "second-rate," but in view of the relative clause, "who were active etc.," it seems that the *Suda* or his source is talking chronologically.

ii "Door-Maker": Aristomenes the comic poet was so called in jest.[1]

[1] The force of the nickname is not clear. Was it his father's occupation (cf. the jokes at Euripides' mother), his own occupation, or (more probably) from something in his comedy?

iii [third entry on the list of victors at the Lenaea]

Aristomenes 2

iv The play [*Knights*] was produced at the Lenaea in the archonship of Stratocles [425/4] by Aristophanes in his own person. It was first. Cratinus won the second prize with *Satyrs*, Aristomenes the third with *Wood-Bearers*.

v [*Wealth*] was produced in the archonship of Antipatros [389/8]. Competing poets were Nicochares with *Laconians*, Aristomenes with *Admetus*, Nicophon with *Adonis*, and Alcaeus with *Pasiphae*.

vi [from a second-century AD list of comic poets and their plays]

Aristome]nes'/*Assistant*]s/*Magician*]s

vii Andocides *On the Mysteries* 1.13

τούσδε Ἀνδρόμαχος ἐμήνυσεν· Ἀλκιβιάδην, Νικι-
άδην, Μέλητον, Ἀρχεβιάδην, Ἄρχιππον, Διογένη,
Πολύστρατον, Ἀριστομένη, Οἰωνίαν, Παναίτιον.

viii *IG Urb. Rom.* 216.10–14

——ἐ]πὶ Διοφάντου Διονύ[σῳ——
——ἐν ἄσ]τει ἐπὶ Νικοτέλους [——
——]ε ἐπὶ Λυσιμάχου [——
——ἐν ἄστε]ι ἐπὶ Μοριχίδου [——
—ἐπὶ Στρατοκλέο]υς Κολεοφόροις [——

Fragments

ΑΔΜΗΤΟΣ

vii Andromachus named the following men [as involved in the "celebration" of the Mysteries]: Alcibiades, Nicides, Meletus, Archebiades, Archippus, Diogenes, Polystratus, Aristomenes, Oionias, Panaitius.

viii [a Roman inscription listing comic poets and their plays, grouped in order of their placings]

. . . in the archonship of Diophantus (395/4) with *Dionys*[*us* . . .

. . . at the Dionysia in the archonship of Nicoteles (391/0) . . .

. . . in the archonship of Lysimachus (436/5) . . .

. . . at the Dionysia in the archonship of Morychides (440/39) . . .

. . . in the archonship of Stratocl]es with *Sheath-Bearers* . . .

Fragments

ADMETUS

Only the title is known for this play, which competed against Aristophanes' Wealth in 388. Admetus will have been a character in Alcestis *by Phrynichus (the early tragedian, and not the comic poet), perhaps a satyr play, and certainly in Euripides' extant* Alcestis, *staged in 438 in the fourth position (where the spectators would be expecting a satyr play). Theopompus wrote a comedy called* Admetus; *Admetus was a character in a lost tragedy (or more probably satyr play) by Sophocles (fr. 851). There is no guarantee that these plays followed the story dramatised in*

129

ΒΟΗΘΟΙ

1 Macrobius *Satires* 5.20.12

ἔνδον γὰρ ἡμῖν ἐστιν ἀνδρῶν γάργαρα.

2 Priscian *Grammatical Foundations* 17.169

{A.} εὖ γάρ, εὖ
πράττειν σε βούλομαί <τι>. {B.} πῶς λέγεις; {A.}
  ὅπως;
μετ᾽ ἐμοῦ ξυνέσῃ.

3 Priscian *Grammatical Foundations* 18.254

μισῶ σ᾽ ὁτιὴ λέγεις με ταἰσχρά.

4 Priscian *Grammatical Foundations* 18.277

ἐπειδὴ τοὺς πρυτάνεις προσήλθομεν

ΓΟΗΤΕΣ

Alcestis. *Admetus figured in other stories: that of the Argo, his wooing of Alcestis, and the tale told in Callimachus 5, that Admetus was the erōmenos of Apollo.*

ASSISTANTS

The word means "helper" or "supporter," and at Plato Republic 566b something like "bodyguard." Certainly a chorus of bodyguards, or even overenthusiastic would-be helpers could provide good comic material.

1 We have heaps of men in there.

2 (A) I want to make you happy, really happy. (B) How?
(A) How? Well, you will be with me.

3 I hate you because you say shameful things about me.

4 When we approached the presiding officials . . .

WIZARDS

The word is usually pejorative, implying trickery, enchantment, and deceit, but in Symposium Plato uses it more positively to describe the nature of Eros as something of a rogue. It is used in oratory of clever (suspiciously too clever) opponents, and in Bacchae of the newly arrived priest of Dionysus. Can we imagine a chorus of such characters, new to Athens and clearly up to no good? F 5 sounds as if something a little underhanded is being devised.

5 Σ Aristophanes *Thesmophoriazusae* 258

παντευχίαν δὲ τοῦ θεοῦ ταύτην λαβεῖν
καὶ περίθετον πρόσωπον, ὃ λαβὼν ἔσταθι.

6 Athenaeus 658a

ἁλίπαστον αἰεὶ τὸν θεράποντ᾽ ἐπεσθίειν.

7 Athenaeus 287d

βεμβράδας φέρων ὀβολοῦ

ΔΙΟΝΥΣΟΣ ΑΣΚΗΤΗΣ

11 Athenaeus 650cd

ὁ Χῖος οὐκ οἶσθ᾽ ὡς ἀμαμηλίδας ποιεῖ;

12 Athenaeus 658a

ἁλίπαστα ταῦτα παρατίθημί σοι κρέα.

5 To take this outfit of the god and this mask and having taken them, stand.

6 The servant always to eat salted meat.

7 Carrying an obol's worth of sprats.

Brief fragments: (F 8) "boiled meats," (F 9) "bookseller," (F 10) "hide" (of human skin).

DIONYSUS IN TRAINING

If the comic poet on the Roman inscription (T 8) is Aristomenes, this may have been his winning play at the Dionysia of 394. "Dionysus as antihero" is a favourite and recurring theme in Old Comedy, in which Dionysus finds himself in ludicrous and inappropriate situations, thereby providing the humour for the spectators. We may compare his learning the rules of war from Phormion, the great Athenian admiral, in Eupolis' Officers, *pretending to be a Trojan shepherd in* Dionysalexander, *and disguising himself as Heracles and being taught how to row by Charon in* Frogs. *In Aeschylus' satyr play* Spectators or Isthmian Athletes, *the satyrs abandon Dionysus to train as athletes themselves. The comic poet Metagenes wrote the intriguingly titled comedy,* Homer or the Athletes.

11 Don't you know that Chios produces medlars?

12 I am placing these salted meats before you.

Brief fragment: (F 13) "ball boxing."

ΚΟΛΕΟΦΟΡΟΙ Η ΥΛΟΦΟΡΟΙ

ΑΔΗΛΩΝ ΔΡΑΜΑΤΩΝ

14 Athenaeus 11d

ἀκρατιοῦμαι μικρόν, εἶθ’ ἥξω πάλιν
ἄρτου δὶς ἢ τρὶς ἀποδακών.

15 Pollux 6.167

φιλακόλουθος ἄρχεται.

16 Harpocration p.204.4 Dindorf

ὅτι δὲ καὶ οἱ δοῦλοι ἀφεθέντες ὑπὸ τῶν δεσποτῶν
ἐτέλουν τὸ μετοίκιον ἄλλοι τε τῶν κωμικῶν δεδηλώ-
κασι καὶ Ἀριστομένης.

SHEATH-BEARERS OR
WOOD-BEARERS

T 4 gives the name of Aristomenes' third-place comedy at the Lenaea of 424 (archonship of Stratocles) as Hylophoroi (Wood-Bearers). *But if the poet of T 8 is Aristomenes, then he produced a* Koleophoroi (Sheath-Bearers) *in the archonship of a man named —es. Capps and Geissler make a strong case for identifying the two.*

UNASSIGNED FRAGMENTS

14 I'll have a little breakfast, then come back later, having had two or three bites of bread.[1]

[1] *Akratismon* (breakfast) was a light early meal usually consisting of bread dipped into unmixed (*akratēs*) wine. The main meal (*ariston*) of the day was at lunch.

15 He leads from the rear.

16 The comic poets, including Aristomenes, have made it clear that slaves freed by their masters also paid the metic tax.

ΑΡΙΣΤΩΝΥΜΟΣ

Testimonium

i *Suda* α 3936

Ἀριστώνυμος, κωμικός. τῶν δραμάτων αὐτοῦ ἐστιν
Ἥλιος ῥιγῶν, ὡς Ἀθήναιος ἐν Δειπνοσοφισταῖς.

Fragments

ΘΗΣΕΥΣ

*As one would expect, Theseus was a popular character
in Athenian drama, both in tragedy and comedy. In trag-
edy he was a character in Euripides'* Suppliant Women,
Heracles, *the Hippolytus plays,* Aigeus, *and* Theseus—*it is
sometimes thought that* Theseus *was a satyr play—and in
Sophocles'* Oedipus at Colonus *and his lost* Phaedra. *The*

136

ARISTONYMUS

Described in T 1 merely as "a comic poet," F 3 records that he, Ameipsias, and Sannyrion made fun of Aristophanes for entrusting the production of his comedies to others (e.g., Philonides and Callistratus), who, it is alleged, took the credit for Aristophanes' work. This should place Aristonymus in the later years of the fifth century BC. No other reference in the nine brief fragments helps with a date.

Testimonium

i Aristonymus, a comic poet. Among his plays is *The Sun is Cold,* according to Athenaeus in *The Learned Banqueters* [287c].

Fragments

THESEUS

early tragedian, Achaeus, also wrote a Theseus. *In Old Comedy he appears to have been a character in Cratinus'* Run-Aways *(F 53), and a comedy called "Theseus" is attested for Theopompus. It has been suggested that F 1 describes the meal set before Theseus by Hecale or the search by Theseus for Minos' ring (see Bacchylides 17).*

137

1 Athenaeus 87a

κόγχος ἦν λεπτῶν ἁλῶν ὁμοίως[1]

[1] βάπτων ἄλλων A; λεπτῶν Meineke, ἁλῶν Porson.

ΗΛΙΟΣ ΡΙΓΩΝ

2 Athenaeus 287cd

ὅ γε τοι Σικελὸς ταῖς βεμβραφύαις προσέοικεν ὁ
καρκινοβήτης

ὥστ᾽ οὔτ᾽ ἀφύη νῦν ἐστ᾽ ἔθ᾽ ἁπλῶς οὔτ᾽ αὖ βεμβρὰς
κακοδαίμων

3

(a) Σ (Arethas) Plato *Apology* 19c

Ἀριστώνυμος δ᾽ ἐν Ἡλίῳ Ῥιγοῦντι καὶ Σαννυρίων ἐν
Γέλωτι "τετράδι" φασιν αὐτὸν "γενέσθαι", διό⟨τι⟩ τὸν
βίον κατέτριψεν ἑτέροις πονῶν.

(b) *Life of Aristophanes* I.7

διὸ καὶ ἔσκωπτον αὐτὸν Ἀριστώνυμός τε καὶ Ἀμει-
ψίας "τετράδι" λέγοντες "γεγονέναι" κατὰ τὴν παρ-
οιμίαν ⟨ὡς⟩ ἄλλοις πονοῦντα.

1 In like manner there was a conch shell of fine salt.

THE SUN IS COLD

It is not clear what the title implies about the comedy.
Comedy titles such as Dionysos in Training *(Aristomenes)*
and Zeus Badly Treated *(Platon), suggest that this play fea-*
tured the Sun God (Helios) far from his natural warm and
comfortable home and suffering accordingly.

2 Well, that Sicilian crab walker looks rather like a dish of
minnow and smelt.

And so there is simply neither a minnow nor a misera-
ble smelt.

3

(a) Aristonymus in his *The Sun is Cold* and Sannyrion in
his *Laughter* [F 5] says that he [Aristophanes] was "born
on the fourth," because he had spent his life toiling for
others.[1]

(b) And so Aristonymus and Ameipsias [F 27] would
make fun of him, saying that he was "born on the fourth" in
accordance with the proverb "working for others."

[1] The point of "working for others" refers to the fact that
Aristophanes had many of his plays produced through others,
such as Callistratus and Philonides.

4 The Antiatticist p. 81.26

ἀπόδειξιν δοῦναι

ΑΔΗΛΩΝ ΔΡΑΜΑΤΩΝ

4 To provide a demonstration

Brief fragments: (F 5) "lambskin," (F 6) "silent."

UNASSIGNED FRAGMENTS

Brief fragments: (F 7) "of the North," (F 8) "morsels."

ΑΥΤΟΚΡΑΤΗΣ

Testimonia

i *Suda* α 4500

Αὐτοκράτης· Ἀθηναῖος, κωμικὸς ἀρχαῖος. τῶν δραμά-
των αὐτοῦ Τυμπανισταί. ἔγραψε δὲ καὶ τραγῳδίας
πολλάς.

ii P. Oxy. 2659 F 1 col. ii 5

Αὐτοκρ[άτους
Τυμπα[νισταί

Fragments

ΤΥΜΠΑΝΙΣΤΑΙ

1 Aelian *On the History of Animals* 12.9

οἷα παίζουσιν φίλαι
πάρθενοι Λυδῶν κόραι
κοῦφα πηδῶσαι <ποδοῖν
κἀνασείουσαι> κόμαν
5   κἀνακρουουσαι χέροιν

142

AUTOCRATES

i Autocrates, of Athens, poet of Old Comedy. Among his plays is the *Drummers*. He also wrote many tragedies.[1]

[1] This last sentence is clearly an error.

ii [from a second-century AD papyrus list of comic poets and their plays]

Autocr[ates'/*Drum*[mers

Fragments

DRUMMERS

A tympanon was a handheld drum, like a modern tambou-rine, and with the aulos was part of the orgiastic worship of gods such as Dionysus and the Great Mother. Sophocles wrote a play with this title, perhaps a satyr play?

1 Just as the maidens play, dear daughters of the Lydians, lightly leaping ‹on their feet, shaking out› their hair with

Ἐφεσίαν παρ' Ἄρτεμιν
† καλλίσταν καὶ τοῖν ἰσχίοιν
τὸ μὲν κάτω, τὸ δ' αὖ
εἰς ἄνω ἐξαίρουσα †
10 οἷα κίγλος ἄλλεται.

    3–4 supp. van Leeuwen.

3 Photius (b, z) α 113

ἀμνοὶ δὲ βληχάζουσιν ὑπ' ἀγαλακτίας

their hands, in the presence of Artemis of Ephesus, and most pleasingly dropping their hips down, now raising them up again, just as a wagtail hops.

3 The lambs bleat for lack of milk.

Brief fragment: (F 2) "it is considered."

ΚΑΛΛΙΑΣ

*Callias' career is usually placed in the 440s and 430s, but
he could have been active until the mid-410s (see under
Men-in-Chains). He is identified at T 3 as one of the rivals
of Cratinus (career: 454–423) and very likely won at the
Dionysia in 446 (T 4). A strong case can be made for identi-
fying Callias as the poet whose works appear on the Roman
inscription (T 6). The list, admittedly very fragmentary, re-
cords quite a number of plays that finished in third to fifth
place. Add in the first- and second-place winners, and we
need a poet with a respectable career who was active in the
440s and 430s and whose play produced in 434 begins
"Cy–." The only known comic title to fit this last criterion is*
Cyclopes *by Callias. If T 5 does refer to Callias, then he*

Testimonia

i *Suda* κ 213

Καλλίας· Ἀθηναῖος, κωμικός, υἱὸς Λυσιμάχου· ὃς
ἐπεκλήθη Σχοινίων διὰ τὸ σχοινοπλόκου εἶναι
πατρός. οὗ δράματα Αἰγύπτιος, Ἀταλάντη, Κύκλωπες,
Πεδῆται, Βάτραχοι, Σχολάζοντες.

CALLIAS I

won two victories at the Dionysia. The plural titles suggest a comedy with an active chorus, and of the forty fragments eight make fun of contemporary figures. Some titles (Atalantas, Cyclopes) suggest the burlesque of myth which was popular in the 430s. T 1 and 2 record that Callias was nicknamed "Ropey"; Sonnino argues that Callias himself is the speaker of F 18, speaking perhaps in a parabasis.

More controversial is whether the lengthy fragments of what has been called The Tragedy *(or* Spectacle*) of the* Letters *belongs to this Callias. For those fragments and the attendant controversy see the entry on Callias II.*

Recent bibliography: O. Imperio, in Tessere *189–254; M. Sonnino,* Phoenix *53 (1999) 330–31.*

Testimonia

i Callias: of Athens, comic poet, son of Lysimachus, who was nicknamed "Ropey" because he was the son of a rope maker. His plays are *Egyptian, Atalanta, Cyclopes, Men-in-Chains, Frogs, Men at Leisure.*

ii Cratinus F 361 (*ap.* Hephaestion *Handbook* 15.21)

πλὴν Ξενίου νόμοισι καὶ Σχοινίωνος, ὦ Χάρων.

iii Σ Aristophanes *Knights* 528b

τοὺς ἐχθρούς· τοὺς περὶ Καλλίαν φησί.

iv *IG* ii² 2318.76–78

   κωμ[ῳδῶν
   Ἀνδ[ἐχορήγει
   Καλ[λίας ἐδίδασκεν

v *IG* ii² 2325.53

   Καλλία]ς ΙΙ

vi *IG Urb. Rom.* 216.1–6

—Γ΄ ἐν ἄστει——ἐ]πὶ Ἀντιοχίδου Κύ[κλωψιν——
—Λήναια————]ς κωμῳδίᾳ. Δ΄ ἐν ἄ[στει ἐπὶ——
————————κω]μῳδίᾳ· ἐπὶ Τιμοκλέ[ους——
————————Λήναια] ἐπὶ Θεοδώρου Σατύροις [——

ii Except, Charon, the tunes of Xenius and Ropey.[1]

[1] Hephaestion quotes three lines in the cratinean metre, all with a metatheatrical context. "Ropey" could in view of T 1 refer to Callias, but who Xenius (or Xenias) is we are not certain, although it has been suggested that it too is a nickname for a comic poet accused of being a foreigner (i.e., Aristophanes or Phrynichus).

iii By "rivals" [of Cratinus] he means Callias and his lot.

iv [from the results of the contests for 446]
com[edies/And[. . . . was *chorēgus*/Cal[lias produced

v [from the list of victors at the Dionysia]
Callia]s 2[1]

[1] Not as far-fetched a supplement as it might seem. We have the names of Cratinus, Diopeithes, Crates, Teleclides, Pherecrates, and Hermippus elsewhere on the list, and we need a comic poet whose name fits the available space with known success in the 440s. Callias fits the bill admirably.

vi [from a Roman inscription listing comic poets and their plays in order of their placings]

 . . . in the archonship of Antiochides (435/4) with *Cy[clopes* . . .
 . . . comedy. 4th place: at the Dionysia . . .
 . . . comedy; in the archonship of Timocle[s (440/39) . . .
 . . . in the archonship of Theodorus (438/7) with *Satyrs*
 . . .

———————'Υπ]έροις Σιδηροῖς· ἐπὶ Πυ[θοδώρου——
——Βατράχ]οις. Ε′ ἐπὶ Ἀντιοχίδου [——

Fragments

ΑΙΓΥΠΤΙΟΣ

ΑΤΑΛΑΝΤΑΙ

*Atalanta was a popular subject for both tragedy and com-
edy (the Sicilians Epicharmus and Phormus), but the de-
tails of her story are not easy to unravel. Gantz postulates
two women of that name in early Greek myth: (1) the
daughter of Schoineus of Boeotia, who in order to avoid
marriage for his daughter set up a fatal footrace, which
was won by Hippomenes, and (2) an Arcadian huntress
who was ultimately wooed and won by Milanion "through
labours." We cannot tell which details of her story pro-*

. . . with . . .] *of Iron;* in the archonship of Py[thodorus (432/1) . . .

. . . with *Frog]s.* 5th place: in the archonship of Antiochides (435/4) . . .

Fragments

THE EGYPTIAN

Plural titles (Egyptians) *are known for Aeschylus (from his trilogy* Daughters of Danaus), *for Phrynichus, and for later poets of Middle Comedy. Foreign ethnic titles are not rare in fifth-century drama:* Phoenician Women *by Phrynichus and Euripides;* Trojan Women, Cretan Women, *and* Cretans *by Euripides;* Persians *by Aeschylus and by Pherecrates. A singular title might suggest a parody of the myth of Aegyptus, brother of Danaus, or of some other myth with Egyptian connections.*

ATALANTAS

vided tragedy or comedy with their material. Aeschylus and Aristias each wrote a tragedy about Atalanta, but whether these in any way affected Callias' comedy is uncertain.*

The exact title and authorship present some difficulties. Of the four fragments in K.-A., one (F 1) is cited as "in Atalanta," another (F 2) as "in Atalantas," and two others (F 3–4) as by "the author of the Atalantas." A chorus of Arcadian huntresses would not be out of place in an Old Comedy.

151

1 Zenobius *Popular Proverbs* 4.67

κέρδος αἰσχύνης ἄμεινον· ἕλκε μοιχὸν ἐς μυχόν.

2 *Lexicon Patmense* on Demosthenes 18.242

κίναδος· θηρίον κακουργότατον, οὗ τὸ δέρμα εἰς περι-
κεφαλαίας πεποίηται, ὥς φησι Καλλίας ἐν Ἀταλάν-
ταις.

3 Hesychius δ 1890

τὸν γὰρ Διονύσ‹ι›ον κουρέα ὄντα κωμῳδεῖ· κουρεὺς δὲ
ἦν πρὸς πάππου, ὡς δηλοῖ ὁ τὰς Ἀταλάντας συνθείς.

4 Σ Aristophanes *Birds* 1294

ὡς τοιούτου τὴν ὄψιν ὄντος μνημονεύει αὐτοῦ καὶ μέγα
ῥύγχος ἔχοντος καὶ ὁ τὰς Ἀταλάντας γράψας, καὶ
Εὔπολις ἐν Ταξιάρχοις.

BATPAXOI

KYKΛΩΠΕΣ

1 "Gain ahead of shame"—drag the adulterer into the back room.

2 Fox: a very nasty creature, whose skin is made into caps, as Callias says in his *Atalantas*.

3 Cratinus makes fun of Dionysius for being a barber. He was a barber because of his grandfather, as the author of *Atalantas* makes clear.

4 The man who wrote *Atalantas,* as well as Eupolis in *Officers* [F 282], mentions this feature of his face [Opountius had one eye] and that he had a large nose.

FROGS

The title is known only from the entry in the Suda *(T 1) but has been restored on line 6 of the Roman inscription (T 6) since of Callias' known titles only it will yield a dative plural in –ois (unless the actual title of* Egyptian *is* Egyptians*). If* Frogs *is the correct supplement, it was produced after the Lenaea of 431. The most famous comic* Frogs *is, of course, Aristophanes' masterpiece of that title at the Lenaea of 405. Magnes at* Knights *523 is said "to have dyed himself frog-green," which may indicate that he wrote a comedy with performers costumed as frogs.*

CYCLOPES

How does one "tame a monster"? By making him a figure of fun or by making him a sympathetic and unrequited lover, artists can remove the terror from the frightening creature

of Odyssey 9. *Cratinus'* Odysseus and Company, *probably
performed between 439 and 436, certainly parodied the
story of Odysseus and Polyphemus from Homer, as did Euripides' satyr play,* Cyclops *(date unknown, but almost certainly later than Cratinus' comedy). While the fragments
of Callias' play reveal a dinner (F 6–7, 10), drinking (F 9),
cottabus playing (F 12), and dancing (F 7), nowhere is
there any connection to the story of Odysseus and the*

5 *Suda* α 3750

ὥσπερ ἀράχνηκες τὴν ὁδὸν προφορούμενα

6 Athenaeus 286ab

κίθαρος ὀπτὸς καὶ βατὶς θύννου τε κεφάλαιον τοδί,
ἐγχέλεια, κάραβοι, λινεύς, ἀχαρνὼς οὑτοσί.

7 Athenaeus 140e

φυλλὰς ἡ δείπνων κατάλυσις ἥδε καθάπερ
    σχημάτων.

8 Athenaeus 524f

τί γὰρ ἡ τρυφερὰ καὶ καλλιτράπεζος Ἰωνία εἴφ' ὅ
τι πράσσει.

9 Athenaeus 487a

καὶ δέξαι τηνδὶ μετανιπτρίδα τῆς Ὑγιείας.

Cyclops. In fact the mention of bronze-working (F 11) suggests that the Cyclopes may not be the monsters of Homer, but the craftsmen of the gods, who are usually mentioned in the plural. The comedy could have turned on these rough craftsmen being introduced to the finer things in life. On three occasions Athenaeus (140e, 524f, 667d) attributes Cyclopes to "Callias or Diocles," but there is no other evidence for a Cyclopes by Diocles.

5 Making their way up and down along the road, like spiders.

6 Roasted flatfish and skate and here's a head of tuna, eel, crayfish, mullet, and here's a sea bass.

7 This branch of leaves marks the end of the dinner and of the dancing as well.

8 And what about Ionia, land of luxury and fine dining? Tell me how it is doing.

9 Take this after-washing cup of Health.

10 Athenaeus 285e

πρὸς τῆς ἀφύης τῆς ἡδίστης

11 Pollux 7.105

καταχαλκεύεσθαι τοίνυν ἐς πέδας

12 Athenaeus 667d

ὅτι δὲ ἆθλον προὔκειτο τῷ εὖ προεμένῳ τὸν κότταβον προείρηκε μὲν καὶ ὁ Ἀντιφάνης· ᾠὰ γάρ ἐστι καὶ πεμμάτια καὶ τραγήματα. ὁμοίως δὲ διεξέρχονται Κηφισόδωρος ἐν Τροφωνίῳ καὶ Καλλίας ἢ Διοκλῆς ἐν Κύκλωψι καὶ Εὔπολις Ἕρμιππός τε ἐν τοῖς Ἰάμβοις.

ΠΕΔΗΤΑΙ

The best-known of Callias' comedies, it is usually dated to the late 430s on the basis of F 21, the comic allegation that Aspasia taught Pericles how to speak in public. But the kōmōidoumenoi can be placed equally well in the 410s— several are made fun of in Birds *(D-414), Melanthius (F 14), Socrates (F 15), Acestor (F 17), Lampon (F 20)—and there is no need for a joke at Aspasia's influence over Pericles to be limited to its victim's lifetime. In the fourth century Aspasia will be elevated to the status of wise woman and appear in Plato's* Menexenus *and the lost* Aspasia *by*

10 In the name of this the most delicious of sprats.

11 Bronze accordingly forged into chains.

12 Antiphanes [F 57] has already been cited that there was a prize for the winner in *cottabus:* eggs and buns and cheese. Cephisodorus [F 5] gives a similar list in *Trophonius,* also Callias (or Diocles) in *Cyclopes,* Eupolis [F 399], and Hermippos in his *Iambs* [F 7 West].

Brief fragment: (F 13) "wagon tracks."

MEN-IN-CHAINS

Aeschines the Socratic. Comedy clearly has much to do with the establishment of this tradition.

The title remains a mystery. It has been suggested that the "men-in-chains" are slaves, the Spartans captured at Pylos (425), or the Athenians under the "tyranny" of Pericles, but we have no way of knowing how overtly political any of Callias' comedies may have been.

Recent bibliography: Storey, Hermes *116 (1988) 379–83; Olson 225, 235–36, 445.*

14 Σ Aristophanes *Birds* 151.

{A.} τί δ᾿ ἆρα; τοὺς Μελανθίου τῷ γνώσομαι;
{B.} οὓς ἂν μάλιστα λευκοπρώκτους εἰσίδῃς.

15 Diogenes Laertius 2.18

{A.} τί δὴ σὺ σεμνὴ καὶ φρονεῖς οὕτω μέγα;
{B.} ἔξεστι γάρ μοι. Σωκράτης γὰρ αἴτιος.

16 Orus *Orthography* fol. 281ᵛ 11

ἴσως ξυνῳδὸς τῷ χρόνῳ γενήσεται.
† τῆς δὴ γὰρ ἀγαθὸν χρῆμα καὶ ξυνῳδικόν.

17 Σ Aristophanes *Birds* 31.

καὶ Σάκαν οἱ χοροὶ μισοῦσι.

18 Photius (b, z) α 1110

ὅτ᾿ ἀμαλλείῳ παῖς ὢν ἐδέθην.

14 (A) So then, how will I recognize the sons of Melanthius?

(B) They'll be the ones you see with the whitest butts.[1]

[1] Melanthius (*PAA* 638270) was a favourite target of comedy for gluttonous behaviour, alleged effeminacy, and a leprous appearance (see Aristophanes *Peace*, *Birds;* Eupolis F 43, 178; Pherecrates F 148; Leucon F 3; Platon F 140; and Archippus F 28.) The joke here turns on a pun between *Melan*thios (black) and *white*-assed, carrying also the overtone of leprosy.

15 (A) Why are you [fem.] so haughty and have such high-and-mighty thoughts?

(B) Because I can—and Socrates is why.[1]

[1] The second speaker has been identified as Euripides in female guise or as Euripides' muse. Perhaps the personification of tragedy? Comedy linked the cleverness of Euripidean tragedy to the influence of Socrates (Aristophanes F 392). For the arrogance of Socrates see *Clouds* 362–63.

16 . . . will perhaps become harmonious in time

for . . . is indeed a good and harmonious thing.

17 And choruses do hate Sacas.[1]

[1] Sacas is a nickname for the tragic poet Acestor (*PAA* 116685, *TrGF* 25), made fun of for his poetry and for being allegedly an illegal alien (*Wasps* 1220–21, *Birds* 31, Eupolis F 172.15–16, Cratinus F 92, Metagenes F 14, Theopompos F 61).

18 When I was a boy I was tied up with a sheaf band.

19 Pollux 7.113

τῆς πατρικῆς ἀρίδος

20 Athenaeus 344e

καὶ Λάμπωνα δὲ τὸν μάντιν ἐπὶ τοῖς ὁμοίοις κωμῳδοῦσι Καλλίας Πεδήταις καὶ Λύσιππος Βάκχαις.

21 Σ Plato *Menexenus* 235e

ἐπεγήματο δὲ μετὰ τὸν Περικλέους θάνατον Λυσικλεῖ τῷ προβατοκαπήλῳ, καὶ ἐξ αὐτοῦ ἔσχεν υἱὸν ὀνόματι Ποριστήν, καί τὸν Λυσικλέα ῥήτορα δεινότατον κατεσκεύασατο, καθάπερ καί Περικλέα δημηγορεῖν παρεσκεύασεν, ὡς Αἰσχίνης ὁ Σωκρατικὸς ἐν διαλόγῳ Ἀσπασίᾳ καὶ Καλλίας ὁμοίως Πεδήταις.

ΣΑΤΥΡΟΙ

19 Of my father's auger.

20 Callias in *Men-in-Chains* and Lysippus in *Bacchae* [F 6] make fun of Lampon the soothsayer for the same reason [gluttony].[1]

  [1] Lampon (*PAA* 601665) was a major figure in Athenian affairs in the late fifth century. He took part in the colonisation of Thurii in the 440s and the expedition to Sicily in 415. Comedy portrays him as the self-serving expert bent mainly on satisfying his own wants.

21 After the death of Pericles she [Aspasia] married Lysicles the sheep merchant and by him had a son named Poristes, and she turned Lysicles into a very skilful speaker, just as she had taught Pericles how to speak in public, as Aeschines the Socratic says in his dialogue *Aspasia* and Callias likewise in his *Men-in-Chains*.

Brief fragments: (F 22) "we were going inside," (F 23) "boxwood pipes."

SATYRS

At least five comedies in the late fifth century either were called "Satyrs" (by Callias, Ecphantides, Phrynichus, and Cratinus [L-424]) or had a chorus of satyrs (Cratinus' Dionysalexander). Callias' comedy is dated by T 6 to 437, a year after Euripides had put on a satyr play without a chorus of satyrs (Alcestis). Was Satyrs Callias' (and comedy's) way of responding to tragedy's omission of the satyrs?

ΣΧΟΛΑΖΟΝΤΕΣ

ΥΠ]ΕΡΑ ΣΙΔΗΡΑ

ΑΔΗΛΩΝ ΔΡΑΜΑΤΩΝ

24 Pollux 2.102

τραυλὴ μέν ἐστιν, ἀλλ᾽ ἀνεστομωμένη.

25 Clement of Alexandria *Miscellanies* 6.12.5

μετὰ μαινομένων φασὶν χρῆναι μαίνεσθαι πάντας
ὁμοίως.

26 Athenaeus 57a

ἔτνος, πῦρ, γογγυλίδες, ῥάφανοι, δρυπεπεῖς,
ἐλατῆρες

CALLIAS I

MEN AT LEISURE

Another comedy known only from the entry in the Suda.
We might compare the chorus in Eupolis' Spongers *(L-
421) where the spongers describe their expertise (F 172).*

. . .] OF IRON

The fifth line of the Roman inscription (T 6) gives . . .]erois
siderois, *the dative plural for " . . . of iron," for a comedy
produced between 436 and 432. Suggestions for the title
have been* Entera Sidera *(Guts of Iron) and* Hypera Sidera
*(Pestles of Iron). Neither title helps us with the nature of
the comedy.*

UNASSIGNED FRAGMENTS

24 She may have a lisp, but doesn't keep her mouth shut.

25 They say that with madmen everyone should act
madly.

26 Soup, fire, turnips, radishes, tree-ripened olives, flat-
cakes.[1]

[1] "Fire" (*pyr*) seems odd here in a list of edibles. Could some
form of *pyros* (wheat) be the correct reading or *pyriatē* (curdled
beestings)?

27 Pollux 3.25

†δυαδελφίδην† ταὐτῷ μυχῷ

28 Hesychius μ 486

Μεγαρικαὶ σφίγγες

40 Athenaeus 577b

Ἀριστοφῶν δ᾽ ὁ ῥήτωρ ὁ τὸν νόμον εἰσενεγκὼν ἐπ᾽
Εὐκλείδου ἄρχοντος, ὃς ἂν μὴ ἐξ ἀστῆς γένηται νόθον
εἶναι, αὐτὸς ἀπεδείχθη ὑπὸ Καλλιάδου τοῦ κωμικοῦ ἐκ
Χορηγίδος τῆς ἑταίρας παιδοποιησάμενος, ὡς ὁ αὐτὸς
ἱστορεῖ Καρύστιος ἐν τρίτῳ Ὑπομνημάτων.

27 Two sisters [nieces?] in the same nook.

28 Sphinxes from Megara [referring to prostitutes].

40 Aristophon, the politician who introduced the law in the archonship of Euclides [403/2] that anyone born of a non-Athenian mother was illegitimate, was himself shown by Calliades [or Callias] the comic poet to have passed off his children by his mistress Choregis, as Carystius records in Book 3 of his *Memoirs* [F 11].[1]

[1] Calliades was a poet of New Comedy active in the late 4th c., in a time when personal humour was rare and in any case Aristophon (*PAA* 176170) would have been dead for years. Callias, on the other hand, is the right sort of poet, but the dating is rather too late. The name of Aristophon's mistress, Choregis ("she who sponsors choruses"), is suspicious, and I suspect that some meta-theatrical joke has been misunderstood.

Brief fragments: (F 29) "the mouth of a mine," (F 30) "Bolbus" (a dancer), (F 31) "with a swollen groin," (F 32) "wrinkle," (F 33) "earth movement," (F 34) "a legend in his own mind," (F 35) "to be on hellebore," (F 36) "food," (F 37) "with a harsh voice," (F 38) "swinish behaviour," (F 39) "vessel."

ΚΑΛΛΙΑΣ Ο ΑΘΗΝΑΙΟΣ

This is the name given by Athenaeus (453c) to the author of the grammatikē tragōidia *(The Tragedy of Letters), also called* The Spectacle of Letters, *the fragments of which reveal a strange, even bizarre, work based on the letters of the Greek alphabet. If this was indeed a performed comedy of the Old (or Middle) period, it says a great deal about comic imagination and the readiness of the spectators to accept the unusual. The title is best explained if we regard the play as a comedy with the word "tragedy" in its title. Much of what Athenaeus has to say about this work has come through Clearchus of Soli, a pupil of Aristotle, who wrote* About Riddles.

Testimonia

i Athenaeus 276a

καὶ γὰρ Καλλίαν ἱστορεῖ τὸν Ἀθηναῖον γραμματικὴν συνθεῖναι τραγῳδίαν, ἀφ' ἧς ποιῆσαι τὰ μέλη καὶ τὴν διάθεσιν Εὐριπίδην ἐν Μηδείᾳ καὶ Σοφοκλέα τὸν Οἰδίπουν.

CALLIAS II ("THE ATHENIAN")

There is a problem of dating. The speaker in Athenaeus claims that this comedy had an influence on Euripides' Medea (431) and Sophocles' Oedipus (usually dated to the early 420s), in which case it could be dated to the 430s, a dating which fits well the career of Callias the comic poet. But the twenty-four letters are those of the Ionic alphabet which became official at Athens in 403/2, and thus a date at the end of the century might be preferable, especially if the author was having some fun with the newly added letters to the alphabet (eta, xi, psi, omega). For Callias the comic poet to be the author, we would have to push his career as late as 400, not impossible but something of a stretch.

Recent bibliography: R. Rosen, CPh 94 (1998) 147–67; C. J. Ruijgh, Mnemosyne 54 (2001) 257–335; J. A. Smith, CPh 98 (2003) 313–29.

Testimonia

i He [Clearchus] records that Callias the Athenian composed *The Tragedy of Letters*, from which Euripides made both songs and order of words in his *Medea* and from which Sophocles made his *Oedipus*.

167

THE POETS OF OLD COMEDY

ii Athenaeus 448b

ὥρα ἡμῖν, ἄνδρες φίλοι, ζητεῖν τι καὶ περὶ γρίφων, ἵνα
τι κἂν βραχὺ διαστῶμεν ἀπὸ τῶν ποτηρίων, οὐ κατὰ
τὴν Καλλίου τοῦ Ἀθηναίου ἐπιγραφομένην γραμμα-
τικὴν τραγῳδίαν. ἀλλ᾽ ἡμεῖς ζητήσωμεν πρότερον μὲν
τίς ὁ ὅρος τοῦ γρίφου, τίνα δὲ Κλεοβουλίνη ἡ Λινδία
προὔβαλλεν ἐν τοῖς αἰνίγμασιν—ἱκανῶς γὰρ εἴρηκε
περὶ αὐτῶν ὁ ἑταῖρος ἡμῶν Διότιμος ὁ Ὀλυμπηνός,
ἀλλὰ πῶς οἱ κωμῳδιοποιοὶ αὐτῶν μέμνηνται,

Fragment

1 Athenaeus 453c–54a

ὁ δὲ Ἀθηναῖος Καλλίας (ἐζητοῦμεν γὰρ ἔτι πρότερον
περὶ αὐτοῦ) μικρὸν ἔμπροσθεν γενόμενος τοῖς χρόνοις
Στράττιδος ἐποίησε τὴν καλουμένην γραμματικὴν
τραγῳδίαν οὕτω διατάξας. πρόλογος μὲν αὐτῆς ἐστιν
ἐκ τῶν στοιχείων, ὃν χρὴ λέγειν διαιροῦντας κατὰ τὰς
παραγραφὰς καὶ τὴν τελευτὴν καταστροφικῶς ποι-
ουμένους εἰς τἄλφα·

⟨τὸ ἄλφα⟩, βῆτα, γάμμα, δέλτα, θεοῦ γὰρ εἶ,
ζῆτ᾽, ἦτα, θῆτ᾽, ἰῶτα, κάππα, λάβδα, μῦ,
νῦ, ξεῖ, τὸ οὖ, πεῖ, ῥῶ, τὸ σίγμα, ταῦ, ⟨τὸ⟩ ὖ,
παρὸν ⟨τὸ⟩ φεῖ, ⟨τὸ⟩ χεῖ, τε τῷ ψεῖ εἰς τὸ ὦ.

ὁ χορὸς δὲ γυναικῶν ἐκ τῶν σύνδυο πεποιημένος αὐτῷ
ἐστιν ἔμμετρος ἅμα καὶ μεμελοποιημένος τόνδε τὸν

ii "It is time, my friends, to turn our inquiries also to the subject of riddles, to give us a short rest from our cups, but not along the lines of so-called *Tragedy of Letters* by Callias the Athenian. Let us consider first the definition of a riddle, but what Cleobulina of Lindos proposed in her *Puzzles* has already been sufficiently discussed by our comrade Diotimus of Olympene. Let us consider also how the comic poets mention them."

Fragment

1 Callias the Athenian (we were enquiring about him earlier), who was active a little before the time of Strattis, composed *The Tragedy of Letters* as it is called, arranging it in the following manner. The prologue consists of the letter names of the alphabet, which one has to speak by dividing off all the letters and pronouncing each separately starting with alpha:

⟨alpha⟩, beta, gamma, delta, "ei" of the god,
zeta, eta, theta, iota, kappa, lambda, mu,
nu, xi, the "ou," pi, rho, the sigma, tau, ⟨the⟩ "u,"
then there's ⟨the⟩ phi, ⟨the⟩ chi, with the psi, and on
    to the "ō."[1]

The entry chorus of women has been arranged by him in pairs and sung in the following manner:

[1] In the classical period the letter we call "epsilon" was called "ei" (pronounced as a short "e"), and that which we call "omicron" was "ou" (pronounced as a short "o").

τρόπον· βῆτα ἄλφα βα, βῆτα εἶ βε, βῆτα ἦτα βη,
βῆτα ἰῶτα βι, βῆτα οὖ βο, βῆτα ὖ βυ, βῆτα ὦ βω, καὶ
πάλιν ἐν ἀντιστρόφῳ τοῦ μέλους καὶ τοῦ μέτρου
γάμμα ἄλφα, γάμμα εἶ, γάμμα ἦτα, γάμμα ἰῶτα,
γάμμα οὖ, γάμμα ὖ, γάμμα ὦ, καὶ ἐπὶ τῶν λοιπῶν
συλλαβῶν ὁμοίως ἑκάστων τό τε μέτρον καὶ τὸ μέλος
ἐν ἀντιστρόφοις ἔχουσι πᾶσαι ταὐτόν. ὥστε τὸν Εὐρι-
πίδην μὴ μόνον ὑπονοεῖσθαι τὴν Μήδειαν ἐντεῦθεν
πεποιηκέναι πᾶσαν, ἀλλὰ καὶ τὸ μέλος αὐτὸ μετενη-
νοχότα φανερὸν εἶναι. τὸν δὲ Σοφοκλέα διελεῖν φασιν
ἀποτολμῆσαι τὸ ποίημα τῷ μέτρῳ τοῦτ' ἀκούσαντα
καὶ ποιῆσαι ἐν τῷ Οἰδίποδι οὕτως·

ἐγὼ οὔτ' ἐμαυτὸν οὔτε σ' ἀλγυνῶ. ⟨τί⟩ ταῦτ'
⟨ἄλλως⟩ ἐλέγχεις;

διόπερ οἱ λοιποὶ τὰς ἀντιστρόφους ἀπὸ τούτου παρ-
εδέχοντο πάντες, ὡς ἔοικεν, εἰς τὰς τραγῳδίας. καὶ
μετὰ τὸν χορὸν εἰσάγει πάλιν ἐκ τῶν φωνηέντων
ῥῆσιν οὕτως (ἣν δεῖ κατὰ τὰς παραγραφὰς ὁμοίως
τοῖς πρόσθεν λέγοντα διαιρεῖν, ἵν' ἡ τοῦ ποιήσαντος
ὑπόκρισις σῴζηται κατὰ τὴν δύναμιν)·

{Α.} ἄλφα μόνον, ὦ γυναῖκες, εἶ τε δεύτερον
λέγειν μόνον χρὴ. {ΧΟ.} καὶ τρίτον μόνον γ'
ἐρεῖς

---

[2] The explanation for this absurd claim may be that ingenious
scholars found letter names in the text of tragedy, e.g., in the lines
quoted we have "ou" in *out'*, "tau" in *tauta*, and "chei" (the Greek
for chi) in *elengcheis*. Smith points out that Oedipus dramatises a
search (*zētēsis*) for the murderer of Laius son of *Labda*chus.

beta alpha "ba," beta ei "be," beta eta "bē," beta iota
"bi," beta ou "bo," beta u "bu," beta ō "bō,"

and again in the antistrophe of the song:

gamma alpha, gamma ei, gamma eta, gamma iota,
gamma ou, gamma u, gamma ō.

and similarly for the rest of the syllables each has the same
metre and music in response. As a result one may sus-
pect that Euripides not only composed all of his *Medea* on
this basis, but also it is clear that he took over the lyric it-
self. They say also that Sophocles, on hearing this, took the
bold step of dividing his poetry by metre and wrote in his
Oedipus [332–33]:

Egō out' emauton oute s' algynō. ‹ti› tauta/‹allōs›
elengcheis?
[I am not hurting myself or you. Why ask me these
useless questions?][2]

And so from this model all the other ‹poets› adopted anti-
strophic responsion in their tragedies.

After the entry chorus he introduces a speech by the
vowels, which the speaker must divide off all the letters
just as before so that the intention of the author with re-
spect to pronunciation may be preserved:

(A) You must say "alpha" by itself, women, then sec-
ondly "ei" by itself.

(CHORUS) Then third you will say by itself?

{A.} ἦτ᾽ ἄρα φήσω {ΧΟ.} τὸ τέταρτόν τ᾽ αὖ μόνον
ἰῶτα, πέμπτον οὗ, τό θ᾽ ἕκτον ὖ μόνον
λέγε. {Α.} λοίσθιον δὲ φωνῶ σοι τὸ ὦ
τῶν ἑπτὰ φωνῶν, ἑπτὰ δ᾽ ἐν μέτροις μόνον.
καὶ τοῦτο λέξασ᾽ εἶτα δὴ σαυτῇ λάλει.

δεδήλωκε δὲ καὶ διὰ τῶν ἰαμβείων γράμμα πρῶτος
οὗτος ἀκολαστότερον μὲν κατὰ τὴν διάνοιαν, πεφρα-
σμένον δὲ τὸν τρόπον τοῦτον·

κύω γάρ, ὦ γυναῖκες. ἀλλ᾽ αἰδοῖ, φίλαι,
ἐν γράμμασι σφῶν τοὔνομ᾽ ἐξερῶ βρέφους.
ὀρθὴ μακρὰ γραμμή ᾽στιν· ἐκ δ᾽ αὐτῆς μέσης
μικρὰ παρεστῶσ᾽ ἑκατέρωθεν ὑπτία.
ἔπειτα κύκλος πόδας ἔχων βραχεῖς δύο.

(A) I will say "eta" then.

(CHORUS) Then fourth by itself ‹say› "iota," fifth "o," sixth "u" by itself.

(A) Last of the seven vowels I tell you ‹to say› "ō," seven in only seven lines. When you have spoken each, then say them to yourself.

Callias was the first to reveal a word through iambic lines, a rather vulgar word, but phrased in the following manner:

Dear ladies, I am pregnant, but for modesty's sake I will spell out the name of my child for you in letters. A great upright stroke, and from its middle stands a little slanting stroke on each side. Then a circle with two little feet.[3]

[3] The letters described are psi and omega ("ō"), yielding *pso*, perhaps related to *psoa* (foul smell). The speaker is not pregnant, then, but suffering from gas.

173

ΚΑΝΘΑΡΟΣ

Testimonia

i *Suda* κ 309

Κάνθαρος, Ἀθηναῖος, κωμικός. μνημονεύεται τούτου δράματα Μήδεια, Τηρεύς, Συμμαχίαι, Μύρμηκες, Ἀηδόνες.

ii *IG* ii² 2318.115

Κάνθα]ρος ἐδ[ίδασκε

CANTHARUS

A minor poet of Old Comedy, active in the 420s and 410s. His name has been plausibly restored on two inscriptions (T 2–3), the first of which would give him a victory at the Dionysia of 422. The Suda (T 1) has five titles, but only two are cited by the ancients. These may be the only two genuine comedies by Cantharus, as Alliance and Ants are also the titles of comedies by Platon, evidence of confusion or collaboration between the poets? Nightingales could be an alternative title for Tereus. In that case both his comedies would have been burlesques of myth, or even of tragedy. As far as we can gather, only Strattis and Aristophanes wrote play-length burlesques of tragedy.

Testimonia

i Cantharus: of Athens, comic poet. Recorded plays by him are: *Medea, Tereus, Alliances, Ants, Nightingales.*

ii [results at the Dionysia of 422]

Cantha]rus pro[duced.

175

iii *IG* ii² 2325.60

Κά[νθαρος¹

¹ Κάνθαρος Capps, Καλλίστρατος Wilhelm.

Fragments

ΑΗΔΟΝΕΣ

ΜΗΔΕΙΑ

iii [from the list of victors at the Dionysia—in the late 420s]

Ca[ntharus[1]

[1] Some restore this name as Ca[llistratus and see the victory as that of Aristophanes' *Babylonians,* produced through Callistratus at the Dionysia of 426. But the creators of the list (or their sources) seem quite able to distinguish the actual poet from the producer pro tempore, and unlike Aristophanes' other producer, Philonides, there is no evidence that Callistratus ever wrote comedy.

Fragments

NIGHTINGALES

The title is known only from T 1 and may be an alternative title for Tereus, *since in that myth Procne was turned into a nightingale. If the play was produced after* Birds *(414), Cantharus might have got the idea from the brief appearance of the nightingale at the close of the first part of that comedy.*

MEDEA

Of Old Comic poets only Strattis is credited with a Medea, *although Eupolis (F 106) does parody certain lines from Euripides' powerful version (431) of that theme. The comedy by Cantharus is very probably his winning entry at the Dionysia of 422. It will have been later than Euripides' play and was presumably influenced by it, although none of the fragments shows any sign of influence.*

1 *Suda* α 3729

κιθαρῳδὸν ἐξηγείρατ' Ἀράβιον † τὸν τοῦτον χορόν.

ΜΥΡΜΗΚΕΣ

ΣΥΜΜΑΧΙΑΙ

1 You have awakened an Arabian musician in this chorus.[1]

[1] There was a proverb about the "Arabian *aulos* player," who would "play for a drachma, and stop for four," in other words someone who did not know when to cease. We may imagine that the chorus of Cantharus' play (in its parodos?) just went on and on, prompting this comment.

Brief fragments: (F 2) "heavy-weighted," (F 3) "we will sing," (F 4) "to drive."

ANTS

No other reference to or citation from this comedy exists. Platon wrote a play of this name, while Pherecrates wrote an Ant-Men. *A chorus of ants would be well within the spirit of Old Comedy—compare* Birds, Fishes, *and* Beasts, *also* Wasps, *where the chorus is not composed of anthropomorphised creatures, but of humans metaphorically identified with wasps.*

ALLIANCES

Platon wrote an Alliance, *of which seven fragments are cited with his name only as the author and five others cited as "Platon or Cantharus." One fragment (= Platon F 170) is cited only as "Cantharus in* Alliance." *The question is (1) whether we have two plays with similar titles:* Alliance *by Platon, and* Alliance(s) *by Cantharus, (2) a single play about whose authorship there was some confusion, or (3) Cantharus perhaps acting as producer of this play for Platon.*

ΤΗΡΕΥΣ

5 Photius (b, z) α 466

γυναῖκ' Ἀθηναίαν καλήν τε κἀγαθήν

6 Athenaeus 81d

Κυδωνίοις μήλοισιν ἴσα τὰ τιτθία

εἰς τὰ Α, ἴσα τὰ Meineke.

7 Photius (b) α 1301

καὶ πρότερον οὖσα παρθένος
ἀμφηγάπαζες αὐτόν.

8 Photius (b, z) α 1118

ἀμαξιαῖα κομπάσματα.

ΑΔΗΛΩΝ ΔΡΑΜΑΤΩΝ

10 Athenaeus 11c

{Α.} οὐκοῦν ἀκρατισώμεθ' αὐτοῦ. {Β.} μηδαμῶς·
Ἰσθμοῖ γὰρ ἀριστήσομεν.

CANTHARUS

TEREUS

The story of Tereus, his wife Procne, and her sister Philomela was dramatised first by Sophocles (in the 430s?) and then by Philocles. Tereus appears as a character in Birds, *where the gory details of the story have been played down and Tereus and Procne become a happily married couple. Is Cantharus' comedy earlier or later than* Birds, *and which poet first saw the comic possibilities in the tragic story? F 5–7 should refer to one or both of the female figures in the story.*

5 A fine and noble Athenian lady.

6 Breasts like Cydonian apples.

7 And before, when you were unmarried, you would embrace him warmly.

8 Inflated words the size of wagons.

Brief fragment: (F 9) "to persuade."

UNASSIGNED FRAGMENTS

10 (A) Shall we have breakfast here? (B) Not at all, for we shall be having lunch at the Isthmus.[1]

[1] As Euripides' *Medea* was set in Corinth (on the Isthmus), it is a fair bet that this comes from Cantharus' *Medea*.

Brief fragments: (F 11) "the human body," (F 12) "a magadis harp," (F 13) "pulse porridge."

ΚΗΦΙΣΟΔΩΡΟΣ

Testimonia

i *Suda* κ 1565

Κηφισόδωρος· Ἀθηναῖος, κωμικὸς τῆς ἀρχαίας κωμῳ-
δίας. ἔστιν αὐτοῦ τῶν δραμάτων Ἀντιλαΐς, Ἀμαζόνες,
Τροφώνιος, Ὗς.

τραγῳδίας codd., κωμῳδίας Kuster.

ii Lysias 21.4

ἐπὶ δὲ Εὐκλείδου ἄρχοντος κωμῳδοῖς χορηγῶν Κηφι-
σοδώρῳ ἐνίκων, καὶ ἀνήλωσα σὺν τῇ τῆς σκευῆς
ἀναθέσει ἑκκαίδεκα μνᾶς.

Κηφισοδότῳ X, Κηφισοδώρῳ Clinton.

CEPHISODORUS

The Suda *(T 1) gives us four play titles; we have citations from three. T 2 gives a firm date of 402 for a victory, perhaps that recorded on the victors' list for the Dionysia (T 3). Cephisodorus thus belongs to the very late fifth century and early fourth. If MacDowell is correct in his identification that three of the men (Archippus, Aristomenes, Cephisodorus) named in the violation of the Mysteries in 415 (T 4) were comic poets, then Cephisodorus was absent from Athens from 415 to c. 405 and may not have begun his comic career until after his return. In the case of Cephisodorus this identification is made less likely than the others by the very common occurrence of the name and the fact that the Cephisodorus of the Mysteries was a metic (resident alien).*

Testimonia

i Cephisodorus: of Athens, poet of Old Comedy.[1] His plays include *Antilaïs, Amazons, Trophonius, The Sow.*

[1] The text has "tragedy," but this must be corrected to "comedy."

ii In the archonship of Euclides [403/2] I was the victorious *chorēgus* in comedy for Cephisodorus. Along with the dedication of the equipment I spent sixteen minas.

iii *IG* ii² 2325.69

Κ[η]φισόδ[ωρος

iv Andocides 1.15

τούσδε Τεῦκρος ἐμήνυσεν· Φαῖδρον, Γνιφονίδην, Ἰσό-
νομον, Ἡφαιστόδωρον, Κηφισόδωρον, ἑαυτόν, Δι-
όγνητον, Σμινδυρίδην, Φιλοκρατη, Ἀντιφῶν, Τείσαρ-
χον, Παντακλη.

Fragments

ΑΜΑΖΟΝΕΣ

1 Photius p. 337.19

σκώπτεις μ᾽, ἐγὼ δὲ τοῖς λόγοις ὄνος ὕομαι.

2 Athenaeus 629c

τὴν δ᾽ ἀπόκινον καλουμένην ὄρχησιν

184

CEPHISODORUS

iii [from the list of victors at the Dionysia]

C[e]phisod[orus

iv Teucer named the following [as involved in the "celebration" of the Mysteries]; Phaedrus, Gniphonides, Isonomus, Hephaestodorus, Cephisodorus, himself, Diognetus, Smindyrides, Philocrates, Antiphon, Teisarchus, Pantacles.

Fragments

AMAZONS

While Athenian art of the fifth century delighted to show Greek male heroes defeating the Amazon women (most notably the mural in the Painted Stoa), Attic drama did not make much use of the myth of the Amazons. Tragedy does mention their invasion of Athens (Eumenides), *one of Heracles' labours is to subdue them* (Heracles), *and Theseus was the father of Hippolytus by "that Amazon woman." In* Lysistrata *the women do refer to the Amazons as examples of those who stood up to men, but on the whole Amazons are avoided as a comic subject. Epicrates, a poet of Middle Comedy, did write a later* Amazons.

1 You make fun of me, but I am the donkey in the rain of your words.

2 The bugger-off dance.

ΑΝΤΙΛΑΙΣ

ΤΡΟΦΩΝΙΟΣ

3 Athenaeus 689ef

{Α.} ἔπειτ᾽ ἀλείφεσθαι τὸ σῶμά μοι πρίω
μύρον ἴρινον καὶ ῥόδινον, ἄγαμαι, Ξανθία·
καὶ τοῖς ποσὶν χωρὶς πρίω μοι βάκχαριν.
{ΞΑΝΘΙΑΣ.} ὦ λακκόπρωκτε, βάκχαριν τοῖς σοῖς
    ποσὶν
ἐγὼ πρίωμαι; λαικάσομ᾽ ἆρα. βάκχαριν;

---

[1] Asarabacca (or baccharis) was a powder derived from a cycla-
men (sowbread) which was sprinkled on or rubbed into the body.
The point of the joke is that such care of the feet was considered
very sensual and sexually provoking. Xanthias fears that by having
to apply the powder he will thus arouse the sexual interest of his
master.

CEPHISODORUS

RIVAL OF LAÏS

*Laïs was a famous courtesan of the late fifth and early
fourth centuries. Taken from Sicily to Athens as a young
girl in 415 (Plutarch* Nicias *15), she became the most fa-
mous hetaera of her day and was frequently alluded to in
comedy. The title suggests that a fictional rival to Laïs was
a character in the play, perhaps in the same way that a
rival to Paphlagon (Cleon) was sought in* Knights.

TROPHONIUS

*Trophonius was a hero whose oracle in Boeotia was one
of the most respected and consulted in the Greek world.
Pausanias (9.39) gives us a lengthy description of the pro-
cess of consultation, which he himself claims to have un-
dergone. Cratinus had written a comedy with the same
title some years earlier. Do we have a scene describing an
experience at the oracle like that at the shrine of Asclepius
in* Wealth? *The anointing with scent in F 3 and the use of
fuller's earth (F 6) might have something to do with the
ritual of purification involved in consulting the oracle.*

3 (A) And then, Xanthias, please buy for me some iris-
and-rose scent to anoint my body with. And for my feet
also buy some asarabacca.

(XANTHIAS) Me, buy asarabacca for your feet? You
asshole! I'll be buggered. Asarabacca?[1]

4 Pollux 7.87

> σανδάλιά τε τῶν λεπτοσχιδῶν,
> ἐφ᾽ οἷς τὰ χρυσᾶ ταῦτ᾽ ἔπεστιν ἄνθεμα.
> νῦν δ᾽, ὥσπερ ἡ θεράπαιν᾽, ἔχω περιβαρίδας.

5 Athenaeus 667d

ὅτι δὲ ἆθλον προύκειτο τῷ εὖ προεμένῳ τὸν κότταβον προείρηκε μὲν καὶ ὁ Ἀντιφάνης· ᾠὰ γάρ ἐστι καὶ πεμμάτια καὶ τραγήματα. ὁμοίως δὲ διεξέρχονται Κηφισόδωρος ἐν Τροφωνίῳ καὶ Καλλίας ἢ Διοκλῆς ἐν Κύκλωψι καὶ Εὔπολις Ἕρμιππός τε ἐν τοῖς Ἰάμβοις.

ΥΣ

7 Herodian *Singular Vocabulary* p. 944.13 L

ὦ καὶ λέων καὶ μυγαλῆ καὶ σκορπίος

8 Athenaeus 119d

κρεᾴδιόν τι φαῦλον ἢ ταρίχιον

9 Athenaeus 345f

οὐδ᾽ ὀψοφάγος οὐδ᾽ ἀδολέσχης

4 Sandals with the narrow slits on which there are those flowers made of gold. But at the moment I am wearing shoes just like my maid.

5 Antiphanes [F 57] has already been cited that there was a prize for the winner in *cottabus,* eggs and buns and cheese. Cephisodorus gives a similar list in *Trophonius,* also Callias (or Diocles) in *Cyclops* [F 12], Eupolis [F 399], and Hermippos in his *Iambs* [F 7 West].

Brief fragment: (F 6) "fuller's earth."

THE SOW

*It has been suggested that this title has something to do with the proverb about "Boeotian pigs" or that it was a nickname for a prostitute. Plutarch (*Theseus 9*) knows a story that the sow of Crommyon, killed by Theseus, was in fact a notorious she-bandit with unclean personal habits. Alternatively since the so-called "Goose play" (V 4–5) seems to have had a goose at the centre of its plot, perhaps a sow played a crucial role in this comedy.*

7 You lion, you shrew mouse, you scorpion.

8 A bit of inferior meat or a little herring.

9 Neither a gourmand nor a chatterbox.

10 Pollux 10.109

σπονδὴ δὲ παρὰ τῶν ὁλκάδων καὶ †καταφαντισγός†

σπονδὴ van Herwerden; περὶ Headlam; καταφαντισγός F, καταφατισγός S, κάμητα φύστης L, φρυγανισμός van Herwerden.

ΑΔΗΛΩΝ ΔΡΑΜΑΤΩΝ

13 Athenaeus 459d

ἄγε δή, τίς ἀρχὴ τῶν λόγων γενήσεται;

10 Enthusiasm on the part of the cargo ships and a forage for grain.[1]

[1] Pollux is citing comic authors for the use of *phrygeus* and *phrygetron* (barley roaster) as cooking vessels, but his citation from Cephisodorus is heavily corrupt and does not seem to mention cooking vessels at all, unless we are to see a pun on ὁλκάδων (cargo ships) and ὁλκείων (bowls) or read ὁλκείων in the text. I have translated van Herwerden's conjecture.

Brief fragments: (F 11) "lamp lighting," (F 12) "weighings."

UNASSIGNED FRAGMENTS

13 Well then, what shall be the opening of my speech?

Brief fragment: (F 14) "Atticism."

ΧΙΟΝΙΔΗΣ

Testimonia

i *Suda* χ 318

Χιωνίδης· Ἀθηναῖος, κωμικὸς τῆς ἀρχαίας κωμῳδίας,
ὃν καὶ λέγουσι πρωταγωνιστὴν γενέσθαι τῆς ἀρχαίας
κωμῳδίας, διδάσκειν δὲ ἔτεσιν ὀκτὼ πρὸ τῶν Περ-
σικῶν. τῶν δραμάτων αὐτοῦ ἐστι καὶ ταῦτα· Ἥρως,
Πτωχοί, Πέρσαι ἢ Ἀσσύριοι.

ii Aristotle *Poetics* 1448a33

Ἐπίχαρμος ὁ ποιητὴς πολλῷ πρότερος ὢν Χιωνίδου
καὶ Μάγνητος.

---

[1] Aristotle's statement raises a problem, since the *Suda* (μ 20)
makes Epicharmus and Magnes active at the same time, admit-
tedly Magnes as a young poet and Epicharmus as an older man,
while the anonymous writer on comedy (Koster III.15–16) dates
Epicharmus' activity in the 73rd Olympiad (488–485), which is
not "much earlier" than either Chionides or Magnes.

CHIONIDES

T 1 is usually taken to mean that Chionides was the victor at the first competition for comedy at the Dionysia. "Eight years before the Persian Wars" would place the debut of Comedy in 486, assuming that "Persian Wars" refers to the year of the great battles, 480/79. Olson's close study of the list of victors yields a date between extremes of the mid-490s and the early 470s for the first comic competition; thus the traditional date is not going to be far out of line. Only three titles are recorded for Chionides, of which the authenticity of Beggars *was debated in antiquity. F 4 also seems to belong later in the century. One wonders just how much evidence Aristotle and other ancient scholars had to go on when they came to consider the earliest Greek comic writers.*

Testimonia

i Chionides: of Athens, poet of Old Comedy, who they also say was the first competitor of Old Comedy and that he produced eight years before the Persian Wars. These are his plays: *Hero, Beggars, Persians or Assyrians.*

ii Epicharmus the poet, who was much earlier than Chionides and Magnes.[1]

193

Fragments

ΗΡΩΕΣ

1 Pollux 10.43

πολλοὺς ἐγῷδα κοὐ κατὰ σὲ νεανίας
φρουροῦντας ἀτεχνῶς κἂν σάμακι κοιμωμένους.

2 Photius (b, z) α 220

καὶ μὴν μὰ τὸν Δί᾽ οὐδὲν ἔτι γέ μοι δοκῶ
ἄγνου διαφέρειν ἐν χαράδρᾳ πεφυκότος.

ΠΕΡΣΑΙ Η ΑΣΣΥΡΙΟΙ

CHIONIDES

Fragments

HEROES

The Suda *(T 1) gives the title as* Hero, *but all three fragments are cited from the* Heroes *by Chionides. A "hero" (in Greek,* hērōs*) was not what we understand the term to be, i.e., as "lead character," "dashing person of action," but was a person who after his death was worshipped with rituals and honours. His place of death was considered especially worthy of veneration. Both Crates and Aristophanes wrote comedies with this title.*

1 I know of many young men, not at all like you, who go on real guard duty and sleep on a reed mat.

2 By Zeus, I don't consider myself to be any different from a bullrush growing in a fast-flowing stream.

Brief fragment: (F 3) "seven-year-old."

PERSIANS OR ASSYRIANS

In view of the importance of Persia in fifth-century Greek history, we will not be surprised if comedy found them a theme to exploit. In tragedy we have Phrynichus' Phoenician Women *(476), which covered similar ground to Aeschylus'* Persians *(472). Dionysus in* Frogs *(405) says that he enjoyed watching the Persians lament in good barbarian fashion, while Eupolis certainly employed a Persian theme in his* Maricas *(421). Pherecrates wrote a* Persians, *in which a utopian existence is described. Metagenes combined two fabulously affluent cultures in his* Thurio-Persians.

195

ΠΤΩΧΟΙ

4 Athenaeus 638d

ταῦτ᾽ οὐ μὰ Δία Γνήσιππος οὐδ᾽ ὁ Κλεομένης
ἐν ἐννέ᾽ ἂν χορδαῖς κατεγλυκάνατο.

5 Athenaeus 119e

ἆρ᾽ ἂν φάγοιτ᾽ ἂν καὶ ταρίχους, ὦ θεοί;

6 Athenaeus 119e

ἐπὶ τῷ ταρίχει τῷδε τοίνυν κόπτετον.

7 Athenaeus 137e

τυρὸν καὶ φυστὴν δρυπεπεῖς τ᾽ ἐλάας καὶ πράσα

CHIONIDES

BEGGARS

Two problems arise over this comedy. First, Athenaeus cites this play three times and twice assigns it to "the man who wrote the Beggars *attributed to Chionides." Second, F 4 mentions Gnesippus, a poet whom comedians of the 430s made fun of, and one wonders how such a reference can be assigned to Chionides, a poet of the 480s. Perhaps a later comedy called* Beggars *was confused with the play of that name by Chionides, or (less likely) Chionides' play was revived and revised in the 430s.*

4 By Zeus, not even Gnesippus or Cleomenes on their nine strings could have produced anything this sweet.[1]

[1] Gnesippus (see Cratinus F 17) seems to have been a writer of erotic mimes, while Cleomenes of Rhegium is listed by Epicrates (F 4) with Sappho and others for writing erotica.

5 Gods, would you eat even some salted fish?

6 The pair of them are certainly munching away on this salted fish.

7 Cheese and barley cake and tree-ripened olives and leeks.

ΑΔΗΛΩΝ ΔΡΑΜΑΤΩΝ

8 Vitruvius 6 Preface 3

pauca sapientibus fortunam tribuere, quae autem maxima
et necessaria sunt, animi mentisque cogitationibus guber-
nari. haec ita etiam plures philosophi dixerunt. non minus
poetae, qui antiquas comoedias graece scripserunt, eas-
dem sententias versibus in scaena pronuntiaverunt, ut
Eu⟨polis⟩, Crates, Chionides, Aristophanes, maxime
etiam cum his Alexis.

UNASSIGNED FRAGMENT

8 Fortune is of little assistance to wise men; rather the things which are most important and essential are controlled by the judgements of the mind and the heart. Many philosophers have said this, and no less have the poets, who wrote Greek Comedy long ago, expressed these sentiments on the stage in their verses: Eu⟨polis⟩ [F 494], Crates [F 60], Chionides, Aristophanes [F 924], and especially along with these Alexis.

ΚΡΑΤΗΣ

For Crates the testimonia provide as much, if not more, information as the fragments. He is placed after Cratinus (debut 454) and his career is presumably over by the time of Knights *(L-424), since Aristophanes regards him as a figure of the past. Athenaeus, citing F 16–17, states that Crates'* Beasts *was later than Cratinus'* Wealth-Gods, *a comedy which has been plausibly dated to the 430s. We shall not be far wrong if we date Crates' career with his seven or so comedies to 450–430.*

As well as allegedly being the first to bring drunken characters on stage (T 4), Crates is credited by Aristotle (T 12) as "the first to abandon the iambic mode and create whole stories and plots." Add to this the comment by the anonymous writer (T 4) that Pherecrates followed the example of Crates and "refrained from personal insult," and we have evidence for a sort of Old Comedy different from the politically and topically charged farces of Aristophanes and Eupolis, although Norwood overstates the case by postulating "the school of Crates." Comparing the remains of Crates and Archippus, each with about sixty fragments, in Crates we find no instance of personal humour, but at least a dozen by Archippus. Aristotle with the advantage of

CRATES I

hindsight saw in Crates the ancestor of the structured comedy of wit and manners prevalent in his own day. In his view Aristophanes and the great days of Old Comedy may have been a detour on the straight course to New Comedy.

Aristophanes praises Crates (T 13, 16) for his comedy, although one must always be careful of compliments in comedy, which build up only to bring down later. There is more than a hint of patronising in his description of Crates "giving a good lunch . . . on a tight budget" and "yet sometimes he crashed, sometimes he didn't." The word order here is significant. Most important is his comment, "some quite witty concepts from his very delicate palate," where "witty" is asteios (of the city, urbane) and "very delicate" a guess at the meaning of krambotatos ("sweet," "dry" suggests the scholiast). With some condescension Aristophanes is describing Crates' comedy as "really quite decent stuff, not the roughhouse of Cratinus, who swept all before him, but with some clever and innovative ideas and a pleasant enough style." In F 347 (T 16) Aristophanes commends the ingenuity of Crates' creation of the "ivory salt fish," but we note that this "and a million other such jokes" were only "giggled at." I suspect that F 32 confused the ancient spectators as much as it has confused us.

THE POETS OF OLD COMEDY

Testimonia

i *Suda* κ 2339

Κράτης, Ἀθηναῖος, κωμικός· οὗ ἦν ἀδελφὸς Ἐπίλυκος, ποιητὴς ἐπῶν. δράματα δὲ αὐτοῦ εἰσιν ζ´· Γείτονες, Ἥρωες, Θηρία, Λάμια, Πεδῆται, Σάμιοι. ἔγραψε δὲ καὶ καταλογάδην τινά.

ii Diogenes Laertius 4.23

γεγόνασι δὲ Κράτητες δέκα· πρῶτος ὁ τῆς ἀρχαίας κωμῳδίας ποιητής.

iii *Canons of the Comedians*, tab. M cap. 4

κωμῳδοποιοὶ ἀρχαίας ζ´· Ἐπίχαρμος, Κρατῖνος, Εὔπολις, Ἀριστοφάνης, Φερεκράτης, Κράτης, Πλάτων.

iv Anonymous *On Comedy* (Koster III.11–13, 26–30)

τούτων δέ εἰσιν ἀξιολογώτατοι Ἐπίχαρμος, Μάγνης, Κρατῖνος, Κράτης, Φερεκράτης, Φρύνιχος, Εὔπολις, Ἀριστοφάνης.

Κράτης Ἀθηναῖος. τοῦτον ὑποκριτὴν φασι γεγονέναι τὸ πρῶτον, ὃς ἐπιβέβληκε Κρατίνῳ, πάνυ γελοῖος καὶ ἱλαρὸς γενόμενος, καὶ πρῶτος μεθύοντας ἐν κωμῳδίᾳ προήγαγεν. τούτου δράματά ἐστιν ἑπτά.

Φερεκράτης Ἀθηναῖος . . . γενόμενος {ὅ} δὲ ὑποκριτὴς ἐζήλωσε Κράτητα, καὶ αὖ τοῦ μὲν λοιδορεῖν ἀπέστη.

202

CRATES I

Testimonia

i Crates: of Athens, comic poet; his brother was Epilycus the epic poet. There are seven plays by him: *Neighbours, Heroes, Beasts, Lamia, Men-in-Chains, Samians*. [He also wrote some prose works.][1]

[1] *Men-in-Chains* (*Pedetai*) is likely an error for *Games* (*Paidiai*), and we also know of *Daring Deeds* (*Tolmai*), which would make up the total of seven. The business about "prose works" is a confusion with a later writer of that name.

ii There were ten men named Crates. The first is the poet of Old Comedy.

iii There are seven poets of Old Comedy: Epicharmus, Cratinus, Eupolis, Aristophanes, Pherecrates, Crates, Platon.

iv The most noteworthy of these [poets of Old Comedy] are Epicharmus, Magnes, Cratinus, Crates, Pherecrates, Phrynichus, Eupolis, Aristophanes.

Crates of Athens: they say that he was at first an actor who overlapped with Cratinus, very funny and entertaining, the first to bring drunken characters on stage in a comedy. His plays are seven in number.

Pherecrates of Athens: having been first an actor, he followed the example of Crates, and likewise refrained from personal insult.

THE POETS OF OLD COMEDY

v Eusebius (Jerome) *Chronicles*, p. 112.15 Helm

Crates comicus et Telesilla ac Bacchylides lyricus clari
habentur. Praxilla quoque et Cleobulina sunt celebres.

Eusebius (Armenian version), p. 193 Harst

Krates der Komiker und Telesilla waren gekannt.

vi Syncellus p. 297.5–7 Mosshammer

Κράτης ὁ κωμικὸς καὶ Τελέσιλλα καὶ Πραξίλλα καὶ
Κλεοβουλίνα ἐγνωρίζοντο. Βακχυλίδης ὁ μελοποιὸς
ἤκμαζεν.

vii Demetrius Lacon *On Poetry*, B col. 38, p. 112 Romeo.

ὁ γ[ὰ]ρ δὴ Κράτης κατὰ [τ]ὸν αὐ[τὸν] χρόνον γε-
[γο]νὼ[ς Αἰσ]χύλῳ, τούτου διὰ τ[ῶ]ν Ἠδωνῶν [εὐ]δο-
κιμηθέν[τος].

viii Synesius *Dio* 18

ἐγὼ δὴ θαμὰ καὶ τραγῳδίαις ἐπετραγῴδησα, καὶ
κωμῳδίαις ἐπιστωμύλλομαι πρὸς τὸν πόνον ἑκάστου
τοῦ γράψαντος. εἴποις ἂν ἡλικιώτην εἶναι νῦν μὲν
Κρατίνου καὶ Κράτητος, νῦν δὲ Διφίλου τε καὶ Φιλή-
μονος.

v [for the year 451/0] The comic poet Crates, and Telesilla, and Bacchylides the lyric poet are recognised as well-known. Praxilla also and Cleobulina are famous.

[for the year 449/8] The comic poet Crates and Telesilla were well-known.

vi Crates the comic poet as well as Telesilla and Praxilla and Cleoboulina were becoming well-known; the lyric poet Bacchylides was at his height.

vii For Crates in fact lived around the same time as Aeschylus, who was well-regarded for his *Edonians*.[1]

[1] Not strictly true since Aeschylus died in 456 and Crates' career begins in the late 450s.

viii In the same way I mourned tragically along with the tragedians and played the fool with comedy according to the style of each author. You might say that I was a contemporary now of Cratinus and Crates, now of Diphilus and Philemon.

ix *The Names and Plays of the Poets of Old Comedy*
(Koster VIII)

Κράτητος δράματα η′

x *IG* ii² 2325.52

Κρά]της III

xi *PSI* 144.20–26

Κράτητα μ[έντοι τὸν κω-
μικὸν ποιη[τὴν γε-
γραφότα τὸν[
τον ἐν τῇ ἀ[ρχῇ τῆς ἀν-
τεπιρρήσεως[
πλειον[
δε καὶ μ[

xii Aristotle *Poetics* 1449b5

τὸ δὲ μύθους ποιεῖν τὸ μὲν ἐξ ἀρχῆς ἐκ Σικελίας ἦλθε,
τῶν δὲ Ἀθήνησιν Κράτης πρῶτος ἦρξεν ἀφέμενος τῆς
ἰαμβικῆς ἰδέας καθόλου ποιεῖν λόγους καὶ μύθους.

xiii Aristophanes *Knights* 537–40

οἵας δὲ Κράτης ὀργὰς ὑμῶν ἠνέσχετο καὶ
στυφελιγμούς,
ὃς ἀπὸ σμικρᾶς δαπάνης ὑμᾶς ἀριστίζων
ἀπέπεμπεν,

CRATES I

ix Of Crates eight plays.

x [from the list of victors at the Dionysia, c. 450]

Cra]tes 3

xi [from a second-century AD papyrus containing bits of
a *Life of Demosthenes*]

Crates h[owever the co-]
mic poe[t . . . who has wri-]
tten the [
in the b[eginning of the an-]
tepirhhema [
more [
and also [

xii The creation of plots came originally from Sicily; of
those at Athens Crates was the first to abandon the iambic
mode and write whole stories and plots.

xiii And the angry reception and the insults that Crates
had to put up with. He would send you home, serving a

ἀπὸ κραμβοτάτου στόματος μάττων ἀστειοτάτας
  ἐπινοίας·
χοῦτος μέντοι μόνον ἀντήρκει, τοτὲ μὲν πίπτων,
  τοτὲ δ' οὐχί.

μόνος codd., μόνον Sommerstein.

xiv Σ Aristophanes *Knights* 537a

οἵας δὲ Κράτης ὀργάς· οὗτος κωμῳδίας ποιητής, ὃς
πρῶτον ὑπεκρίνατο ⟨τὰ⟩ Κρατίνου, καὶ αὐτὸς ποιητὴς
ὕστερον ἐγένετο, καὶ ἐξωνεῖτο τοὺς θεατὰς καὶ τὴν
τούτων εὔνοιαν.

xv Σ Aristophanes *Knights* 539a

ἀπὸ κραμβοτάτου· ἡδυτάτου, ξηροτάτου. ἔπαιξε δὲ
ἀπὸ τῆς τοῦ λαχάνου ἐπινοίας. αὐτοσχέδιος γὰρ ἦν
περὶ τὰ δράματα.

xvi Aristophanes F 347 (*Thesmophoriazusae* β)

ἦν μέγα τι βρῶμ' ἔτι τρυγῳδοποιομουσική,
ἡνίκα Κράτης τό τε τάριχος ἐλεφάντινον
λαμπρὸν ἐνόμιζεν ἀπόνως παραβεβλημένον,
ἄλλα τε τοιαῦθ' ἕτερα μυρί' ἐκιχλίζετο.

ΓΕΙΤΟΝΕΣ

nice lunch on a small budget, kneading some quite witty concepts from his very delicate palate. However, he just did all right, sometimes he crashed, sometimes he didn't.

xiv "The insults of Crates": Crates was a comic poet, who was first an actor in the plays of Cratinus and later became a poet himself. He would buy off the spectators and their approval.

xv *"apo krambotatou"*: "very sweet," "very dry." He is playing on an idea from green vegetables, since he was rather offhand about his plays.

xvi Making comic song was still marvellous fare, when Crates would describe salt fish as "ivoried," "splendid," and "effortlessly called up" [F 32]. A million other such jokes were giggled at.

NEIGHBOURS

The plural title suggests that the chorus in this comedy was composed of "neighbours," for which we might compare Friends *(Eupolis),* Demesmen *(Hermippus), or* Banqueters *(Aristophanes). The speaker of F 1 may be an Ionian.*

THE POETS OF OLD COMEDY

Testimonium

i Athenaeus 429a

ἀγνοοῦσί τε οἱ λέγοντες πρῶτον Ἐπίχαρμον ἐπὶ τὴν
σκηνὴν παραγαγεῖν μεθύοντα, μεθ᾽ ὃν Κράτητα ἐν
Γείτοσι.

Fragments

1 Athenaeus 396d

νῦν μὲν γὰρ ἡμῖν † παιδικῶν δαις †
ὅκωσπερ ἀρνῶν ἐστι γαλαθηνῶν τε καὶ
χοίρων.

2 Athenaeus 690d

γλυκύτατον δ᾽ ὦζε βασιλείου μύρου.

δ᾽ ὦζε Porson, δὲ ὦ Ζεῦ A.

3 Pollux 10.118

οὐκ ἔστι μοι λυχνίδιον.

4 Photius (b, Sᶻ) α 1434

σὲ δὲ χρὴ σιγᾶν μηδ᾽ ἀναγρύζειν.

5 Bekker's *Lexicon* p. 144.27

εἰ σοφὸς ᾖ

CRATES I

Testimonium

i Those who say that Epicharmus was the first to bring a drunken person on stage, and after him Crates in *Neighbours,* do not realize this.

Fragments

1 For now we have a feast (?) of boy friends, like suckling lambs and young piglets.[1]

[1] *Wasps* 572–73 shows that "lambs" (boys) and "piglets" (girls) can be used in a suggestively sexual context.

2 And had the sweetest smell of royal myrrh.

3 I do not have a lampstand.

4 You must be quiet and not utter a peep.

5 If you [masc.] are wise.

6 Photius p. 633.21

ὗς διὰ ῥόδων

ΕΟΡΤΑΙ

ΗΡΩΕΣ

Fragments

10 Hesychius o 1658

οὐκ ἀσκίῳ μεντἄρ' ἐμορμολύττετο
αὐτούς, ἐπεὶ τάδ' ἔστ' ἀληθῆ.

11 Photius (b, z) α 452

οὐκοῦν ἔτνους χρὴ δεῦρο τρύβλιον φέρειν
καὶ τῆς ἀθάρης.

12 Photius (b, z) α 1797

τὸν αὐχέν' ἐκ γῆς ἀνεκὰς, εἰς αὐτοὺς βλέπων.

6 A pig through roses.

Brief fragments: (F 7) "you led astray," (F 8) "scooping out a trough," (F 9) "to play at pessoi."

FEASTS

F 40 of Daring Deeds is attributed in two manuscripts to "Crates in Feasts," while F 41 in all manuscripts is attributed to "Crates in Feasts." But Feasts is otherwise unknown for Crates—it is the title of a comedy by Platon, confusion with which may have caused the misattribution.

HEROES

Both Chionides and Aristophanes wrote comedies of this title, the latter of which had some sort of celebration in honour of heroes. Characters returning from the dead were not uncommon in satyr play or Old Comedy, e.g., Solon's ghost in Cratinus' F 246, the four political leaders in Eupolis' Demes, and a chorus of heroes could have made for an arresting spectacle.

Fragments

10 If this is true, then he wasn't frightening them with a wineskin.

11 So you must bring here a bowl of soup and porridge.

12 ⟨Lifting⟩ your neck up from the ground, looking at them.

13 Pollux 3.155

ἀλτῆρσι θυλάκοισι χρῆσαι τὸ μέγεθος.

14 Pollux 10.90

ὁ κάνης δὲ τῆς κοίτης ὑπερέχειν μοι δοκεῖ.

15 Pollux 10.175

ῥιπίδι κοπραγωγῷ

ΘΗΡΙΑ

Theria *(beasts) has the overtones of "wild," "unsocial," and "antihuman." Part of the folklore surrounding a harmonious "utopia" in the past was the notion that "in those days" beasts could talk and associated freely and easily with men (see Empedocles F 130). Old Comedy featured a number of plays where the interaction between humans and creatures formed the basis of the action:* Birds *where birds used to rule the world and where a man-bird will regain that sovereignty,* Fishes *by Archippus where a formal treaty is needed to achieve peace and reciprocity between Athenians and the fishes, and here in* Beasts *the chorus is calling for an end to eating meat as part of a new order (F 19).*

This comedy presents two recurring themes in Old Comedy: the prominence of animal choruses which some have seen as part of the origins of the genre, and the realisation of an ideal world, whose key description is automatos *(of its own accord—see F 17.8). There will be no need to work or prepare food in such an ideal world. Aristoph-*

13 To use jumping-weights, the size of grain sacks.

14 The mattress seems to me to stretch over the end of the bed.

15 In a wicker dung basket.

BEASTS

anes did not write comedies of this sort, although the theme does lie beneath the agon in Wealth—there Poverty will argue that work is morally beneficial and to have it too easy is not good for human character.

   In a lengthy excursus on comic utopias (267e–70a) Athenaeus claims that F 16–17 are by two different speakers, and implies that F 17 follows F 16 "immediately after this." But the metres of the two fragments are different: F 16 in iambic tetrameter catalectic, a metre that is found in an Aristophanic agon, and F 17 in the basic iambic trimeter. Either F 17 followed F 16 in the next scene, or Crates composed an agon with two different metres, one the "ordinary" iambics of comedy. The two speakers do not seem to be opposed to a new and ideal order, but perhaps on how to achieve it or what features it will stress, the kitchen or the bathroom, or whether it will be an "automatic" utopia or a luxurious excess. Perhaps the two speakers (who?) are trying to outdo one another once the utopian theme has been

Fragments

16 Athenaeus 267e

{A.} ἔπειτα δοῦλον οὐδὲ εἷς κεκτήσετ᾽ οὐδὲ δούλην,
ἀλλ᾽ αὐτὸς αὑτῷ δῆτ᾽ ἀνὴρ γέρων διακονήσει;
{B.} οὐ δῆθ᾽· ὁδοιποροῦντα γὰρ τὰ πάντ᾽ ἐγὼ
ποιήσω.
{A.} τί δῆτα τοῦτ᾽ αὐτοῖς πλέον; {B.} πρόσεισιν αὔθ᾽
ἕκαστον
5 τῶν σκευαρίων, ὅταν καλῇ τις "παρατίθου, τράπεζα.
αὐτὴ παρασκεύαζε σαυτόν. μάττε θυλακίσκε.
ἔγχει κύαθε. ποῦ ᾽σθ᾽ ἡ κύλιξ; διάνιζ᾽ ἰοῦσα
σαυτήν.
ἀνάβαινε μᾶζα. τὴν χύτραν χρῆν ἐξερᾶν τὰ τεῦτλα.
ἰχθύ βάδιζ᾽." "ἀλλ᾽ οὐδέπω ᾽πὶ θάτερ᾽ ὀπτός εἰμι."
10 "οὔκουν μεταστρέψας σεαυτὸν ἁλὶ πάσεις ἀλείφων;"

216

*established. Do we have a protagonist in search of an ideal
society who is given a choice by two gods or heroes as to
what sort of utopia he would choose? The chorus of beasts
will have assisted in his search and choice.*

*Athenaeus says also that the first three comedies that
he mentions, Cratinus'* Wealth-Gods, *Crates'* Beasts, *and
Teleclides'* Amphictyons, *are discussed in the order that
they were performed. A date for* Beasts *in the late 430s
seems indicated.*

Recent bibliography: M. Farioli, Aevum (ant.) *12 (1999)
17–59; J. Wilkins, in* Rivals *347–48; Ceccarelli, in* Rivals
453–55; I. Ruffell, in Rivals *481–82; Pellegrino* (Utopie)
55–69; Olson 75, 100–101, 427.

Fragments

16 (A) So no one will have a slave boy or slave girl, and ev-
ery old man will have to work on his own for himself?

(B) Not at all, for I shall make everything self-mobile.

(A) What advantage will they get from that?

(B) Why, every utensil will appear when someone calls.
"Table, put yourself in place here, and set all the places on
your own. Grain sack, start kneading. Pitcher, start pour-
ing. Where is that cup? Come and rinse yourself out. Bar-
ley loaf, up on the table. The cook pot should be ladling out
the beets by now. Fish, get a move on. 'But I'm not done
yet on the other side.' Well, flip yourself over and baste
yourself in salt and oil."

17 Athenaeus 268a

ἐξῆς δὲ μετὰ ταῦτα ὁ τὸν ἐναντίον τούτῳ παραλαμβάνων λόγον φησίν·

ἀλλ' ἀντίθες τοι· 'γὼ γὰρ αὖ τραπέμπαλιν
τὰ θερμὰ λουτρὰ πρῶτον ἄξω τοῖς ἐμοῖς
ἐπὶ κιόνων, ὥσπερ διὰ τοῦ Παιωνίου
ἀπὸ τῆς θαλάττης ὥσθ' ἑκάστῳ ῥεύσεται
5   εἰς τὴν πύελον. ἐρεῖ δὲ θὕδωρ "ἀνέχετε."
εἶθ' ἀλάβαστος εὐθέως ἥξει μύρου
αὐτόματος ὁ σπόγγος τε καὶ τὰ σάνδαλα.

18 Harpocration p. 241.8 Dindorf

ἔχοντες εὐπαθῆ βίον
παρουσίαν τε χρημάτων.

19 Athenaeus 119c [lines 1–2], Pollux 6.53 [lines 3–4]

{Α.} καὶ τῶν ῥαφάνων ἕψειν χρὴ
ἰχθῦς τ' ὀπτᾶν τούς τε ταρίχους, ἡμῶν δ' ἄπο
χεῖρας ἔχεσθαι.
{Β.} οὐκ ἄρ' ἔτ' οὐδὲν κρέας, ὡς ὑμεῖς λέγετ', οὐδ'
ὁτιοῦν ἐδόμεσθα,
οὐδ' ἐξ ἀγορᾶς, οὐδὲ τάκωνας ποιησόμεθ' οὐδ'
ἀλλᾶντας;

4 ἐξ ἀγορᾶς codd., οὐδ' ἔτι χορδὰς Kock.

ΛΑΜΙΑ

17 Then right after this the person taking up the counter-argument says:

But just consider the other side. I shall do the exact opposite and provide hot baths for my people, straight from the sea on columns, just like at the House of Healing, so that it will flow into everyone's bathtubs. The water will say, "Turn me off now, people," and immediately will arrive on its own a jar full of scented oil, a sponge, and sandals.

18 Having a pleasant life and lots of money.

19 (A) Also you may boil cabbages and roast fresh and salted fish, but keep your hands away from us.
(B) So, as you [pl.] say, we won't be eating meat any more, no tripe any more, no meat pies, no sausages? [1]

[1] I translate Kock's reading.

LAMIA

The Lamia was a Greek bogey figure, used by nurses and parents to scare children. Having lost her own offspring, she would steal the children of others, had foul personal habits (perhaps hermaphroditic), and could remove her eyes from their sockets. Yet behind this witchlike creature lay a myth with the potential for tragedy (see Σ Peace 758): Lamia was the beautiful daughter of Belus and Libya, with whom Zeus fell in love. Hera punished Lamia by killing her children and making her sleepless so that her grief could never be interrupted. Zeus took pity on her and gave her the ability to remove her eyes and thus not notice what was going on around her. He also gave her the power to change her shape. Thus this figure of conventional myth, with reminiscences of Io, Niobe, Europa, and Semele, became a hideous child-stealing bogey woman. Other versions of the story make her the daughter of Poseidon, and mother of either Scylla the monster or the Sibyl.

Stesichorus (c. 600 BC) knows the myth of Lamia, while Euripides (F 472m) refers to "my name, most reviled by

Fragments

20 Σ Aristophanes *Assemblywomen* 77

σκυτάλην ἔχουσα ἐπέρδετο

21 Athenaeus 418c

ἐπὴ τριπήχη Θετταλικῶς τετμημένα

22 Pollux 9.62

ἡμίεκτόν ἐστι χρυσοῦ (μανθάνεις;) ὀκτὼ ὀβολοί.

23 Photius (Sᶻ) α 3396

καὶ μάλιστ᾽ ἀφροδισίοις ἀθύρμασιν· ἡδὺ γὰρ κἀκεῖνο τὸ δρᾶν, λέγεσθαι δ᾽ οὐ καλόν.

24 Photius (b, z) α 1759

ἀνδριστὶ μιμεῖσθαι φωνήν

mortals, Lamia of Libya." We do not know whether the Lamia that Euripides and Crates brought on stage was the ill-fated mortal or the monster of popular lore (or both), but comedy does seem to have made capital with her stick, foul personal habits, and her defence against capture by breaking wind (Crates F 20, Wasps 1035 = Peace 758, Wasps 1177, and a very puzzling passage at Assembly-Women 77).

Fragments

20 With stick in hand she [Lamia] would break wind.

21 Words sliced three-feet thick, Thessalian style.

22 A hemiect of gold—do you understand?—eight obols.

23 And especially with the playthings of love. Sweet it is to do this, but not nice to talk about.[1]

[1] The Greek has been arranged in various metrical forms.

24 To imitate the sound of a man's voice.

25 Σ Plato *Philebus* 14a

ὁ μῦθος ἀπώλετο

ΜΕΤΟΙΚΟΙ

Fragment

26 *Etymologicum Genuinum* AB

λιποπωγωνία

ΠΑΙΔΙΑΙ

25 The story was lost.

METICS

The lexicographer attributes F 26 to "Crates in his Metics," the only mention of such a comedy by Crates—it is not included by the Suda (T 1) among the titles. A Metics is assigned to Pherecrates, again with one fragment extant, while four fragments are known for a Metics by Platon (F 80–83). It is thus not clear whether we have one, two, or three plays with this title. Crates and Pherecrates could easily be confused, but Platon's Metics certainly seems secure. Metics (metoikoi) were the formally registered non-Athenian residents of Athens, and were seen as part of the community (see Acharnians 508). They could certainly have formed an appropriate comic chorus.

Fragment

26 Lack of a beard.

GAMES

Games (Paidiai) *is probably the comedy which the* Suda *(T 1) cites as* Men-in-Chains (Pedetai) *through a confusion with Callias' comedy of that name. If the plural title denotes the chorus, then perhaps the chorus members represented various Athenian games, of which Pollux gives a list at 9.110–17, entering (as Bergk suggested) bearing recognizable implements of their game. But the one game mentioned, the kissing game in F 27, seems to have had no recognizable symbol, and perhaps the title reflects the playing of various games during the play—by children (cf. Theopompus'* Children*) or by party guests.*

Fragments

27 Pollux 9.114

παί-
ζειν δ' ἐν ἀνδρικοῖς χοροῖσι
τὴν κυνητίνδ', ὥσπερ εἰκός,
τοὺς καλοὺς φιλοῦσα.

28 Photius (b, z) a 1010

τοῖς δὲ τραγῳδοῖς ἕτερος σεμνὸς πᾶσιν λόγος
ἄλλος ὅδ' ἔστιν.

ΠΕΔΗΤΑΙ

ΡΗΤΟΡΕΣ

Fragment

30 Athenaeus 369c

Κηφισιακαῖσι γογγυλίσιν ὅμοια πάνυ

ΣΑΜΙΟΙ

Fragments

27 She plays the kissing game among the groups of men, kissing, as you would expect, the good-looking ones.

28 This is a different sort of story, a serious one, for all the tragic poets.

Brief fragment: (F 29) "cup."

MEN-IN-CHAINS

See the note for Games.

POLITICIANS

Athenaeus attributes F 30 to "Crates in Politicians," *another instance of a play known by only one attribution. The easiest solution is to regard this title as a garbled form of either* Neighbours *(Retorsin ~ Geitosin) or* Heroes *(Retorsin ~ Erosin).*

Fragment

30 Quite like Cephisian turnips.

SAMIANS

Is there any connection between a play called "Samians" by a poet of the 430s and the critical revolt of Samos (440/ 39) from the Athenian archē? *But since Crates seems to have been an apolitical and nontopical comic poet, we*

Fragments

31 Bachmann's *Lexicon* p. 419.6

ἥξει δὲ ταχέως ἀργυρίου χλῆδον λαβών

32 Athenaeus 117b

σκυτίνη πότ᾽ ἐν χύτρᾳ τάριχος ἐλεφάντινον
ἧψε ποντιὰς χελώνη πευκίνοισι κύμασιν,
καρκίνοι ποδάνεμοί τε καὶ τανύπτεροι λύκοι
† υσοριμαχειν † ἄνδρες οὐρανοῦ καττύματα.
παῖ ἐκεῖνον, ἄγχ᾽ ἐκεῖνον. ἐν Κέῳ τίς ἡμέρα;

33 Zenobius 3.15

ἵππῳ γηράσκοντι τὰ μείονα κύκλ᾽ ἐπίβαλλε.

34 Σ Hippocrates *Epidemics* 5.7

ἔπαιξαν γυναῖκες ἅτ᾽ ὀρχηστρίδες καλαί,
ἐπὶ κοχωνῶν τὰς τρίχας καθειμέναι.

35 Pollux 7.63

ἱμάτια περιπόρφυρα

might ask what other aspects of Samians might have been useful for comedy. Perhaps the known luxury of Ionian states, or their distinct dialect, or reputation for cleverness.

Fragments

31 He will come quickly, having acquired a heap of silver.

32 Once in a leather cooking pot a sea turtle boiled up an ivory salt fish with pine-wood waves, while wind-swift crabs and long-winged wolves . . . [corrupt] . . . men little bits of the sky. Hit him, choke him! What day is it on Chios?[1]

[1] Aristophanes (T 16) thought the concept of "ivory salt fish" to be excellent "comic fare," but the passage as transmitted does not yield its meaning readily. It is probably best regarded as nonsense verse, with inappropriate adjectives for the nouns and arresting nonsequiturs.

33 Set out smaller circuits for an aging horse.

34 The lovely dancing girls darted out naked, their hair let down to their bums.[1]

[1] Text and metre are uncertain. I have preferred Dübner's γυμναί (naked) to the received text γυναῖκες (women) and Fritzsche's ἐπῆιξαν (darted out) to ἔπαιξαν (sported).

35 Clothes with purple trim.

ΤΟΛΜΑΙ

Fragments

36 Pollux 9.53

πρῶτα μὲν ταλαντιαῖος ὅστις ἔστ' αὐτῶν λέγε.

37 Athenaeus 247f

ποιμαίνει δ' ἐπισίτιον,
ῥιγῶν δ' ἐν Μεγαβύζου,
†δέξετ' ἐπὶ μισθῷ σῖτος†.

1 ἐπισίτιος Dalecampio.

38 Photius p. 337.10

ὄνος ἐν μελίτταις

ΑΔΗΛΩΝ ΔΡΑΜΑΤΩΝ

43 Athenaeus 50e

πάνυ γάρ ἐστιν ὡρικὰ
τὰ τιτθί' ὥσπερ μῆλα ἢ μιμαίκυλα.

44 Σ Aratus 1, p. 45 Martin

ἐξ Ἑστίας ἀρχόμενος εὔχομαι θεοῖς.

DARING DEEDS

*Unless we are to imagine a female chorus representing
"daring deeds" (how costumed?), we have a comedy whose
title reflects a continuing theme within the play.*

Fragments

36 First tell me which of them weighs [is worth?] a talent.

37 He is looking after a man who works for board only,
freezing in the house of Megabyzus, † food as well as wage
will receive†.[1]

> [1] The text and metre (probably from a song) are corrupt.
> Megabyzus is a known Persian name (Herodotus 7.82), but here is
> probably used to carry overtones of grandeur.

38 A donkey among the bees.

*Brief fragments: (F 39) "ever since the time," (F 40) "a
whip set with bones," (F 41) "stockings three layers thick,"
(F 42) "songs of bath men."*

UNASSIGNED FRAGMENTS

43 Her breasts are very fine, like apples or the fruit of the
strawberry tree.

44 Beginning with Hestia I pray to the gods.

45 Photius (b) α 2066

ἀντάκουε νῦν ἐμοῦ

46 Pollux 4.183

ἀλλὰ σικύαν ποτιβαλῶ τοι καὶ τὺ λῇς ἀποσχάσω

47 *Etymologicum Magnum* cod. Vb (Gaisford) col. 193C

ἄναλτος χύτρα

60 Vitruvius 6 Preface 3

pauca sapientibus fortunam tribuere, quae autem maxima et necessaria sunt, animi mentisque cogitationibus gubernari. haec ita etiam plures philosophi dixerunt. non minus poetae, qui antiquas comoedias graece scripserunt, easdem sententias versibus in scaena pronuntiaverunt, ut Eu⟨polis⟩, Crates, Chionides, Aristophanes, maxime etiam cum his Alexis.

45 Now, you [sing.] hear me!

46 I will place this cupping glass on you, and if you agree, will draw some blood.[1]

[1] The dialect is Doric, and the speaker may be a stereotypical comic doctor, who today would be presented as speaking in a thick German accent.

47 A pot that can't be filled.

60 Fortune is of little assistance to wise men; rather the things which are most important and essential are controlled by the judgements of the mind and the heart. Many philosophers have said this, and no less have the poets, who wrote Greek Comedy long ago, expressed these sentiments on the stage in their verses: Eu‹polis›, Crates, Chionides [F 8], Aristophanes [F 924], and especially Alexis.

Brief fragments: (F 48) "one unjustly rich," (F 49) "strange ‹dream›," (F 50) "force-fed," (F 51) "I will stand up," (F 52) "I came back to life," (F 53) "worth ten drachmas," (F 54) "to say falsely," (F 55) "half-chewed," (F 56) "back in court again."

ΚΡΑΤΗΣ ΙΙ

Testimonium

i *Suda* κ 2340

Κράτης, Ἀθηναῖος, κωμικὸς καὶ αὐτὸς τῆς ἀρχαίας κωμῳδίας. φέρεται αὐτοῦ δράματα τρία, Θησαυρός, Ὄρνιθες, Φιλάργυρος.

CRATES II

The entry in the Suda *to Crates (κ 2339) is followed immediately by κ 2340, where another Crates of Old Comedy is recorded with three titles, none of which is ever mentioned or cited elsewhere. Diogenes Laertius (see above T 2) knows of only one comic poet of that name. Of the three titles preserved,* Treasure *is a common title in Middle and New Comedy, but nothing like it appears in Old Comedy, while* Money-Lover *sounds like the type of character again frequent in later comedy. The easiest explanation is that a poet named Crates from the fourth century has been erroneously described as a "poet of Old Comedy."*

Testimonium

i Crates: of Athens, himself also a poet of Old Comedy. Three plays by him are preserved: *Treasure, Birds, Money-Lover.*

ΚΡΑΤΙΝΟΣ

One of the canonical Three of Old Comedy along with Eupolis and Aristophanes, Cratinus was the great poet of the generation before Aristophanes, and it may well have been he that developed Old Comedy into a vigorous and imaginative dramatic form, employing both political themes and personal jokes against contemporary figures (to onomasti kōmōidein). *The beginning of his career is usually set in the mid-450s (see T 4 and T 7), where his name comes on the list of victors at the Dionysia two places after Euphronius, for whom we can place a victory in 458. The reference to the 85th Olympiad in T 3 is either a mistake or, more likely, reflects his first victory at the Lenaea (see T 8). The joke in Aristophanes' Peace (421–T 3, T 11e) about his death during the first Spartan invasion of 431 is chronologically impossible, but may still indicate that he died soon after his victory in 423 at the Dionysia with Wine-Flask (see T 2 to that comedy).*

The Suda (T 1) assigns him twenty-one plays. We have as many as twenty-nine titles, although the actual existence of some is doubtful, e.g., Dionysuses (confused with Dionysalexander?), Blazers, Men of Laconia, Dramatic Rehearsals, Men of Ida (for some an alternative title of Dionysalexander). We have fragments assigned for twenty-two plays, plus two titles known only from the records of the

CRATINUS

festivals preserved in the hypotheses to plays by Aristophanes (T 9a, 9b). We can work with a total of twenty-four comedies in a career that lasted from c. 454–423.

Aristophanes treats Cratinus with an apparent mixture of respect and disdain, although we must always be careful of compliments in comedy, as they are often made in irony to set up the later joke. Thus in Knights *(T 11d) the underlying point is that Cratinus used to be a great comic poet, expressed in terms of a common image in Greek poetry, the writer as a flowing river, but now—as he is competing with Aristophanes at L-424—he is past his prime and should be sitting as a spectator, not producing inferior comedies. Cratinus would make a devastating reply with* Wine-Flask *the next year, in 423, turning Aristophanes' dismissal on its head, making himself his own chief character in a comedy about Comedy, and thus winning the first prize. Some later sources see his comedy as effective and vigorous, but roughly shaped and not maintaining a coherent plot or consistent comic level (see T 25, 31, 35). What we know of* Dionysalexander *and* Wine-Flask *suggests otherwise.*

Cratinus is particularly associated with personal humour. As Platonius puts it (T 25), he is "an emulator of Archilochus," and notice the term "enemies" in T 11d. This is more than just a conclusion drawn from the first title al-

phabetically in the corpus, Archilochuses, *since parodies of and allusions to Archilochus can be found throughout the fragments. Archilochus was the first and greatest of the iambic poets, whose poems contained abusive language, colloquial and obscene language, and a "target" or victim of the poet's alleged wrath. Old Comedy and iambic poetry have much in common, and it was very probably Cratinus who first developed this feature into a fine art in comedy. One of Cratinus' targets was Pericles, and on one school of thought Pericles and his political policies are the target of what can only be called "satire." Cratinus called Pericles "Zeus" (F 73, 258), and on this reading just about any mention of Zeus is meant to stand for Pericles and whole comedies are reconstructed with a political subtext (e.g., Dionysalexander, Nemesis). I would be more cautious here. I do not see Cratinus as out to "get" Pericles in the same way that Aristophanes attacks Cleon, and I suspect that political comedy on a larger and ad hominem scale had to wait for the new poets of the 420s, in particular for Aristophanes with his* Knights *(424).*

Cratinus was fond of the mythological burlesque, as one-third of the titles suggest a comedy of this sort. He would take a familiar story from myth and recast in comic fashion, examining, as Lucian would centuries later, the "logical" comic consequences of such a story. For instance, what would happen if Paris were not available for the Judgement of Paris and Hermes had to replace him with Dionysus (Dionysalexander)? *Or take the story that Helen was hatched from an egg resulting from the union of Zeus and Nemesis, what happens when Leda of Sparta is given that egg to incubate and hatch* (Nemesis)? *Unlike Aristophanes, Cratinus does not seem to indulge in large-scale parodies of specific tragic plays, although Bakola has argued persuasively that some plays* (Wealth-Gods *and* Run-Aways) *are engaging with earlier tragedy, and that Cratinus is especially fascinated by Aeschylus (see T 3). But in these I would regard Cratinus' principal aim as creating a humorous burlesque of the myth, with any serious or topical elements reduced to incidental songs and jokes.*

We see also the expression of a consistent poetic persona in his plays. His Wine-Flask *(D-423) responds to comments made the previous year by Aristophanes in* Knights, *but Biles and Bakola have argued that the picture of the poet as the dramatic genius inspired by wine may be partly the personality that he has developed in his own comedies. Indeed all of Aristophanes' descriptions of Cratinus (T 11) may derive from Cratinus' own earlier self-presentation. We see only the final exchanges in a "war between the poets," but Cratinus may have been responsible also for the conscious metatheatricality of Old Comedy, for the great game that involved poet, rivals, and spectators.*

Recent bibliography: G. Bona, in La Polis e il suo teatro *(1988) 181–211;* M. Heath, G&R 37 *(1990) 143–58;* S. Beta, QUCC 69 *(1992) 95–108;* K. Sidwell, GRBS 34 *(1993) 365–89, in* J. Griffith (ed.), Stage Directions *(1995) 56–80;* M. Farioli, Aevum (ant.) 7 *(1994) 119–36;* Aevum (ant.) 9 *(1996) 73–105;* C. Neri, AFLB 37–38 *(1994–1995) 261–88;* M. de F. Silva, Humanitas 49 *(1997) 3–23;* M. Clavo, Itaca 12–13 *(1996–1997) 19–40;* R. Quaglia, Acme 51 *(1998) 23–71;* I. Ruffell, CQ 52 *(2002) 138–63;* Z. Biles, AJPh 123 *(2002) 169–204;* Storey & Allan 198–201; G. Guidorizzi, in ΚΩΜΩΙΔΟΤΡΑΓΩΙΔΙΑ *119–35;* A. Melero Bellido, in CGA *117–31;* Revermann *299–311;*

Testimonia

i *Suda* κ 2344

Κρατῖνος, Καλλιμήδους, Ἀθηναῖος, κωμικός· λαμ-
πρὸς τὸν χαρακτῆρα, φιλοπότης δὲ καὶ παιδικῶν
ἡττημένος. ἦν δὲ τῆς ἀρχαίας κωμῳδίας. ἔγραψε δὲ
δράματα κα΄, ἐνίκησε δὲ θ΄.

ii *Canons of Comedy*

κωμῳδοποιοὶ ἀρχαίας ζ΄· Ἐπίχαρμος, Κρατῖνος, Εὔ-
πολις, Ἀριστοφάνης, Φερεκράτης, Κράτης, Πλάτων.

iii Anonymous *On Comedy* (Koster III.12–14, 20–27)

τούτων δέ εἰσιν ἀξιολογώτατοι Ἐπίχαρμος,
Μάγνης, Κρατῖνος, Κράτης, Φερεκράτης, Φρύνιχος,
Εὔπολις, Ἀριστοφάνης.

Κρατῖνος Ἀθηναῖος νικᾷ μετὰ τὴν πε΄ Ὀλυμπιάδα,
τελευτᾷ δὲ Λακεδαιμονίων εἰς τὴν Ἀττικὴν εἰσβαλόν-
των τὸ πρῶτον, ὥς φησιν Ἀριστοφάνης·

ὡρακιάσας· οὐ γὰρ ἐξηνέσχετο
ἰδεῖν πίθον καταγνύμενον οἴνου πλέων.

γέγονε δὲ ποιητικώτατος, κατασκευάζων εἰς τὸν
Αἰσχύλου χαρακτῆρα. φέρεται δὲ δράματα αὐτοῦ κα΄.

E. *Bakola*, PCPhS *54 (2008) 1–29;* Cratinus and the Art of Comedy *(Oxford 2010);* W. *Luppe,* Lustrum *48 (2006) 45–72.*

Testimonia

i Cratinus: the son of Callimedes, of Athens, comic poet. Brilliant in style, but also fond of drink and susceptible to boys. He was a poet of Old Comedy. He wrote twenty-one plays, and won nine times.

ii There were seven poets of Old Comedy: Epicharmus, Cratinus, Eupolis, Aristophanes, Pherecrates, Crates, Platon.

iii The most noteworthy of these [poets of Old Comedy] are: Epicharmus, Magnes, Cratinus, Crates, Pherecrates, Phrynichus, Eupolis, Aristophanes.

Cratinus of Athens won a victory after the 85th Olympiad [440/39–437/6]. He died when the Spartans invaded for the first time [431] as Aristophanes says:

He just fainted away, because he could not bear to watch a full jar of wine being smashed. [*Peace* 702–3]

He was a very creative poet, composing in the style of Aeschylus. Twenty-one plays of his are preserved.

Κράτης Ἀθηναῖος. τοῦτον ὑποκριτήν φασι γεγο-
νέναι τὸ πρῶτον, ὃς ἐπιβέβληκε Κρατίνῳ,

Εὔπολις Ἀθηναῖος . . . γεγονὼς δυνατὸς τῇ λέξει
καὶ ζηλῶν Κρατῖνον·

iv Eusebius (Jerome)

Cratinus et Plato comoediarum scriptores clari habentur.

Eusebius (Armenian)

Kratinos und Platon, die Komiker, gingen um diese Zeit
auf.

v Syncellus *Chronography* p. 297.3 Mosshammer.

Κρατῖνος καὶ Πλάτων οἱ κωμικοὶ ἤκμαζον.

vi Lucian *Long-Lives* 25.

Κρατῖνος δὲ ὁ τῆς κωμῳδίας ποιητὴς τέσσαρα πρὸς
τοῖς ἐνενήκοντα ἔτεσιν ἐβίωσε, καὶ πρὸς τῷ τέλει τοῦ
βίου διδάξας τὴν Πυτίνην καὶ νικήσας μετ᾽ οὐ πολὺ
ἐτελεύτα.

vii *IG* ii² 2325.50

Κρατῖ]νος Π I

viii *IG* ii² 2325.121

Κρατῖνος III

Crates of Athens: they say that he was at first an actor who overlapped with Cratinus.

Eupolis of Athens . . . very powerful in his writing and an emulator of Cratinus.

iv [for the year 454/3] Cratinus and Platon, writers of comedy, were well known.

[for the year 453/2] Cratinus and Platon, the comic writers, belong to this period.

v The comic poets Cratinus and Platon were at their height.

vi Cratinus, the comic poet, lived for ninety-four years. At the end of his life he produced *Wine-Flask* and won the prize, and died not long after.

vii [list of victors at the Dionysia, from the 450s]
   Crati]nus 6

viii [list of victors at the Lenaea, early 430s]
   Cratinus 3

ix

(a) Hypothesis I *Acharnians*

ἐδιδάχθη ἐπὶ Εὐθύνου ἄρχοντος ἐν Ληναίοις διὰ Καλλιστράτου· καὶ πρῶτος ἦν· δεύτερος Κρατῖνος Χειμαζομένοις. οὐ σῴζονται. τρίτος Εὔπολις Νουμηνίαις.

(b) Hypothesis II *Knights*

ἐδιδάχθη τὸ δρᾶμα ἐπὶ Στρατοκλέους ἄρχοντος δημοσίᾳ εἰς Λήναια δι᾽ αὐτοῦ τοῦ Ἀριστοφάνους. πρῶτος ἦν· ἐνίκα δεύτερος Κρατῖνος Σατύροις, τρίτος Ἀριστομένης Ὑλοφόροις.

(c) Hypothesis V *Clouds*

αἱ πρῶται Νεφέλαι ἐδιδάχθησαν ἐν ἄστει ἐπὶ ἄρχοντος Ἰσάρχου, ὅτε Κρατῖνος μὲν ἐνίκα Πυτίνῃ, Ἀμειψίας δὲ Κόννῳ.

x P. Oxy. 2739

    Π]υλαία
    Δηλιάδ[ες
    Πλοῦτο[ι
    Νέμεσις
    Δραπέτι[δες
    Βουκόλο[ι

ix

(a) It [*Acharnians*] was produced in the archonship of
Euthynus [426/5] at the Lenaea through Callistratus. It
placed first. Cratinus was second with *Tempest-Tossed*—it
has not been preserved. Eupolis third with *New Moons*.

(b) The play [*Knights*] was produced in the archonship
of Stratocles [425/4] at the Lenaea through Aristophanes
himself. It placed first. Cratinus won second prize with *Sa-
tyrs,* and Aristomenes third with *Wood-Bearers*.

(c) The first version of Clouds was produced at the City
Dionysia in the archonship of Isarchus [424/3], when Cra-
tinus won with *Wine-Flask*, then Ameipsias with *Konnos*.

x [from a second-century AD papyrus, listing poets and
their plays]

> *Pylaea/Delian Women/Wealth-Gods/Nemesis/
> Runaways/Cow-Herders*[1]

[1] The titles are not in alphabetical order; are they listed chro-
nologically?

xi

(a) Aristophanes *Acharnians* 848–53

οὐδ' ἐντυχὼν ἐν τἀγορᾷ
　　πρόσεισί σοι βαδίζων
Κρατῖνος ἀποκεκαρμένος
　　μοιχὸν μιᾷ μαχαίρᾳ,
ὁ περιπόνηρος Ἀρτέμων,
ὁ ταχὺς ἄγαν τὴν μουσικήν,
ὄζων κακὸν τῶν μασχαλῶν
　　πατρὸς Τραγασαίου·

(b) *Acharnians* 1168–73

　　ὁ δὲ λίθον λαβεῖν
βουλόμενος ἐν σκότῳ λάβοι
τῇ χειρὶ πέλεθον ἀρτίως κεχεσμένον·
ἐπάξειεν δ' ἔχων
τὸν μάρμαρον, κἄπειθ' ἁμαρ-
τὼν βάλοι Κρατῖνον.

(c) *Knights* 400

εἴ σε μὴ μισῶ, γενοίμην ἐν Κρατίνου κῴδιον

(d) *Knights* 526–36

εἶτα Κρατίνου μεμνημένος, ὃς πολλῷ ῥεύσας ποτ'
　　ἐπαίνῳ

xi

(a) Nor in *your* marketplace will Cratinus happen to come up and bump into you, hair trimmed on a straight blade in the adulterer's cut, a thorough-going scoundrel Artemon, poetry far too hastily composed, armpits stinking, son of a father from Goatland.

(b) Then wanting to chuck a stone may he [Antimachus] in the darkness seize with his hand a freshly shat turd, and may he charge missile in hand, miss, but hit Cratinus.

(c) If I don't hate you, may I become a duvet in Cratinus' house.

(d) Then with Cratinus in mind, who flowed on a wave of

διὰ τῶν ἀφελῶν πεδίων ἔρρει, καὶ τῆς στάσεως
    παρασύρων
ἐφόρει τὰς δρῦς καὶ τὰς πλατάνους καὶ τοὺς
    ἐχθροὺς προθελύμνους·
ᾆσαι δ' οὐκ ἦν ἐν συμποσίῳ πλήν· "Δωροῖ
    συκοπέδιλε,"
καὶ "τέκτονες εὐπαλάμων ὕμνων"· οὕτως ἤνθησεν
    ἐκεῖνος.
νυνὶ δ' ὑμεῖς αὐτὸν ὁρῶντες παραληροῦντ' οὐκ
    ἐλεεῖτε,
ἐκπιπτουσῶν τῶν ἠλέκτρων καὶ τοῦ τόνου οὐκέτ'
    ἐνόντος
τῶν θ' ἁρμονιῶν διαχασκουσῶν· ἀλλὰ γέρων ὢν
    περιέρρει,
ὥσπερ Κοννᾶς, "στέφανον μὲν ἔχων αὖον, δίψῃ δ'
    ἀπολωλώς,"
ὃν χρῆν διὰ τὰς προτέρας νίκας πίνειν ἐν τῷ
    πρυτανείῳ,
καὶ μὴ ληρεῖν, ἀλλὰ θεᾶσθαι λιπαρὸν παρὰ τῷ
    Διονύσῳ.

(e) *Peace* 700–703

{ΕΡ.} τί δαὶ Κρατῖνος ὁ σοφός; ἔστιν; {ΤΡ.}
    ἀπέθανεν,
ὅθ' οἱ Λάκωνες ἐνέβαλον. {ΕΡ.} τί παθών; {ΤΡ.} ὅ
    τι;
ὡρακιάσας· οὐ γὰρ ἐξηνέσχετο
ἰδὼν πίθον καταγνύμενον οἴνου πλέων.

praise, coursing through the open plains, sweeping head-long from their roots oaks and plane trees and enemies. Singing at a party had to include "Goddess of bribes with fig-wood shoes" and "Makers of clever hymns." He was great then. But now you look on and have no pity for him in his dotage—his frets have fallen out, his strings have lost their tuning, and his harmonies are full of holes. An old man, he stumbles about like Connas, "with withered crown and dying of thirst," when because of his previous victories he should be having a lifetime of free drinks in the Council House, and instead of spouting nonsense he should be sitting splendidly beside Dionysus.

(e) (HERMES) So what about the great Cratinus? Is he still alive?

(TRYGAEUS) He died, when the Spartans invaded.

(HERMES) What happened?

(TRYGAEUS) What happened? He just fainted away, because he could not bear to watch a full jar of wine being smashed.

THE POETS OF OLD COMEDY

(f) *Frogs* 354–57

εὐφημεῖν χρὴ κἀξίστασθαι τοῖς ἡμετέροισι
   χοροῖσιν,
ὅστις ἄπειρος τοιῶνδε λόγων ἢ γνώμην μὴ
   καθαρεύει,
ἢ γενναίων ὄργια Μουσῶν μήτ᾽ εἶδεν μήτ᾽
   ἐχόρευσεν,
μηδὲ Κρατίνου τοῦ ταυροφάγου γλώττης Βακχεῖ᾽
   ἐτελέσθη

xii Horace *Satires* 1.4.1–5

Eupolis atque Cratinus Aristophanesque poetae
atque alii, quorum comoedia prisca virorum est,
siquis erat dignus describi, quod malus ac fur,
quod moechus foret aut sicarius aut alioqui
famosus, multa cum libertate notabant.

xiii Persius 1.123–25

   audaci quicumque adflate Cratino
iratum Eupolidem praegrandi cum sene palles,
aspice et haec, si forte aliquid decoctius audis.

xiv Velleius Paterculus 1.16.3

una priscam illam et ueterem sub Cratino Aristophaneque
et Eupolide comoediam.

CRATINUS

(f) All must be silent and all must withdraw from our songs and dances, those who do not understand such words, whose intellect is not pure, who have not seen nor danced in the rites of the noble Muses, who have not been initiated into the Bacchic speech of bull-eating Cratinus.

xii Eupolis, Cratinus, and Aristophanes and indeed any of the other poets of Old Comedy would with great freedom call attention to anyone who was worthy of being pointed out, for being a wicked man or a thief, an adulterer or a pickpocket or notorious for any other reason.

xiii You who get off on bold Cratinus, who are thrilled by Eupolis as well as the grand old man [Aristophanes], turn your attention also to this, if you would hear something more distilled.

xiv One [generation brought to brilliance] that early Old Comedy under Cratinus, Aristophanes, and Eupolis.

xv Quintilian 10.1.65–66

antiqua comoedia cum sinceram illam sermonis Attici
gratiam prope sola retinet, tum facundissimae libertatis, et
si est <in> insectandis uitiis praecipua, plurimum tamen
uirium etiam in ceteris partibus habet. Nam et grandis et
elegans et uenusta . . . plures eius auctores, Aristophanes
tamen et Eupolis Cratinusque praecipui.

xvi Dion of Prusa 16.9

Ἀθηναῖοι γὰρ εἰωθότες ἀκούειν κακῶς, καὶ νὴ Δία ἐπ᾽
αὐτὸ τοῦτο συνιόντες εἰς τὸ θέατρον ὡς λοιδορη-
θησόμενοι, καὶ προτεθεικότες ἀγῶνα καὶ νίκην τοῖς
ἄμεινον αὐτὸ πράττουσιν, οὐκ αὐτοὶ τοῦτο εὑρόντες,
ἀλλὰ τοῦ θεοῦ συμβουλεύσαντος, Ἀριστοφάνους μὲν
ἤκουον καὶ Κρατίνου καὶ Πλάτωνος, καὶ τούτους οὐδὲν
κακὸν ἐποίησαν.

xvii [Plutarch] *Table-Talk* 711f

τῶν δὲ κωμῳδιῶν ἡ μὲν ἀρχαία διὰ τὴν ἀνωμαλίαν
ἀνάρμοστος ἀνθρώποις πίνουσιν· ἥ τε γὰρ ἐν ταῖς
λεγομέναις παραβάσεσιν αὐτῶν σπουδὴ καὶ παρ-
ρησία λίαν ἄκρατός ἐστι καὶ σύντονος, ἥ τε πρὸς τὰ
σκώμματα καὶ βωμολοχίας εὐχέρεια δεινῶς κατάκο-
ρος καὶ ἀναπεπταμένη καὶ γέμουσα ῥημάτων ἀκό-
σμων καὶ ἀκολάστων ὀνομάτων· ἔτι δ᾽ ὥσπερ ἐν τοῖς
ἡγεμονικοῖς δείπνοις ἑκάστῳ παρέστηκε τῶν κατα-

xv Not only is Old Comedy perhaps alone in preserving that pure grace of Attic language, but it also possesses a very potent freedom, and if it is especially good in chasing down vice, it does have a very great deal of power, however, in other areas, for it is lofty, elegant, and full of charm . . . there are many authors but especially Aristophanes, Eupolis, and Cratinus.

xvi The Athenians were accustomed to hearing bad things about themselves and by Zeus they went to the theatre for the very purpose of being insulted. They established a competition and awarded a prize to the one who did this best. This was not their own invention, but rather on the advice of a god did they listen to Aristophanes and Platon and Cratinus and take no action against them.

xvii Of the types of comedy, the Old is unsuitable for men at their drink because of its lack of consistency. For in the so-called parabases the seriousness and freedom to speak are just too uncontrolled and intense, and its readiness for jests and buffoonery is terribly immoderate and brazen and bursting with indecent and uncontrolled expressions. Just as at banquets of the rich and famous each guest has

κειμένων οἰνοχόος, οὕτω δεήσει γραμματικὸν ἑκάστῳ
τὸ καθ᾽ ἕκαστον ἐξηγεῖσθαι, τίς ὁ Λαισποδίας παρ᾽
Εὐπόλιδι καὶ ὁ Κινησίας παρὰ Πλάτωνι καὶ ὁ Λάμ-
πων παρὰ Κρατίνῳ, καὶ τῶν κωμῳδουμένων ἕκαστος,
ὥστε γραμματοδιδασκαλεῖον ἡμῖν γενέσθαι τὸ συμ-
πόσιον ἢ κωφὰ καὶ ἄσημα τὰ σκώμματα διαφέρε-
σθαι.

xviii [Dionysius of Halicarnassus] *Art of Rhetoric* 8.11

ἡ δέ γε κωμῳδία ὅτι πολιτεύεται ἐν τοῖς δράμασι καὶ
φιλοσοφεῖ, ἡ τῶν περὶ τὸν Κρατῖνον καὶ Ἀριστο-
φάνην καὶ Εὔπολιν, τί δεῖ καὶ λέγειν; ἡ γάρ τοι
κωμῳδία αὐτὴ τὸ γελοῖον προστησαμένη φιλοσοφεῖ.

xix Evanthius *On Drama* (Koster XXV.1.24–25)

comodiae veteris pater Eupolis cum Cratino Aristophane-
que esse credatur.

xx Himerius 24 p. 115.14 Colonna

οὐκ ἦν ἀδοξότερος Δαιδάλου Φειδίας . . . οὐκ Ἐπι-
χάρμου Κρατῖνος, οὐ τῶν ἀμφὶ Τισίαν καὶ Κόρακα οἱ
κατὰ Γοργίαν καὶ Πρωταγόραν ἀνθήσαντες

xxi Synesius *Dio* 18

ἐγὼ δὴ θαμὰ καὶ τραγῳδίαις ἐπετραγῴδησα, καὶ κω-
μῳδίαις ἐπιστωμύλλομαι πρὸς τὸν πόνον ἑκάστου τοῦ

his own wine waiter standing beside him, so too we would need a learned scholar beside each guest to explain each reference, e.g., who Laispodias was in Eupolis [F 107], and Cinesias in Platon [F 200], and Lampon in Cratinus [F 62, 125] and so on for each of the people made fun of. So our party would become a classroom and the jokes would fall on deaf and ignorant ears.

xviii It is hardly necessary to state that comedy in the time of Cratinus and Aristophanes and Eupolis engaged with politics and philosophy. For in fact comedy is philosophical when it evokes laughter.

xix Eupolis, along with Cratinus and Aristophanes, is believed to be the father of Old Comedy.

xx Phidias had no less of a reputation than Daedalus . . . nor Cratinus than Epicharmus, nor those who flourished with Gorgias and Protagoras than those at the time of Tisias and Korax.

xxi I mourned tragically along with the tragedians and played the fool with comedy according to the style of each

γράψαντος. εἴποις ἂν ἡλικιώτην εἶναι νῦν μὲν Κρα-
τίνου καὶ Κράτητος, νῦν δὲ Διφίλου τε καὶ Φιλήμονος

xxii Libanius *Letters* 1477.5

ἢ οὐχ ἑώρακας αὐτοὺς πίνοντας μὲν ὑπὲρ τὸν Κρα-
τῖνον, ἐσθίοντας δὲ ὑπὲρ τὸν Ἡρακλέα;

xxiii Zenobius *Common Sayings* 3.81

"Ἐπειοῦ δειλότερος"· οὕτως ἐλέγετο Κρατῖνος ὁ κωμι-
κός, ἴσως διὰ τὸ ταξιαρχῆσαι τῆς Οἰνηίδος φυλῆς καὶ
δειλότερος φανῆναι. καὶ γὰρ Ἐπειὸς δειλὸς ἦν.

xxiv Platonius *On the Different Sorts of Comedy* (Koster
I.2–3, 12–14)

ἐπὶ τῶν Ἀριστοφάνους καὶ Κρατίνου καὶ Εὐπόλιδος
χρόνων τὰ τῆς δημοκρατίας ἐκράτει παρ᾽ Ἀθηναίοις
καὶ τὴν ἐξουσίαν σύμπασαν ὁ δῆμος . . . ἐπὶ τοίνυν
τῆς Ἀριστοφάνους καὶ Κρατίνου καὶ Εὐπόλιδος
κωμῳδίας ἀφόρητοί τινες κατὰ τῶν ἁμαρτανόντων
ἦσαν οἱ ποιηταί.

xxv Platonius *On the Different Sorts of Styles* (Koster
II.1–8)

Κρατῖνος ὁ τῆς παλαιᾶς κωμῳδίας ποιητής, ἅτε δὴ
κατὰ τὰς Ἀρχιλόχου ζηλώσεις, αὐστηρὸς μὲν ταῖς
λοιδορίαις ἐστίν· οὐ γὰρ ὥσπερ Ἀριστοφάνης ἐπι-

author. You might say that I was a contemporary now of Cratinus and Crates, then of Diphilus and Philemon.

xxii Have you not seen them, drinking more than Cratinus, eating more than Heracles?

xxiii "More cowardly than Epeius": this was said of the comic poet Cratinus, perhaps because he had been a taxiarch for the tribe of Oeneis and had shown himself rather cowardly. Epeius was a coward.[1]

[1] Oeneis is a tribe in the political and social order of Athens, and taxiarchs were in charge of the troops of each tribe. But the name "Oeneis" is related to the Greek word for wine (*oinos*), and Cratinus may have described himself (or been described) in comedy as "leader of the men from the Wine-Tribe." Epeius was a figure in the Trojan War, the builder of the Horse, who acquired in later literature a reputation for cowardice.

xxiv In the time of Aristophanes and Cratinus and Eupolis the democracy ruled at Athens and the people possessed supreme authority . . . So then in the time of the comedy of Aristophanes and Cratinus and Eupolis the poets were an irresistible force against wrongdoers.

xxv Cratinus, the poet of Old Comedy, is harsh in his insults—he is, after all, emulating Archilochus. Unlike Aris-

τρέχειν τὴν χάριν τοῖς σκώμμασι ποιεῖ, τὸ φορτικὸν
τῆς ἐπιτιμήσεως διὰ ταύτης ἀναιρῶν, ἀλλ' ἁπλῶς
κατὰ τὴν παροιμίαν γυμνῇ τῇ κεφαλῇ τίθησι τὰς
βλασφημίας κατὰ τῶν ἁμαρτανόντων, πολὺς δὲ καὶ
⟨ἐν⟩ ταῖς τροπαῖς τυγχάνει. εὔστοχος δὲ ὢν ἐν ταῖς
ἐπιβολαῖς τῶν δραμάτων καὶ διασκευαῖς, εἶτα προιὼν
καὶ διασπῶν τὰς ὑποθέσεις οὐκ ἀκολούθως πληροῖ τὰ
δράματα.

xxvi

(a) Tzetzes *Distinctions among Poets* (Koster XXIa.78–
87)

τῆς δευτέρας ἦν ὁ ψόγος κεκρυμμένος,
ἧς ἦν Κρατῖνος, Εὔπολις, Φερεκράτης,
Ἀριστοφάνης, Ἕρμιππός τε καὶ Πλάτων·

(b) Tzetzes *Proem* (Koster XIa.78–79, 97–101)

ἀλλὰ ψήφισμα θέντος Ἀλκιβιάδου κωμῳδεῖν ἐσχημα-
τισμένως καὶ μὴ προδήλως αὐτός τε ὁ Εὔπολις Κρα-
τῖνός τε καὶ Φερεκράτης καὶ Πλάτων, οὐχ ὁ φιλόσο-
φος, Ἀριστοφάνης τε σὺν ἑτέροις τὰ συμβολικὰ
μετεχειρίσαντο σκώμματα, καὶ ἡ δευτέρα κωμῳδία τῇ
Ἀττικῇ ἀνεσκίρτησεν.

tophanes he does not allow charm to flow through his
jokes, thereby lightening the vulgarity of his criticism, but
rather makes his jokes at evildoers "full speed ahead," so to
speak. He is rather lavish in figures of speech. He is suc-
cessful in the conception and layout of his plays, but his
plots fall apart and he does not flesh out his plays consis-
tently.

xxvi

(a) Concealed insult was characteristic of second ‹com-
edy›, of which there were Cratinus, Eupolis, Pherecrates,
Aristophanes, Hermippus, and Platon.

(b) But when Alcibiades passed a law to make fun of peo-
ple indirectly and not plainly, Eupolis and Cratinus and
Pherecrates and Aristophanes with the rest fashioned
their jokes allusively and so second comedy was at its
height at Athens.

(c) Tzetzes *Prolegomena to Lycophron* (Koster XXIIb.39–41)

κωμῳδοὶ πραττόμενοι εἰσιν οὗτοι, οἷοι Ἀριστοφάνης Κρατῖνος Πλάτων Εὔπολις Φερεκράτης καὶ ἔτεροι

xxvii Σ Aristophanes *Knights* 537a

"οἵας δὲ Κράτης ὀργάς"· οὗτος κωμῳδίας ποιητής, ὃς πρῶτον ὑπεκρίνατο ‹τὰ› Κρατίνου, καὶ αὐτὸς ποιητὴς ὕστερον ἐγένετο.

xxviii Σ Aristophanes *Knights* 400a

ὡς ἐνουρητὴν δὲ καὶ μέθυσον διαβάλλει τὸν Κρατῖνον. ὁ δὲ Κρατῖνος καὶ αὐτὸς ἀρχαίας κωμῳδίας ποιητής, πρεσβύτερος Ἀριστοφάνους, τῶν εὐδοκίμων ἄγαν.

xxix Σ Aristophanes *Peace* 741

τινές φασι καὶ εἰς Κρατῖνον αἰνίττεσθαι ὡς τοιαῦτα ποιοῦντα δράματα.

xxx Σ Aristophanes *Frogs* 357

εἴρηται δὲ παρὰ τὸ Σοφοκλέους ἐκ Τυροῦς "Διονύσου τοῦ ταυροφάγου." ἢ ὅτι φίλοινος ἦν καὶ διὰ τοῦτο ἐπίθετον τοῦ Διονύσου αὐτῷ περιτιθέασιν. οἱ δὲ ἔτι περιεργότερον ὅλον τὸν λόγον ἀποδιδόασι . . . ἢ

(c) The comic poets that are studied are those such as Aristophanes, Cratinus, Platon, Eupolis, Pherecrates and the others.

xxii "The insults at Crates": this man was a comic poet, who at first acted in plays by Cratinus, and later became a poet himself.

xxviii He accuses Cratinus of being a drunk and incontinent. Cratinus was himself a poet of Old Comedy, earlier than Aristophanes, one of the most highly regarded.

xxix Some say that this is also an allusion to Cratinus, who wrote such plays.

xxx This is parodied from "of Dionysus the bull eater," found in Sophocles' *Tyro* [F 668]. Or because he [Cratinus] was fond of wine and for that reason they attach an epithet of Dionysus to him. Some say that the whole expression is just superfluous. Or "bold," as from the

τολμηρόν· ἀπὸ τῶν βακχῶν. τολμηροὺς γὰρ διέσυρε
τοὺς Ἀθηναίους ἐν τοῖς δράμασι.

xxxi Anonymous *On Comedy* (Koster V.12–21)

καὶ αὐτὴ δὲ ἡ παλαιὰ ἑαυτῆς διαφέρει. καὶ γὰρ οἱ ἐν
Ἀττικῇ πρῶτον συστησάμενοι τὸ ἐπιτήδευμα τῆς
κωμῳδίας—ἦσαν δὲ οἱ περὶ Σαννυρίωνα—καὶ τὰ
πρόσωπα εἰσῆγον ἀτάκτως, καὶ μόνος ἦν γέλως τὸ
κατασκευαζόμενον. ἐπιγενόμενος δὲ ὁ Κρατῖνος κατ-
έστησε μὲν πρῶτον τὰ ἐν τῇ κωμῳδίᾳ πρόσωπα μέχρι
τριῶν στήσας τὴν ἀταξίαν καὶ τῷ χαρίεντι τῆς κωμῳ-
δίας τὸ ὠφέλιμον προστέθεικε τοὺς κακῶς πράττοντας
διαβάλλων καὶ ὥσπερ δημοσίᾳ μάστιγι τῇ κωμῳδίᾳ
κολάζων. ἀλλ᾽ ἔτι μὲν καὶ οὗτος τῆς ἀρχαιότητος
μετεῖχε καὶ ἠρέμα πως τῆς ἀταξίας.

xxxii Diomedes *Art of Grammar* (Koster XXIV.46–52)

poetae primi comici fuerunt Susario, Mullus et Magnes. hi
veteris disciplinae iocularia quaedam minus scite ac ve-
nuste pronuntiabant . . . secunda aetate fuerunt
Aristophanes, Eupolis et Cratinus, qui et principum vitia
sectati acerbissimas comeodias composuerunt.

xxxiii Σ Dionysius Thrax (Koster XVIIIa.1–2, 37–41)

κωμῳδία λέγεται τὰ τῶν κωμικῶν ποιήματα, ὡς τὰ τοῦ
Μενάνδρου καὶ Ἀριστοφάνους καὶ Κρατίνου καὶ τῶν

bacchae, for he [Cratinus] attacked the Athenians boldly
in his plays.

xxxi Old Comedy has differences within itself. For those
at Athens who first put together the business of comedy—
these were Sannyrion[1]and his people—would bring char-
acters on haphazardly and the humour lay in the perfor-
mance. But when Cratinus followed these, he first fixed
the number of characters at three, thereby stopping the
disorder, and to the fun of comedy he added a usefulness
by attacking those who behaved badly and punishing them
by using comedy as a sort of public whip. But he too did
share partly in the old style and in some degree of its lack
of order.

[1] "Sannyrion" is clearly an error for "Susarion."

xxxii The first comic poets were Susarion, Mullus, and
Magnes. They were of the old style and delivered their
jokes rather less skilfully and elegantly . . . To the second
age belonged Aristophanes, Eupolis, and Cratinus, who
wrote very fierce comedies attacking the vices of the lead-
ing men.

xxxiii By "comedy" is meant the plays of the comic poets,
those by Menander, Aristophanes, Cratinus, and the like

ὁμοίων . . . διὸ καὶ τρεῖς διαφορὰς ἔδοξεν ἔχειν ἡ
κωμῳδία· καὶ ἡ μὲν καλεῖται παλαιά, ἡ ἐξ ἀρχῆς
φανερῶς ἐλέγχουσα, ἡ δὲ μέση, ἡ αἰνιγματωδῶς, ἡ δὲ
νέα, ἡ μηδ᾽ ὅλως τοῦτο ποιοῦσα πλὴν ἐπὶ δούλων ἢ
ξένων. καὶ τῆς μὲν παλαιᾶς πολλοὶ γεγόνασιν, ἐπί-
σημος δὲ Κρατῖνος ὁ καὶ πραττόμενος, μετέσχον δέ
τινος χρόνου τῆς παλαιᾶς κωμῳδίας Εὔπολίς τε καὶ
Ἀριστοφάνης

xxxiv Σ Thucydides 1.30.1

ἡ παλαιὰ Ἀτθίς, ἧς ἐστιν Εὔπολις Κρατῖνος Ἀρι-
στοφάνης Θουκυδίδης.

xxxv *Life of Aristophanes* (Koster XXVIII.1–5)

Ἀριστοφάνης . . . πρῶτος δοκεῖ τὴν κωμῳδίαν ἔτι
πλανωμένην τῇ ἀρχαίᾳ ἀγωγῇ ἐπὶ τὸ χρησιμώτερον
καὶ σεμνότερον μεταγαγεῖν, πικρότερόν τε καὶ
αἰσχρότερον Κρατίνου καὶ Εὐπόλιδος βλασφημούν-
των ἢ ἔδει.

xxxvi Rufinus *On the Metres of Terence* (GrL VI p. 564.7)

ad Probum de metris comoediarum sic dicit: "nam quod
de metris comoediarum requisisti, et ego scio plurimos
existimare Terentianas vel maxime fabulas metrum non
habere comoediae graecae, id est Menandri Philemonos
Diphili et ceterorum, quae trimetris versibus constat.

. . . Comedy appears to have had three forms. What is called "Old Comedy" is comedy which from the start attacks openly, "Middle" that ‹which attacks› allusively, and "New" that which does do not do this at all except for slaves and foreigners. There were many poets of Old Comedy, especially Cratinus, who is still studied. For a while Eupolis and Aristophanes were part of Old Comedy.

xxxiv The Old Attic, to which belong Eupolis, Cratinus, Aristophanes, Thucydides.

xxxv Aristophanes . . . seems to have been the first to steer comedy, which was wandering about in the old style, to something more useful and more serious, when Cratinus and Eupolis were using bad language more bitterly and more shamelessly than they needed to.

xxxvi He [Firmianus] writes to Probus as follows about comic metres: "Now about what you have asked about the metres of comedy, I do know that very many people believe that Terence's plays in particular do not possess the metre of Greek Comedy, that is the comedy of Menander, Philemon, and Diphilus, which consists of verses in tri-

nostri enim veteris comediae scriptores in modulandis fa-
bulis sequi maluerunt, Eupolin Cratinum Aristophanem."

xxxvii "Marius Victorinus" (Aphthonius) *Art of Grammar*
3.15 (*GrL* VI p. 124.8)

illa anapesticorum species de fonte dactylici versus
veniens apta admodum comicis quae aristophanios nuncu-
pata est, non quia conditor eius Aristophanes fuit (nam et
Aeschylus et Cratinus, priscae comoediae scriptor, ea usi
sunt), sed quia plurimus in hoc metro Aristophanes in-
venitur.

xxxviii Fragmenta Bobiensia *On Metres* (*GrL* VI p.
622.12)

comicum, quod praecipue dactylos et anapestos admittat,
ut est apud Cratinum "super aquosis fontibus ipsa sederat
ales Ceycis"; satyricum, quod complures habeat solutions
et tribrachyn pedem ⟨frequenter admittat⟩, ut est item
apud Cratinum "qualis aquila cita celeribus rapida pinnis
transvolat."

xxxix Hephaestion *Handbook* 15.21

τούτου δὲ μεῖζόν ἐστι συλλαβῇ τῇ τελευταίᾳ τὸ κα-
λούμενον Κρατίνειον· ἔστι γὰρ ἐκ χοριαμβικοῦ ἐπι-
μίκτου, τοῦ τὴν δευτέραν ἰαμβικὴν ἔχοντος καὶ
τροχαϊκοῦ ἐφθημιμεροῦς . . . τὸ μὲν οὖν καθαρὸν

mesters. For our writers preferred to follow the poets of
Old Comedy in composing their verse, such as Eupolis,
Cratinus, and Aristophanes."

xxxvii That form of anapaests which comes from a dac-
tylic source is quite suitable for comedy. It is called the
"aristophanean," not because Aristophanes was its inven-
tor—in fact Aeschylus and Cratinus, the poet of Old Com-
edy, used it—but because this metre is found so often in
Aristophanes' work.

xxxviii [The tetrameter catalectic] a metre, which in
comedy allows particularly dactyls and anapaests, as in
Cratinus "above the springs of water had perched the bird
of Ceyx," and which in satire permits several resolutions
and ‹often allows› a tribrach, as again in Cratinus "like a
swift eagle flies quickly on rapid wings."

xxxix Longer than this by one syllable at the end is the
metre called the cratinean, which is composed of that ad-
mixed choriamb whose second syzygy is iambic, plus a tro-
chaic hephtheminer [quoting F 361]. Such is the cratinean

Κρατίνειον τοιοῦτόν ἐστι· πολυσχημάτιστον δὲ αὐτὸ
πεποιήκασιν οἱ κωμικοί. τοὺς γὰρ σπονδείους τοὺς
ἐμπίπτοντας ἐν τοῖς ἰαμβικοῖς καὶ τοῖς τροχαϊκοῖς
παρὰ τάξιν παραλαμβάνουσιν ἐν ταῖς μέσαις συζυ-
γίαις, τῇ τροχαϊκῇ καὶ τῇ ἰαμβικῇ.

xl Galen *On his own Books* 17

τῶν παρὰ τοῖς Ἀττικοῖς συγγραφεῦσιν ὀνομάτων
τεσσαράκοντα ὀκτώ· τῶν παρ' Εὐπόλιδι πολιτικῶν
ὀνομάτων τρία· τῶν παρ' Ἀριστοφάνει πολιτικῶν ὀνο-
μάτων πέντε· τῶν παρὰ Κρατίνῳ πολιτικῶν ὀνομάτων
δύο· τῶν ἰδίων κωμικῶν ὀνομάτων παραδείγματα, ἕν·
'εἰ χρήσιμον ἀνάγνωσμα τοῖς πεπαιδευομένοις ἡ
παλαιὰ κωμῳδία'.

xli [Dionysius of Halicarnassus] *Art of Rhetoric* 11.10

κωμικὸν τοῦτο Ἀριστοφάνειον, κωμικὸν τοῦτο Κρα-
τίνειον, τοῦτο Εὐπολίδειον, τοῦτο Μενάνδρου.

xlii Σ Aristophanes *Wasps* 151b

ἐν δὲ τοῖς περὶ Κρατίνου διώρισται

xliii Nicaenus *Epigram* 5 (= *AP* 13.29)

οἰνός τοι χαρίεντι πέλει ταχὺς ἵππος ἀοιδῷ·
    "ὕδωρ δὲ πίνων οὐδὲν ἂν τέκοις σοφόν."
τοῦτ' ἔλεγεν, Διόνυσε, καὶ ἔπνεεν οὐχ ἑνὸς ἀσκοῦ
    Κρατῖνος, ἀλλὰ παντὸς ὠδώδει πίθου.

in its pure form, but the comic poets have made it multiform, by using spondees that occur in iambic and trochaic metra against the order in the central syzygies, the trochaic and the iambic.

xl Forty-eight books of political terms in the Attic historians, three books of political terms in Eupolis, five books of political terms in Aristophanes, and three books of political terms in Cratinus. Examples of particular comic expressions, one book. *Is Old Comedy Useful Reading for Educated Men?*

xli This comic expression is Aristophanic, this one Cratinean, this one Eupolidean, and this one of Menander.

xlii The distinction is made in the work *On Cratinus.*

xliii Wine is a swift steed for a poet of charm, and "you will never create anything great by drinking water." Cratinus used to say this [F 203], Dionysus, and from him wafted the scent, not of just one wineskin, but of an entire

τοιγὰρ ὑπὸ στεφάνοις μέγας ἔβρυεν, εἶχε δὲ κισσῷ
μέτωπον ὥσπερ καὶ σὺ κεκροκωμένον.

xliv Christodorus *AP* 2.357–60

καὶ τύπος ἁβρὸς ἔλαμπεν ἀριστονόοιο Κρατίνου,
ὅς ποτε δημοβόροισι πολισσούχοισιν Ἰώνων
θυμοδακεῖς ἐθόωσεν ἀκοντιστῆρας ἰάμβους,
κῶμον ἀεξήσας, φιλοπαίγμονος ἔργον ἀοιδῆς.

ΑΡΧΙΛΟΧΟΙ

*The title should mean something like "Archilochus and his
followers" or "poets like Archilochus." Old Comedy owed
much to the iambic tradition of personal abuse poets such
as Archilochus, Semonides, and Hipponax, both in the lan-
guage and metre of their verse, but also in the literary per-
sona of the poet ranged against his targeted victim. F 6 and
11 both contain references to Archilochus and his poetry.
T 1 suggests that Homer and Hesiod, or their support-
ers, were characters in the play—these will have been the
"swarm of sophists" of F 2. We may well have had two half-
choruses, as in Lysistrata and Eupolis' Maricas. The plural
"you" in F 2 are probably the human protagonists whose
great idea has sparked off the plot.*

*F 7 plays on a phrase "the vote of Zeus" in reference to
the contest between Athena and Poseidon for the patron-
age of Athens. This suggests that we may have had a contest*

268

jar. Crowns of victory weighed the great man down, and his forehead was as yours, golden with ivy.

xliv Also shone forth the elegant form of great-minded Cratinus, who once sharpened the soul-biting javelin-tips of his iambs against the leaders of Athens who became fat off the people and made comedy something greater, the product of song that loves laughter.[1]

[1] The Greek text has "people-devouring guardians of Ionians." Athens saw itself as the mother city of the Ionian Greeks. This is part of a series of poetic descriptions by Christodorus of Egyptian Thebes (6th c. AD) of the statues in a public gymnasium in Constantinople.

ARCHILOCHUSES

in this play, perhaps between proponents of heroic epic and those of the poetry of blame (iambic or comedy). F 6–8 are in dactylic hexameter, the metre of epic, F 10 can with a small emendation be made to fit the metre of Archilochus F 196, and F 11 is in one of the fifteen-syllable metres used by comedy in its parabases. Might we consider a metatheatrical setting with comedy (or Cratinus himself) choosing or defending the literary model for his work?

The play had been dated (overconfidently) to the early 440s by the mention of Cimon's "gone and left me" (F 1). Cimon died in 450/49. But the reference to his death does not have to be recent, and if Hermann's πρὸ τοῦ *is accepted for the unmetrical* πρώτῳ *in line 3, then* Archilochuses *could be much later. We are not certain which Callias (F 12) was made fun of in the play, the Callias of the last part of the century (target of Eupolis in* Spongers *and of*

269

Fragments

1 Plutarch *Cimon* 10.1

κἀγὼ γὰρ ηὔχουν Μητρόβιος ὁ γραμματεὺς
σὺν ἀνδρὶ θείῳ καὶ φιλοξενωτάτῳ
καὶ πάντ᾽ ἀρίστῳ τῶν Πανελλήνων † πρώτῳ
Κίμωνι λιπαρὸν γῆρας εὐωχούμενος
αἰῶνα πάντα συνδιατρίψειν. ὁ δὲ λιπὼν
βέβηκε πρότερος.

3 πρώτῳ MSS, πρὸ τοῦ Hermann, πρόμῳ Muretus.

2 Clement of Alexandria *Miscellany* 1.24.1–2

οἷον σοφιστῶν σμῆνος ἀνεδιφήσατε.

3 Photius p. 28.27

εὕδοντι δ᾽ αἱρεῖ πρωκτός.

4 Athenaeus 375a

ἤδη δέλφακες, χοῖροι δὲ τοῖσιν ἄλλοις.

the other comic poets, antagonist of Andocides, erastēs of
Autolycus) or his grandfather, active politically in the 440s
(see PCG VIII F 696). If F 12 does refer to the younger
Callias, then Archilochuses *must belong to the 420s, since*
he came into his inheritance in the late 420s and only then
his way of life became comic material. Bakola (71) follows
Luppe (Philologus 1973) in dating the play between 435
and 432.

Recent bibliography: M. Ornaghi, in Zanetto et al. Mo-
menti della ricezione omerica *(Milan 2004) 197–228.*

Fragments

1 And I, Metrobius the secretary, was confident that I
would live a very long time, enjoying a splendid old age, in
the company of Cimon, a godlike and most hospitable
man, by far the best of all Greeks. But he's gone first and
left me.

2 What a swarm of sophists you people have stirred up.[1]

[1] Diogenes Laertius (1.12) records that "clever people were
called 'sophists' . . . poets also are 'sophists' as Cratinus in
Archilochuses so calls Homer, Hesiod, and such like as a compli-
ment."

3 His bottom does the catching while he sleeps.

4 Full-grown pigs now, but to others piglets.[1]

[1] There may well be a *sensus obscaenus* at work here, distin-
guishing the female genitalia of a mature woman (*delphax*) from
that of an immature girl (*choiros*).

5 Stephanus of Byzantium p. 248.14

Δωδωναίῳ κυνὶ, βωλοκόπῳ τίτθη γεράνῳ
προσεοικώς.

6 Athenaeus 164de

εἶδες τὴν Θασίαν ἅλμην οἷ᾽ ἄττα βαΰζει;
ὡς εὖ καὶ ταχέως ἀπετείσατο καὶ παραχρῆμα.
οὐ μέντοι παρὰ κωφὸν ὁ τυφλὸς ἔοικε λαλῆσαι.

7 Photius (Sᶻ) δ 659

ἔνθα Διὸς μεγάλου θᾶκοι πεσσοί τε καλοῦνται.

8 Athenaeus 86e

ἢ μὲν δὴ πίννῃσι καὶ ὀστρείοισιν ὁμοίη.

9 Photius (b, z) α 1325

        εἶτ᾽ ἀμφιετηριζομέναις
ὥραις τε καὶ χρόνῳ μακρῷ

10 Athenaeus 410d

ὠμολίνοις κόμη βρύουσ᾽ ἀτιμίας πλέως.

11 Hephaestion *Handbook* 15.7

Ἐρασμονίδη Βάθιππε τῶν ἀωρολείων.

5 A nurse like a dog from Dodona or an altar-thieving crane?[1]

1 The text and meaning are obscure. I have translated Gronovius' βωμοκλόπῳ (altar-thieving) for the manuscript's βωλοκόπῳ (clod-breaking).

6 Did you notice what the Thasian pickle brine was barking? He well and quickly and immediately got his own back. It's not, however, a blind man talking to a deaf one.[1]

1 Archilochus (of Paros) took part in the colonisation of Thasos, and his poetry was famous for its bitter personal insult (hence "Thasian pickle brine"). The "blind man" could well be Homer.

7 Where are what they call the seat and game board of great Zeus.

8 She is very much indeed like mussels and oysters.

9 As the seasons return year by year and in the length of time.

10 Her hair streaming with coarse linen, a sorry sight.

11 O Bathippus, son of Erasmon, with the smooth chin of a boy.[1]

1 F 168 of Archilochus begins "O Charilaus, son of Erasmon." Bathippus is a documented Athenian name in the 4th c.

12 Σ Lucian *Tragic Zeus* 48

ὁ μὲν Καλλίας οὗτος, ὡς Κρατῖνος Ἀρχιλόχοις φησίν, Ἱππονίκου υἱὸς ἦν τὸν δῆμον Μελιτεύς, ὡς Ἀριστοφάνης Ὥραις πλούσιος καὶ πασχητιῶν καὶ ὑπὸ πορνιδίων διαφορούμενος καὶ κόλακας τρέφων.

13 Σ Lucian *Alexander* 4

"ὑπὲρ τοὺς Κέρκωπας"· οὗτοι ἐν Βοιωτίᾳ διέτριβον Οἰχαλιεῖς ὄντες γένος Σίλλος καὶ Τριβαλὸς ὀνομαζόμενοι, ἐπίορκοι καὶ ἀργοί, ὡς Κρατῖνος Ἀρχιλόχοις.

14 Photius p. 498.10

Σαμιακὸν τρόπον· Κρατῖνος Ἀρχιλόχοις· εἰς ὑηνίαν ἐπισκώπτων †μιννύω†· ναυσὶ γὰρ ἐμφερεῖς εἶχε τὰς πρώρας τὰ τῶν Σαμίων πλοῖα, ὡς Χοιρίλος ὁ Σάμιος.

ΒΟΥΚΟΛΟΙ

The title implies a chorus of rustic cattle herders. Whatever we are to read in the text of F 20, the play appears to have begun with a dithyramb or "from Dithyrambus" (a title of Dionysus—see Bacchae 526). This has suggested to some a connection with Dionysus, even that he was a character in the comedy, and that Cratinus was claiming "Dionysiac poetics" for his comedy. Bakola (42–49) argues that boukoloi was a technical term for "worshippers of Dionysus," but the chain of evidence is weak and not conclusive. F 20 seems to show Cratinus complaining that he did not

12 This Callias, as Cratinus says in *Archilochuses,* was the son of Hipponicus, of Melite by deme, as Aristophanes says in *Seasons* [F 583] a wealthy man and sex-crazed, exploited by prostitutes and supporting spongers.

13 "Beyond the Cercopes": they lived in Boeotia, from Oechalia by race, and were named Sillus and Tribalus. They were liars and lazy, as Cratinus says in *Archilochuses.*

14 "In the Samian way": Cratinus in *Archilochuses,* making fun of Mennion (?) for swinish behaviour. According to Chorilus of Samos [*FGrHist* 696 F 34], Samian boats had prows in the shape of pigs.

Brief fragments: (F 15) "without guile," (F 16) "ithyphallus."

COW-HERDERS

get a chorus from the archon in charge of the festival, and F 17 criticises an archon for refusing Sophocles a chorus, while granting one to the son of Cleomachus, Gnesippus. The speaker of F 17 ("for me") could be the poet speaking through a character or possibly Comedy herself. As most references to Gnesippus seem to belong before the debut of Aristophanes (427), the comedy likely belongs to the 430s or early 420s. The inscription from Aexone (T 1), dated to c. 380, is a record of past successes and does not help us with the date.

Testimonium

i *IG* ii² 3091.3–4

Θρασύβολος χορηγῶν ἐνίκα κωμῳδοῖς
Κρατῖνος ἐδίδασκε Βουκόλος

Fragments

17 Athenaeus 638d

ὃς οὐκ ἔδωκ' αἰτοῦντι Σοφοκλέει χορόν,
τῷ Κλεομάχου δ', ὃν οὐκ ἂν ἠξίουν ἐγὼ
ἐμοὶ διδάσκειν οὐδ' ἂν εἰς Ἀδώνια.

18 Σ Plato *Laches* 187b

ἐν Καρὶ τὸν κίνδυνον· ἐν ἐμοὶ δὴ δοκεῖ
πρώτῳ ποιεῖσθαι πεῖραν.

19 Photius (z) α 2534

καὶ πρὸς τὸν οὐρανὸν σκια-
μαχῶν ἀπο-
κτίννυσι ταῖς ἀπειλαῖς.

20 Hesychius π 4455

†πυρπερέγχει†· Κρατῖνος ἀπὸ <δι>θυράμβου ἐν Βου-
κόλοις ἀρξάμενος, ἐπειδὴ χορὸν οὐκ ἔλαβεν παρὰ τοῦ
ἄρχοντος. ἔστιν οὗ †ἠτήρει

CRATINUS

Testimonium

i [from a list of victorious *chorēgoi,* found at Aexone]

Thrasybulus won as a *chorēgus* for comedy. Cratinus produced his *Cow-Herders.*

Fragments

17 ⟨The archon⟩ who did not grant a chorus to Sophocles when he was applying for one, but did to the son of Cleomachus, whom I wouldn't have considered worthy to perform for me at the festival of Adonis.[1]

[1] This is Gnesippus (*PAA* 279680), made fun of at Chionides F 4; Cratinus F 104, 276; Teleclides F 36; and Eupolis F 148. He is associated with musical innovation, songs about women and love. He has been seen as a poet of private theatre or of erotic mimes.

18 A Carian danger. Well then, it seems it's up to me to make the first attempt.[1]

[1] "A Carian danger" is proverbial for letting someone expendable take the risk.

19 Shaking his fist at the sky, he slays with his threats.

20 "Fire upon spear" (?): Cratinus in *Cow-Herders* begins with a dithyramb, since he did not receive a chorus from the archon to whom he had applied (?).

Brief fragments: (F 21) *"man by man,"* (F 22) *"licence."*

ΒΟΥΣΙΡΙΣ

Fragment

23 Pollux 10.81–82

ὁ βοῦς ἐκεῖνος χἠ μαγὶς καὶ τἄλφιτα.

ΔΗΛΙΑΔΕΣ

BUSIRIS

Apollodorus (2.116ff.) tells the story of Busiris, king in Egypt, who would sacrifice strangers at an altar of Zeus. Heracles, returning from his eleventh Labour (that of the golden apples), slew Busiris, his son, and the attendants at the altar, as depicted on a marvellous late sixth-century vase by the Swing Painter. Epicharmus had previously written a Busiris, *as would several writers of Middle Comedy. Euripides wrote a satyr play of this title, of which little can be ascertained. It would be fascinating to know whether the comic poet influenced the tragedian, or vice versa. Finally Isocrates wrote a* Busiris, *which like his* Encomium of Helen, *attempts to rewrite the myth to the benefit of its subject.*

Fragment

23 That ox and the sacrificial tray and the barley grains.

DELIAN MAIDENS

Thucydides (3.104) records that in 426 the Athenians purified the sacred island of Delos and reestablished rites and games that had fallen into disuse. There were to be celebrated every five years. The chorus at Euripides' Heracles *687–89 (in the 410s) imagines "Delian Maidens" singing a hymn of praise to Apollo. F 24, 32, and 33 do reflect some sort of formal celebration, and if Cratinus' comedy does reflect this action by the Athenians, then it must belong late in his career. We know of productions by him at L-425, L-424, and D-423.*

THE POETS OF OLD COMEDY

Fragments

24 Hesychius α 1869

Ὑπερβορείους αἴθρια τιμῶντας στέφη.

25 Photius p. 26.18

ἐτήσιοι γὰρ πρόσιτ' ἀεὶ πρὸς τὴν τέχνην.

26 Photius p. 481.13

ἵνα σιωπῇ τῆς τέχνης ῥάζωσι τὸν λοιπὸν χρόνον.

σιωπῇ τῆς τέχνης codd., σιωπήσῃς τέχνης Luppe, σιω-
πῶντες τέχνην Kock.

27 Photius p. 481.17

ἔρραζε πρὸς τὴν γῆν, ὁ δ' ἠσκάριζε κἀπέπορδε.

28 Σ Plato *Axiochus* 367b

ἦν ἄρ' ἀληθὴς ὁ λόγος δὶς παῖς ὡς ἔσθ' ὁ γέρων.

29 Athenaeus 396b

τῷ δ' ὑποτρίψας τι μέρος πνῖξον καθαρύλλως.

30 Bekker's *Lexicon* p. 129.9

εἴ τις δ' ὑμῶν κάλλει προκριθῇ.

CRATINUS

Fragments

24 The Hyperboreans who hang decorations of honour on high.[1]

[1] See Herodotus 4.33–35 for the connection between the Hyperboreans and the worship of Apollo at Delos.

25 For you people approach the art differently every year.[1]

[1] The same adjective "differently every year" (*etesioi*) is applied at *Knights* 518 to the short memories of the spectators.

26 So that with silenced art they may snarl in the future.[1]

[1] The first part of the line is suspect. I translate Luppe's emendation. The metre seems to be trochaic tetrameter catalectic, often used in the epirrhematic parts of a parabasis. Are "they" rival poets of Cratinus?

27 Was snarling at the ground, and he was leaping and farting.

28 So the saying is true, that an old man is a child for the second time.

29 Rub down a portion of it in and make a nice casserole.

30 If any of you be judged first in beauty.

281

31 Bekker's *Lexicon* p. 129.12

πρὶν παροῦσα διδάσκῃ.

32 Σ Aristophanes *Birds* 1294

τούτοισι δ' ὄπισθεν ἴτω δίφρον φέρων Λυκοῦργος
ἔχων καλάσιριν.

34 Hesychius β 969

"βοῦς ἐν αὐλίῳ"· παροιμία ἐπὶ τῶν ἀχρήστων.

35 Aristotle *Nicomachean Ethics* 1098a18 + Σ *ad loc.*

μία γὰρ χελιδὼν ἔαρ οὐ ποιεῖ.

ΔΙΔΑΣΚΑΛΙΑΙ

31 Before she gets here and teaches.

32 Let Lycurgus walk behind them, carrying a stool and wearing a long *calasiris*.[1]

[1] The comic poets (*Birds* 1296, Pherecrates F 11) describe Lycurgus (*PAA* 611320), grandfather of the 4th-c. orator and politician, as an Egyptian, either for his ancestry or, more likely, for his fondness for their customs. It has been plausibly argued that he was involved in the establishment of the cult of Isis at Athens. Herodotus 2.81 describes the *calasiris* as an ankle-length linen garment worn by Egyptians.

34 "An ox in a stall." A proverb about those who are useless.

35 Because one swallow does not make a spring.

Brief fragments: (F 33) "branch bearers," (F 36) "to meet up with," (F 37) "immediately."

DRAMATIC REHEARSALS (?)

We have only one citation from this comedy, whose title could mean "List of Dramatic Productions" (the title of a work by Aristotle), "Dramatic Productions," or possibly "Dramatic Rehearsals" (so used by Plato). The last would afford the opportunity for good comedy. Bakola (48–49) sees this fragment as self-referential to the dithyramb in the parodos of Cow-Herders.

Fragment

38 Photius (b, z) α 1650

ὅτε σὺ τοὺς καλοὺς θριάμβους ἀναρύτουσ'
ἀπηχθάνου.

ΔΙΟΝΥΣΑΛΕΞΑΝΔΡΟΣ

*We know more about the plotline of this Old Comedy than
of any other, not from the fragments which are few, but
from the publication in 1904 of most of the hypothesis to
this comedy. Old comedy often placed Dionysus in an un-
usual and potentially comic position, in this case substitut-
ing for Paris (Alexander) in the infamous judgement of the
goddesses, which was also the subject of Sophocles' satyr
play* Judgement *(date unknown).*

*The last sentence has suggested to many that the com-
edy was a thorough-going political allegory by which Dio-
nysus stands for Pericles throughout the play. For in-
stance, the Greeks ravaging the countryside (24–30) while
Dionysus just hides away alludes to Pericles' policy of
Sitzkrieg in 431/0 (see Hermippos F 47). But the last sen-
tence may just mean that at some point in the comedy there
was a skilful and forceful allusion to Pericles and the War
(for which war see below). In view of the play's title should
we not be looking at Alexandros (Paris) for the source of
this comment? By keeping Helen he brings the Trojan War
on his people. The play may well be first and foremost a*

Fragment

38 Since you [fem.] were hated for drawing up fine songs [*thriamboi*] for Dionysus.[1]

[1] The rare verb seems to mean "draw up water," but why should the female figure being addressed have incurred hatred for doing this? Is this a metatheatrical context where "you" could be Comedy or the Muse of Cratinus, and the concept that of poetry as a flowing stream?

DIONYSALEXANDER

burlesque of myth, exploring the comic possibilities of Dionysus in yet again another tight situation. Bakola (181–208) makes a strong case against a primarily political reading of this comedy.

  The date has been widely accepted as 430 or 429 on the assumptions that "the war" is the Peloponnesian War, which broke out in 431, and that the comedy must have been produced before Pericles died in 429. The latter assumption is weakened by the fact that Aristophanes lambastes Pericles for his responsibility for the War in Acharnians *(425) and* Peace *(421). Against the first is that an equally possible candidate for "the war" is the conflict with Samos (440/39). This war was taken very seriously by the Athenians and we know that Pericles was blamed for it because of his Milesian mistress, Aspasia (Plutarch* Pericles *25). The Samian War started when Athens sided against the Samians in a territorial dispute with Miletos. Thus both the Trojan War and the Samian War could be viewed as wars "fought because of a woman."*

  Another unusual, but not unparalleled, feature of this

*play is the chorus of satyrs, whom we would usually expect
to find in a satyr play. In 437 Callias produced a comedy
called* Satyrs, *which has been seen as comedy's response to
Euripides'* Alcestis *(D-438), produced in the fourth posi-
tion where we would anticipate a satyr play, but with no
satyrs. On a date of 437 or 436, the satyrs of* Dionys-
alexander *could be a similar response by Cratinus to*
Alcestis.

*The hypothesis suggests something about the play's
structure. Whether we read "about the poets" or "about
the creation/adoption of sons" at 6–8, the chorus at this
point broke the dramatic illusion and talked directly "to
the spectators." In Aristophanes this usually happens in
a parabasis, in the middle or later on in the play. But if
not much is missing from the hypothesis before we can
make sense of it, then this address is more likely from the
parodos, for which we may compare* Cow-Herders *F 20,*
Wealth-Gods *F 171, and* Frogs *355–72. The principal
break in the comedy surely comes at line 19 when Dionysus
sails off to fetch Helen.*

*The traditional fragments shed some light on the play. F
45 plainly refers to Dionysus disguised as a ram. F 40 de-
scribes the classical portrayal of Dionysus, while he is very
likely the subject of F 41, since grinding one's teeth is often*

HYPOTHESIS (P. OXY. 663)

26 ΔΙΟΝΥΣ[ΑΛΕΞΑΝΔΡΟΣ
27 Η[
28 ΚΡΑΤ[ΕΙΝΟΥ

sign of terror. Dionysus could be reacting to Hermes' or Aphrodite's words or possibly to Paris' angry entry later in the play. F 48 probably refers to Dionysus no longer in the guise of a ram. F 39, 42, and 43 I take as coming from a scene when Dionysus is showing Helen around her new home on Mount Ida, although they could come from an earlier scene when Dionysus confronts the realities of the shepherd's life.

Finally in line 27 of the papyrus we get an H. If this is a number, then this comedy was Cratinus' eighth, very unlikely on a date of 430 but not impossible for 437. But if, as Edmonds suggested, it stands for "or," then Dionysalexander had another title. Some consider that the satyrs formed only a subsidiary chorus and that the "real" chorus consisted of shepherds of Ida and that thus the other title was Men of Ida *(see F 90–91). See also my comments on* Satyrs.

Recent bibliography: P. Lerza, SIFC 54 (1982) 186–93; A. Tatti, Métis 1 (1986) 325–32; M. Revermann, JHS 117 (1997) 197–200; E. Bakola, ZPE 154 (2005) 46–58; I. C. Storey, in Playing around Aristophanes (2006) 105–25; M. Wright, CQ 56 (2006) 593–95; CQ 57 (2007) 412–31; G. Dobrov, CW 100 (2007) 251–65; Olson 71–73, 87–92, 424–25.

HYPOTHESIS

].
]ζητ( )
]παν
]αυτον μη
5   κ]ρίσιν ὁ Ἑρμ(ῆς)
ἀπέρχ]εται κ(αὶ) οὗτοι
μ(ὲν) πρ(ὸς) τοὺς θεατάς
τινα π(ερὶ) ὑῶν ποιή(σεως)
διαλέγονται κ(αὶ)
10   παραφανέντα τὸν
Διόνυσον ἐπισκώ(πτουσι) (καὶ)
χλευάζου(σιν)· ὁ δ(ὲ) πα-
ραγενομένων <
             > αὐτῶι
παρὰ μ(ὲν) Ἥρα[ς] τυραννίδο(ς)
15   ἀκινήτου, πα[ρ]ὰ δ᾽ Ἀθηνᾶς
εὐτυχί(ας) κ(α)τ(ὰ) πόλεμο(ν), τῆς
δ᾽ Ἀφροδί(της) κάλλιστό(ν) τε κ(αὶ)
ἐπέραστον αὐτὸν ὑπάρ-
χειν, κρίνει ταύτην νικᾶν.
20   μ(ε)τ(ὰ) δ(ὲ) ταῦ(τα) πλεύσας εἰς
Λακεδαίμο(να) (καὶ) τὴν Ἑλένην
ἐξαγαγὼν ἐπανέρχετ(αι)
εἰς τὴν Ἴδην. ἀκού(ει) δ(ὲ) με-
τ᾽ ὀλίγον τοὺς Ἀχαιοὺς πυρ-
25   πολ]εῖν τὴν χώ(ραν) (καὶ) [
29   τὸν Ἀλέξαν[δ(ρον). τὴν μ(ὲν) οὖν Ἑλένη(ν)
30   εἰς τάλαρον ὡς τά[χιστα

... seek ... all (?) ... judgement Hermes leaves, while they say some things to the spectators about the poets[1] They joke and make fun of Dionysus when he appears. When ⟨the goddesses and Hermes arrive⟩ and ⟨make promises⟩ to him: from Hera unshaken tyranny, from Athena success in war[2], and Aphrodite that he be as beautiful and sexually attractive as possible,[3] he judges her [Aphrodite] to be the winner. After this he sails off to Sparta, takes Helen away, and returns to Ida. But he hears a little while later that the Greeks are ravaging the countryside ⟨and looking for⟩ Alexander. He hides Helen very quickly in a basket, and

---

[1] The papyrus seems to read περὶ ὑῶν ποιήσεως (about the creation of sons,—and was so defended by Handley citing *PCG* VIII 1109—and by Bakola, about the adoption of sons). Körte's περὶ τῶν ποιητῶν (about the poets) has been accepted by most scholars. Bakola suggests alternatively περὶ ὑῶν ποιητῶν (about adopted sons). [2] Or "courage in war." The papyrus has ευφυκι. The original editors read εὐτυχί(ας), while Austin prefers εὐψυχί(ας). [3] This differs from the usual enticement from Aphrodite, Helen. Changing αὐτὸν to αὐτῷ yields "to provide him with the most beautiful and attractive thing." But it may just be a good comic touch to have the effeminate Dionysus, disguised as a shepherd and wearing the grotesque costume of comedy, offered the gift of beauty.

κρύψας, ἑαυτὸν δ’ εἰς κριὸ[ν
μ(ε)τ(α)σκευάσας ὑπομένει
τὸ μέλλον.   παραγενό-
μενος δ’ Ἀλέξανδ(ρος) κ(αὶ) φωρά-
35 σας ἑκάτερο(ν) ἄγειν ἐπὶ τὰς
ναῦς πρ(οσ)τάττει ὡς παραδώσων
τοῖς Ἀχαιοῖ(ς). ὀκνούσης δ(ὲ) τῆς
Ἑλένη(ς) ταύτην μ(ὲν) οἰκτείρας
ὡς γυναῖχ’ ἔξων ἐπικατέχ(ει),
40 τὸν δ(ὲ) Διόνυ(σον) ὡς παραδοθη-
σόμενο(ν) ἀποστέλλει, συν-
ακολουθ(οῦσι) δ’ οἱ σάτυ(ροι) παρακαλοῦν-
τές τε κ(αὶ) οὐκ ἂν προδώσειν
αὐτὸν φάσκοντες.   κωμωι-
45 δεῖται δ’ ἐν τῶι δράματι Πε-
ρικλῆς μάλα πιθανῶς δι’
ἐμφάσεως ὡς ἐπαγηοχὼς
τοῖς Ἀθηναίοις τὸν πόλεμον.

8 πυωνποιη Pap., π(ερὶ) ὑῶν ποιή(σεως) Rutherford, π(ερὶ)
τῶν ποιη(τῶν) Körte, π(ερὶ) ὑῶν ποιη(τῶν) Bakola.
13 Lacuna indicated by Blass.   16 ευφυκι Pap., εὐτυχίας
ed. pr., εὐψυχίας Austin.   25 [ζητεῖν Austin.

changing himself into a ram awaits developments. Alexander appears and detects each of them, and orders them to be taken to the ships, meaning to give them back to the Greeks. When Helen refuses, he takes pity on her and holds on to her, to keep her as his wife. Dionysus he sends off to be handed over. The satyrs go along with him, encouraging him and insisting that they will not betray him. In the play Pericles is very persuasively made fun of through innuendo[4] for having brought the war on the Athenians.

4 For a useful definition of "innuendo" (*emphasis*) see Quintilian 9.2.65.

THE POETS OF OLD COMEDY

Fragments

39 Pollux 10.140

ἔνεισιν ἐνταυθοῖ μάχαιραι κουρίδες,
αἷς κείρομεν τὰ πρόβατα καὶ τοὺς ποιμένας.

40 Macrobius *Satires* 5.21.6

{A.} στολὴν δὲ δὴ τίν' εἶχε; τοῦτό μοι φράσον.
{B.} θύρσον, κροκωτόν, ποικίλον, καρχήσιον.

41 Photius (b, z) α 629

εὐθὺς γὰρ ἡμώδεις ἀκούων τῶν ἐπῶν
τοὺς προσθίους ὀδόντας.

42 Pollux 7.122

παραστάδας καὶ πρόθυρα βούλει ποικίλα.

43 Σ Aristophanes *Lysistrata* 575

οὔκ, ἀλλὰ βόλιτα χλωρὰ καὶ οἰσπώτην πατεῖν.

44 Athenaeus 119b

ἐν σαργανίσιν ἄξω ταρίχους Ποντικούς.

45 Photius β 130

ὁ δ' ἠλίθιος ὥσπερ πρόβατον βῆ βῆ λέγων βαδίζει.

Fragments

39 And in there are the shearing knives, with which we shear the flocks and the shepherds.

40 (A) What sort of outfit did he have on? Tell me this.
  (B) ‹He had› a thyrsus, saffron robe with lots of decoration, large drinking cup.

41 For as soon as you hear ‹her?› words, you started grinding your front teeth.

42 Do you [sing.] want gateposts and fancy porches?

43 No, but to walk on fresh cowpatties and sheep dung.

44 I shall bring Black Sea salted fish in baskets.

45 And the silly fool just walks about going "baa baa."

46 *Suda* α 2285

† τῶν βδελλολαρύγγων ἀνεπαγγέλτων αὐτῶν
φοιτήσας ἐπὶ δεῖπνον

47 Photius (b) α 1940

οὐ γάρ τοι σύ γε πρῶτος ἄκλητος φοιτᾷς ἐπὶ
δεῖπνον ἄνηστις

48 Pollux 7.28

νακότιλτος ὡσπερεὶ κωδάριον ἐφαινόμην.

49 Athenaeus 384b

χηνοβοσκοί, βουκόλοι

50 Pollux 10.34

κλίνην τε παράπυξον

51 Pollux 7.198

ἡ γελγόπωλις

ΔΙΟΝΥΣΟΙ

Fragment

52 Orus *Orthography* fol. 281ʳ 17

νικῶ μὲν ὁ τῇδε πόλει λέγων τὸ λῷστον.

294

46 Going off to dinner, one of those uninvited leech-throats.

47 You are certainly not the first hungry person to go to dinner uninvited.

48 I appeared shorn, like a fleece.

49 Goose keepers, cow herders.

50 And a bed with boxwood veneer.

51 Woman who sells garlic.

DIONYSUSES

As only one fragment is known for this comedy, we may suspect that Orus, citing F 52, has garbled the title of Dionysalexander. *The metre belongs to choral songs in* Aristophanes, *and if the satyrs in* Dionysalexander *did address the spectators "about the poets," the point about the best advice winning could well refer to the comic poet who best advises the city.*

Fragment

52 Let the winner be the one who says what's best for the city.

ΔΡΑΠΕΤΙΔΕΣ

*The title means "female run-aways," but in F 60 a plural
group is addressed as "sissies," a term for effeminate males,
for which we may compare Eupolis' Draft-Dodgers or
Men-Women and his Dyers, also Cratinus' Poofters. But
who were these "run-aways" and from what or whom were
they running? F 53 is very likely spoken by Theseus, who
should also be the man addressed as "scion of Pandion" (his
grandfather) in F 61. He should also be the person in F 56,
who speaks "when I was alive." We would have either a
scene in the Underworld or a figure returned from the dead
(cf. Solon at F 246).*

*The tragic tone of F 60 suggests that Cratinus is parody-
ing tragedy, and one thinks of Aeschylus' Suppliants (the
daughters of Danaus flee from Egypt and make formal sup-
plication to Pelasgos, king of Argos) or of Aeschylus' Men
of Eleusis, where Adrastus comes to Eleusis and formally
begs Theseus' assistance in burying their dead. The com-*

Fragments

53 Photius (z) α 2602

τὸν Κερκυόνα θ' ἕωθεν ἀποπατοῦντ' ⟨ἐγὼ⟩
ἐπὶ τοῖς λαχάνοις εὑρὼν ἀπέπνιξα.

54 Athenaeus 501d

δέχεσθε φιάλας τάσδε βαλανειομφάλους.

RUN-AWAYS

edy may have had more than a little to do with Eleusis: F 53
occurred there, F 65 refers to the "Sacred Way" between
Eleusis and Athens, Lampon (F 62) proposed a rider to the
"first fruits decree" concerning Eleusis (IG i³ 78), while F
61 mentions the game of pessoi *to which reference is made*
at Euripides' Suppliant Women *409. We usually associate*
paratragedy with the comedy of Aristophanes and Strattis,
but Bakola (ch. 3) makes a good case for Cratinus' strong
engagement with Aeschylus.

Matters are complicated by an implied political theme
in F 59 and the mention of city (polis) in F 61 and by F 58,
which sounds as if Zeus is speaking, and F 62 with its refer-
ence to "mortals." Could there have been a divine theme in
this play? The date is uncertain. If Xenophon (F 58) is the
general of the 430s, he was dead by 429, and the play
should then belong to the 430s. Lampon (F 62) was active
as early as the late 440s and is still a comic target at the end
of the century.

Fragments

53 And I found Cercyon taking a crap at dawn among the
cabbages and I throttled him.[1]

[1] One of Theseus' "labours" on his journey from Troezen to
Athens was to wrestle and kill Cercyon, the ruler of Eleusis.

54 Receive these acorn-navelled cups.

55 Apollonius Dyscolus *Pronouns* (*GrGr* I.1.1, p. 21.12
Schneider)

οὗτος, καθεύδεις; οὐκ ἀναστήσεις † βοτῶν.

56 Photius p. 337.19

οἱ δὲ πυππάζουσι περιτρέχοντες, ὁ δ᾽ ὄνος ὕεται.

57 Photius (z) ined. ἐξελεύθερός

ἦν γὰρ ἐξελεύθερός μοι πατρικός, ἡνίκ᾽ αὐτὸς ἦν.

58 Aelian *On the Nature of Animals* 12.10

φέρε νῦν σοι
ἐξ αἰθρίας καταπυγοσύνην μυὸς ἀστράψω
Ξενοφῶντος.

59 Photius p. 658.14

τοὺς ὧδε μόνον στασιάζοντας καὶ βουλομένους
τινὰς εἶναι.

60 *Suda* α 1499

ποδαπὰς ὑμᾶς εἶναι φάσκων, ὦ μείρακες, οὐκ ἂν
ἁμάρτοιν;

55 Hey you, are you sleeping? Won't you get up?

56 They are running about, shouting "Hey!", while he is just the donkey in the rain.

57 When I was alive, I had a freedman who used to belong to my father.

58 Well then, for you [sing.] I shall out of a clear sky strike down the perverted lust of that mouse, Xenophon.[1]

1 For the ancients (white) mice were proverbial for sexual lust. Xenophon may be the general in the Samian War, who died at Spartolus in 429 (*PAA* 734360).

59 They who only cause internal dissension here and want to be somebody.

60 Where might I say that you sissies were from and not be wrong?

THE POETS OF OLD COMEDY

61 Pollux 9.98–99

Πανδιονίδα πόλεως βασιλεῦ
τῆς ἐριβώλακος, οἶσθ᾽ ἣν λέγομεν,
καὶ κύνα καὶ πόλιν ἣν παίζουσιν.

62 Athenaeus 344e

Λάμπωνα, τὸν οὐ βροτῶν
ψῆφος δύναται φλεγυρὰ δείπνου φίλων ἀπείργειν.
νῦν δ᾽ αὖτις ἐρυγγάνει·
βρύκει γὰρ ἅπαν τὸ παρόν, τρίγλη δὲ κἂν μάχοιτο.

63 Σ Plato *Philebus* 14a

ὁ μῦθος ἀπώλετο.

64 Zenobius *Proverbs* 6.24

ὕδωρ παρρέει

ΕΜΠΙΜΠΡΑΜΕΝΟΙ

61 Scion of Pandion, king of this fertile city, you know the one we mean, and the Dog-and-City game they play.[1]

[1] This refers to a board game, a form of *pessoi* called "City," somewhat like checkers, laid out in squares and employing stones (*psēphoi*) called "dogs" which would block and capture the opponents' pieces.

62 And Lampon, whom no fiery stone [vote?] of mortals can keep from dinner with friends, and now he spews it back up, for he eats everything in sight and would fight with a red mullet.[1]

[1] Lampon (*PAA* 6010665) was an important religious and political figure in the last half of the 5th c. He was involved in the founding of Thurii (440s), was a signatory to the Peace of Nicias (421), and could still be made fun of in comedy c. 400. Athenaeus quotes several comic passages making fun of his appetite. The "fiery stone of mortals" is a mysterious reference, but *psēphos* could refer to the stones in a game of *pessoi* (see F 61) or to the manner of voting by pebbles in the assembly or the law courts.

63 The story was lost.

64 Water rushes in.

Brief fragments: (F 65) "Sacred Way," (F 66) "axe wielder" [of Lampon], (F 67) "you people made a comparison," (F 68) "ground sheets."

THE BLAZERS (see under MEN OF IDA)

ΕΥΜΕΝΙΔΕΣ

Fragments

69 John of Alexandria *Accentuation* p. 29.25 Dindorf

ἐπίσχες αὐτοῦ, μὴ πέρα προβῇς λόγου.

70

(a) Aristophanes *Knights* 529

Δωροῖ συκοπέδιλε.
τέκτονες εὐπαλάμων ὕμνων.

(b) Σ Aristophanes *Knights* 529b, 530a

Δωροῖ συκοπέδιλε· Κρατίνου μέλους ἀρχή.
σκώπτων δὲ τινὰ ἐκεῖνος δωροδόκον καὶ
συκοφάντην τοῦτο εἶπεν.

τέκτονες εὐπαλάμων . . . καὶ τοῦτο δὲ ἐκ τῶν
Εὐμενίδων Κρατίνου.

ΕΥΝΕΙΔΑΙ

EUMENIDES

This comedy may in fact be the same as the next play (Sons of Euneus). Only two fragments are known, and in both cases the citations have been emended (Εὐμένισιν to Εὐνείδαις in F 59; Εὐμενίδων to Εὐνειδῶν in F 60). If Eumenides is in fact a play by Cratinus, it may have been an early one, perhaps influenced by Aeschylus' powerful tragedy of 458.

Fragments

69 Stop here. Go no farther with your speech.

70

(a) Goddess of bribes, with fig-leafed shoes.

Makers of clever hymns.

(b) "Goddess of bribes": the beginning of a song by Cratinus. He said this to poke fun at someone for being a bribe-taker and an informer.

"Makers of clever": . . . this is also from Cratinus' *Eumenides*.

SONS OF EUNEUS (EUNEIDAE)

Euneus was a son of Jason and Hypsipyle, and a character in Euripides' play Hypsipyle. *It is generally thought that the end of that tragedy made a connection between Euneus (the great-grandson of Dionysus) with the clan (genos) of*

Testimonia

i Polemon F 45 *ap.* Athenaeus 698c

κέχρηται δὲ . . . καὶ Κρατῖνος ὁ τῆς ἀρχαίας κωμῳ-
δίας ποιητὴς ἐν Εὐνείδαις.

ii Ptolemy Chennus *ap.* Photius *Library* 190

εὑρεθῆναί φασι . . . τοὺς δὲ Εὐνείδας Κρατίνου πρὸς
τῇ Ἀλεξάνδρου τοῦ βασίλεως Μακεδόνων.

iii Hesychius ε 7007

Εὐνεῖδαι· γένος ἀπὸ Εὔνεω κεκλημένον, τοῦ Ἰάσονος
υἱοῦ, οἷον γένος ὀρχηστῶν καὶ κιθαριστῶν.

iv *IG* ii² 5056

ἱερέως Μελπομένου Διονύσου ἐξ Εὐνειδῶν

musicians at Athens ("sons of Euneus"), who seem to have been in charge of processions in honour of Dionysus Melpomenus ("Dionysus celebrated in song"). Since Euripides' play will have been considerably later than Cratinus' comedy, it is unlikely that the title has anything directly to do with the son of Jason. A guild of dancers and lyre players (T 3), however, would have made for a good comic chorus.

Testimonia

i Cratinus, the poet of Old Comedy, has employed ‹parody› in his *Sons of Euneus*.

ii They say that Cratinus' *Sons of Euneus* was found by the head of Alexander, king of the Macedonians.

iii Sons of Euneus (Euneidae): a clan named for Euneus son of Jason, a clan of dancers and lyre players.

iv [Of a seat in the theatre] Belonging to the priest of Dionysus Melpomenus, from the Euneidae.

Fragments

71 Stobaeus 4.11.11

ἥβης ἐκείνης, νοῦ δὲ τοῦδε καὶ φρενῶν.

72 *Suda* α 1701

ἀμφιανακτίζειν

ΘΡΑΙΤΤΑΙ

Much has been assumed about this comedy, rather too confidently. Some have taken the title along with the references to Pan (F 75), to Bendis (F 85), a wild Thracian goddess, to the Mother Goddess, Cybebe (F 87), and to discordant aulos playing (F 89) to suggest a comedy about the goddess Bendis arriving at Athens with a company of votaries. Here one might cite tragedies such as Bacchae *or Aeschylus' lost* Edonians, *and in comedy Eupolis'* Dyers *(about the goddess Cotyto) and Aristophanes'* Heroes *or* Seasons. *But "Thracian Women" could have other meanings: a chorus of captured Thracian women as in Aeschylus' lost play of that title (about the death of Ajax at Troy), or one of slave girls ("Thratta" is used several times as a generic slave name in Aristophanes). While F 73 does indicate a procession or parade of some sort, we cannot assume that this was a comedy with a religious theme.*

Similarly the joke at Pericles as Zeus (F 73) has been used to see this play as political comedy. Bekker's emendation of the text suggests that Pericles was a character in the play, but how great a role is uncertain. The setting seems to

Fragments

71 Of that time of youth, and this sense and intelligence.

72 To sing the "about me, Lord Apollo" song.[1]

[1] The beginning of a song attributed to Terpander.

THRACIAN WOMEN

be Athens since the jokes at Pericles, Euathlus, and Callias work best in a local context. F 74 may refer to a local prison; F 79 certainly to the Athenian Council (Boule). "Boeotian pigs" was an Attic joke at their neighbours. Revermann 302–5 discusses the unusual architecture of the Odeion, built under the supervision of Pericles, and makes the attractive suggestion that if Pericles (as Zeus?) was a character in the comedy, he would have entered by the eisodos *beneath the odeion.*

The date has been confidently set by some just after the ostracism of Thucydides son of Melesias, taking "now that the ostracon has gone" to mean "now that he has escaped being ostracised." This ostracism is traditionally dated to 443, but a strong case for c. 438 has also been made, making the ostracism a "referendum" on the Samian War. But the verb "has gone" can also mean "be a thing of the past," and Cratinus may be saying that several years have gone by without an ostracism, in which case we need a date rather later than the ostracism of Thucydides. The reference to Pericles in the present tense dates the play to 430 at

THE POETS OF OLD COMEDY

Testimonium

i Athenaeus 495a

Καλλίστρατος ἐν Ὑπομνήμασι Θρᾳττῶν Κρατίνου.

Fragments

73 Plutarch *Pericles* 13.9

ὁ σχινοκέφαλος Ζεὺς ὅδε προσέρχεται
< ὁ > Περικλέης, τᾠδεῖον ἐπὶ τοῦ κρανίου
ἔχων, ἐπειδὴ τοὔστρακον παροίχεται.

1 ὅδε codd., ὁδὶ Bekker.

74 Pollux 10.160

ἐς τὸν καλιόν, ἢν τύχῃ, καθείργνυται.

75 Σ Euripides *Hecuba* 838

{Α.} †πανὶ κακὸν† δεῦρο μαστεύων τινά.
{Β.} ποτὲ χαλκοῦν ἢ ξύλινον; <ἢ> καὶ <τι> χρύσεον
προσῆν;
{Α.} οὐδαμῶς ξύλινος ἐκεῖνος * * *
ἀλλὰ χαλκοῦς ὢν ἀπέδρα. {Β.} πότερα Δαιδάλειος
ἦν
ἢ τις ἐξέκλεψεν αὐτόν;

308

the latest—he died in 429 and was in political hot water for much of 430. Euathlus (F 82) is a kōmōidoumenos *of the 420s (e.g., Acharnians 710) and if F 81 refers to the younger Callias, born c. 450, then even a date of 430 makes him only twenty at the time of his alleged adultery with Phocus' wife—possible, but just barely.*

Since Athenaeus (495a) tells us that Callistratus wrote a commentary to this play (T 45), we may infer that the ancients regarded this comedy with considerable appreciation.

Testimonium

i Callistratus in his *Commentary on Cratinus'* Thracian Women.

Fragments

73 Here comes Pericles, the onion-headed Zeus, with the Odeion on his head, now that the ostracon has gone away.

74 He has been shut up in prison, if it should happen.[1]

[1] Pieters reads attractively Μητίχου for ἦν τύχῃ (the prison of Metichus)—see Pollux 8.121.

75 (A) Come here seeking some . . . to Pan.

(B) Of bronze or wood? Or is there a golden one at hand?

(A) Not that wooden one, not at all . . . but the bronze one has done a runner.

(B) Was it made by Daedalus then, or did someone steal it?

309

76 Pollux 9.91

ὅτι τοὺς κόρακας τὰξ Αἰγύπτου χρυσία κλέπτοντας
ἔπαυσαν.

77 Photius (b, Sᶻ) α 1241

οὗτοι δ᾽ εἰσὶν συοβοιωτοί, κρουπεζοφόρων γένος
ἀνδρῶν.

79 Priscian *Institutes of Grammar* 18.213

τὴν πέρυσι βουλὴν ἐφεστώς.

80 Photius p. 326.19

ὀκτώπουν ἀνεγείρεις.

81 Σ Lucian *Tragic Zeus* 48

εἰς δὲ στιγματίαν αὐτὸν Κρατῖνος κωμῳδεῖ ὡς ἕνα
τῶν κατάχρεων Θρᾴτταις· οἱ γὰρ δανειζόμενοι τὰς
κτήσεις ὑπετίθεσαν καὶ ἐπέγραφον αὐτὰς πρὸς τὸ
γινώσκεσθαι ὅτι ὑποθῆκαί εἰσιν ... κωμῳδεῖ δὲ αὐτὸν
Κρατῖνος καὶ ὡς Φώκου γυναῖκα μοιχεύσαντα καὶ
τρία τάλαντα δόντα εἰς τὸ μὴ κριθῆναι.

82 Σ Aristophanes *Wasps* 592b

Εὔαθλος ῥήτωρ συκοφάντης, οὗ μνημονεύει ... καὶ
Κρατῖνος ἐν Θρᾴτταις.

76 That they stopped those magpies from stealing the golden things from Egypt.

77 These are Boeotian pigs, a clog-wearing race of men.

79 In charge of last year's Council.

80 You are stirring up an octopus.

81 Cratinus makes fun of him [Callias] in *Thracian Women* for being branded as someone who owed money. For people who were in debt would mortgage their houses and have notices written on them so it would be known that they were in debt . . . Cratinus makes fun of him also for having had sex with the wife of Phocus and for paying three talents to avoid going to court.

82 Euathlus was a politician and an informer . . . Cratinus mentions him in *Thracian Women*.

Brief fragments: (F 78) "back the same way," (F 83) "they dismissed," (F 84) "net watcher," (F 85) "with two points" [of Bendis], (F 86) "bad to his slaves" ["with bad slaves"?], (F 87) "possessed by Cybebe," (F 88) "cups," (F 89) "musical chaos."

ΙΔΑΙΟΙ

Fragments

90 Aristophanes *Thesmophoriazusae* 215 + Σ *ad loc.*

{ΚΗ.} ἀτὰρ τί μέλλεις δρᾶν μ'; {ΕΥ.} ἀποξυρεῖν
ταδί,
τὰ κάτω δ' ἀφεύειν.

τὰ γένεια. ταῦτα δὲ ἔλαβεν ἐκ τῶν Ἰδαίων
Κρατίνου.

91 Σ Aristophanes *Assemblywomen* 1121

τὸ ἄνθος, καὶ ὁ Κρατῖνος ἐν τοῖς Ἰδαίοις τὰς θείας
μορφὰς ἐν ἀρχῇ φανείσας.

ἰδίοις codd., Ἰδαίοις Bergk; ἐν ἀρχῇ codd., ἐναργεῖς
Luppe.

MEN OF IDA

Another comedy for which information and remains are scarce. Since the scholiast citing F 90 implies that Aristophanes took material for Thesmophoriazusae *from Cratinus'* Men of Ida *and since Clement of Alexandria (Miscellanies 6.26.4) says that he had done much the same thing in the same play from Cratinus'* Blazers, *some have seen the two as alternative titles for the same comedy. Luppe, on the other hand, argued for* Men of Ida *as the alternative title for* Dionysalexander, *reading the H of the papyrus as "or." Bakola (84–86) develops a revised version of Luppe's argument, accepting the H as "or" and* Idaioi *as the title, but in the sense of* Satyrs of Ida. *F 90 seems to suggest a shaving and singeing scene, part of turning a bearded Dionysus into a pretty, smooth-faced shepherd-prince(?), while F 91, attributed to* Men of Ida *by emending the text of the scholion, mentions "divine shapes appearing at the beginning," or with Luppe's conjecture, "appearing clearly."*

Fragments

90 (RELATIVE) But what are you going to do to me?

(EURIPIDES) Shave these, and then singe away the parts down there.

The cheeks. He took this from Cratinus' *Men of Ida*.

91 "[Losing] the flower." Cratinus in *Men of Ida* . . . divine shapes appearing at the beginning.

313

ΚΛΕΟΒΟΥΛΙΝΑΙ

Testimonium

i Diogenes Laertius 1.89

Κλεόβουλος Εὐαγόρου Λίνδιος . . . γενέσθαι τε αὐτῷ
θυγατέρα Κλεοβουλίνην, αἰνιγμάτων ἑξαμέτρων ποι-
ήτριαν, ἧς μέμνηται καὶ Κρατῖνος ἐν τῷ ὁμωνύμῳ
δράματι, πληθυντικῶς ἐπιγράψας.

Fragments

92 Σ Aristophanes *Birds* 31

      Ἀκέστορα γὰρ ὅμως εἰκὸς λαβεῖν
πληγάς, ἐὰν μὴ συστρέφῃ τὰ πράγματα.

93 Pollux 10.105

ἐπέδωκε βαλάνων ἄβακα τῶν ἐκ Φηγέως.

THE CLEOBULINAS

Cleobulina of Lindus on Rhodes was remembered as a poetess who wrote riddles in epic hexameters. The chorus should then be composed of women riddlers and the comedy based on scenes like those in Knights *and* Wasps *where riddles are posed and answered. Some have used the entry in Jerome for 451/0 (see Crates T 5) to infer a date in the late 450s for Cratinus' play, but Acestor (F 92) is very much a kōmōidoumenos of the 420s and 410s.*

Recent bibliography: E. Matelli, Aevum *(1997) 11–61.*

Testimonium

i Cleobulus the son of Euagoras of Lindos . . . had a daughter named Cleoboulina, a writer of riddling hexameters, whom Cratinus mentions in his play of the same name, using a plural title.

Fragments

92 Acestor is likely to get beaten, if he doesn't get his acts together.[1]

[1] Acestor (*PAA* 116685), the tragic poet (*TrGF* I 25), was nicknamed "Sacas" after a barbarian tribe and alleged to be of foreign birth and hence an illegal citizen. He is made fun of at *Wasps* 1221, *Birds* 31, Eupolis F 172, Metagenes F 14, and Theopompus F 61.

93 He also gave me a tray with acorns from Phigeus.

94 Hephaestion *Handbook* 1.9

ἔστιν ἄκμων καὶ σφῦρα νεανίᾳ εὐτριχι πώλῳ.

95 Hesychius α 1861

ἐκβάλλοντες τοὺς αἰθεῖς πέπλους.

96 Zenobius *Proverbs* 3.149

Μύλλος πάντα ἀκούει

ΛΑΚΩΝΕΣ

Fragment

102 Clement of Alexandria *Miscellanies* 6.5.9–10

Κρατῖνος δ᾽ ἐν τοῖς Λάκωσι·
  φοβερὸν ἀνθρώποις τόδ᾽ αὖ
κταμένοις ἐπ᾽ αἰζηοῖσι καυχᾶσθαι μέγα.

Κρατῖνος δ᾽ ἐν τοῖς Λάκωσι φθονερὸν ἀνθρώποις πέλει/ κταμένοις κτλ. Meineke.

CRATINUS

94 The young colt with flowing mane has an anvil and hammer.[1]

> [1] Perhaps part of a riddle or possibly a *sensus obscaenus*?

95 Throwing off the burning robes.

96 Myllus hears everything. [See the comic poet named Myllus]

Brief fragments: (F 97) "smears," (F 98) "we press down," (F 99) "to buy dainties," (F 100) "blind rat," (F 101) "squirrel."

MEN OF LACONIA

This comedy is known only from the fragment quoted by Clement of Alexandria, and even though not all of Cratinus' plays were well-known and well-cited in antiquity, we might consider whether Clement has assigned this citation to the wrong poet. Comedies of this title are known for Eupolis (doubtful), Platon, and Nicochares. Meineke's reading would make the words "in the Men of Laconia" part of the quotation.

Fragment

102 Cratinus in his *Men of Laconia*:

Moreover, this is a terrible thing, to boast loudly over good men dead,

or with Meineke: "Among the men of Laconia this is a spiteful thing, to boast loudly over good men dead."

THE POETS OF OLD COMEDY

ΜΑΛΘΑΚΟΙ

Testimonium

i Herodian *On Singular Vocabulary* II, p. 945.5

ἔν τισιν ἐν Μαλθακοῖς Κρατίνου· παρεφύλαξε Σύμ-
μαχος.

Fragments

103 Hesychius β 1273

ἄμοργιν ἔνδον βρυτίνην νήθειν τινά.

104 Athenaeus 638e

τίς ἄρ᾽ ἔρωτα † μοιδεν ὦ Γνήσιππε ἐγὼ πολλῇ
  χολη;
οἴομαι ‹   › μηδὲν οὕτως μῶρον εἶναι καὶ κενόν.

105 Athenaeus 685c

παντοίοις γε μὴν κεφαλὴν ἀνθέμοις ἐρέπτομαι·
λειρίοις, ῥόδοις, κρίνεσιν, κοσμοσανδάλοις, ἴοις,

CRATINUS

POOFTERS

The Greek malthakos *means "soft," and hence "cowardly,"*
"unmanly," "effeminate." F 105, in eupolideans and thus
very probably from the parabasis, shows these malthakoi
describing the wreaths they wear, of every sort of flower.
One wonders what the reaction of the spectators would
have been to this sort of "off-side" chorus, and also in come-
dies such as Run-Aways *or Eupolis'* Draft-Dodgers, *de-*
tached amusement or lack of sympathy. Also would such
choruses change their nature and become more "normal,"
or would they continue to the end in their role as "outsid-
ers"? The date is uncertain. The only personal allusion is to
Gnesippus (F 104), who appears to have been active 450–
430.

Testimonium

i For example, in *Poofters* by Cratinus—Symmachus has
a note on this.

Fragments

103 For someone to be inside spinning thread.

104 Who saw me in love, Gnesippus? It makes me really
sick. I don't think . . . to be so foolish and senseless at all.[1]

[1] For Gnesippus see F 17. Many suggestions have been made
to present a coherent text.

105 While I crown my head with every sort of flower:
lilies, roses, white lilies, larkspur, violets, and bergamot

καὶ σισυμβρίοις, ἀνεμωνῶν κάλυξί τ᾽ ἠριναῖς,
ἑρπύλλῳ, κρόκοις, ὑακίνθοις, ἑλιχρύσου κλάδοις,
5   οἰνάνθησιν, ἡμεροκαλλεῖ τε τῷ φιλουμένῳ,
† ἀνθρυσκίσσου φοβῇ
τῷ τ᾽ ἀειφρούρῳ μελιλώτῳ κάρα πυκάζομαι
καὶ < > κύτισος αὐτόματος παρὰ Μέδοντος ἔρχεται.

106 Athenaeus 111e

ἄρτου δ᾽ εἶδός ἐστι καὶ ὁ ἀποπυρίας καλούμενος, ἐπ᾽
ἀνθράκων δ᾽ ὀπτᾶται. καλεῖται δ᾽ οὗτος ὑπό τινων
ζυμίτης. Κρατῖνος Μαλθακοῖς·
πρῶτον ἀποπυρίαν ἔχω ζυμηταμιαδου πλεους κνεφαλ-
λον.

107 Pollux 7.171

λευκοὺς ὑπὸ ποσσὶν ἔχων πίλους.

108 Constantine Porphyrogenitus *Imperial Administra-
tion* 23

Ἴβηρος τραγοπώγων

ΝΕΜΕΣΙΣ

mint, the spring buds of anemones, tufted thyme, cro-
cuses, hyacinths, and sprays of helichryse, vine flowers,
the lovely daylily, and a tuft of narcissus, and with the ever-
watchful honey clover I wreathe my brow. On its own from
Medon comes a medick blossom.[1]

[1] Pollux (6.106) gives a list of flowers used in wreaths, "most of
which Cratinus mentions in *Poofters*," in much the same order as
in Athenaeus. Pollux adds calamint, plantain, narcissus, honey-
suckle, artemisia, and bindweed.

106 There is a type of bread called "apopyria," and it is
roasted over coals. By some it is called "yeast bread."
Cratinus in *Poofters*:

First I have *apopyria* . . . [the rest is corrupt].

107 Having white stockings on his feet.

108 A man from Iberia, with a beard like a goat's.

*Brief fragments: (F 109) "Cabaesus" (of an insatiable
eater), (F 110) "Cyllus' Sack" (on Mount Hymettus), (F
111) "He Who Will Be Sorry," (F 112) "you [sing.] know,"
(F 113) "I am here."*

NEMESIS

*On one level this comedy was a burlesque of the myth of
Zeus and Nemesis, by which Helen is the offspring, not of
Zeus and Leda, but of Zeus and Nemesis. Like Thetis with
Peleus, to avoid Zeus she transformed herself into all sorts
of creatures until finally taking the form of a swan. Zeus*

321

turned himself into a similar form, and the result of their union was an egg, which in some fashion came into the possession of Leda of Sparta. The birth of Helen from that egg was the subject of vase paintings in the fifth century.

The earliest account of Zeus' pursuit and union with Nemesis is found in the Cypria *(seventh/sixth century—F 10–11 West), where we get the details of Zeus' lust for and pursuit of Nemesis, her flight and changes of shape, and finally his assuming the form of a goose, his union with Nemesis, and her laying of the egg from which Helen was born. That Cratinus used this version is made clear by Eratosthenes in his* Constellations *(T 1–3). Hyginus (Astronomica 2.8) expands the story to include Jupiter ordering Venus to adopt the form of an eagle, while he in the shape of a swan takes refuge in the bosom of Nemesis. This is a plotline certainly within the realm of comedy. Cratinus will have seen the comic possibilities in the story, both for the seduction of Nemesis and the hatching of the egg. In F 114 Zeus is told (by whom?—Hermes or Aphrodite?) to "become a large bird" and in F 116 expresses his delight in the food he now consumes. Other references to birds are found at F 120–21. In F 115 Hermes (?) instructs Leda in her role as incubatrix for the egg. Bakola (168–73) points*

Testimonia

i Eratosthenes *Constellations*

(a) Epitome 25

Κύκνου. οὗτός ἐστιν ὁ καλούμενος μέγας, ὃν κύκνῳ εἰκάζουσιν· λέγεται δὲ τὸν Δία ὁμοιωθέντα τῷ ζῴῳ

*out some examples of tragic language and metre in the frag-
ments and speculates that tragic originals may lie behind
this comedy. The fragments do not tell us much about how
the comedy unfolded, but there will have been a change in
the setting, from Rhamnous to Sparta, probably over the
parabasis.*

*So far we have a burlesque of myth, but others, relying
on Plutarch's testimony that F 118 was aimed at Pericles,
have created in* Nemesis *an elaborate political allegory,
like that for* Dionysalexander, *by which Zeus throughout
the comedy was Pericles, Leda Aspasia, while Helen repre-
sents responsibility for the War or Pericles' legitimisation
of his son by Aspasia. Comedy did identify Pericles with
Zeus (as at F 258–59 and* Acharnians *530–34), but a play-
length political allegory seems unlikely. Bakola (224) con-
cludes that, while there may be levels of satire, it "relied on
intermittent suggestion rather than outright allegory."*

*The date is complicated by the evidence of the scholiast
(F 125) that would place* Nemesis *"much later" than* Birds
*(414), but Godolphin argued that the scholiast misidenti-
fied the archonship of Pythodorus (432/1) with that of his
namesake in 404/3. In that case we have an attractive and
reasonable date for the comedy in 431.*

Testimonia

i

(a) The Swan: this is called the Great ⟨Bird⟩, whom they
identify with a swan. The story is told that Zeus turned

τούτῳ Νεμέσεως ἐρασθῆναι, ἐπεὶ αὐτὴ πᾶσαν ἤμειβε
μορφήν, ἵνα τὴν παρθενίαν φυλάξῃ, καὶ τότε κύκνος
γέγονεν· οὕτω καὶ αὐτὸν ὁμοιωθέντα τῷ ὀρνέῳ τούτῳ
καταπτῆναι εἰς Ῥαμνοῦντα τῆς Ἀττικῆς, κἀκεῖ τὴν
Νέμεσιν φθεῖραι· τὴν δὲ τεκεῖν ᾠόν, ἐξ οὗ ἐκκο-
λαφθῆναι καὶ γενέσθαι τὴν Ἑλένην, ὥς φησι Κράτης
ὁ ποιητής.[1]

[1] Κράτης MS, Κρατῖνος Valckenaer.

(b) Vatican fragments (Rehm p. 9)

περὶ τοῦ Ὄρνιθος. οὗτος ὁ μέγας καλεῖται, ὃν κύκνῳ
εἰκάζουσιν. τούτῳ Ζεὺς ὁμοιωθεὶς κατέπτη εἰς Ῥα-
μνοῦντα τῆς Ἀττικῆς κἀκεῖ τὴν Νέμεσιν ἔφθειρεν.
ἐκείνη δὲ ᾠὸν ἔτεκεν, ἐξ οὗ γεννηθῆναι, ὡς Κράτης
ἱστόρησε, τὴν Ἑλένην.

(c) Germanicus, p. 84.19

hic est Cygnus, in quem ferunt Iovem se transfigurasse
et transvolitasse in terram Atticam Rhamnunta ibique
compressisse Nemesin, ut ait Cratinus tragicorum scrip-
tor, eamque edidiise ovum, unde nata sit Helena.

Fragments

114 Athenaeus 373d

ὄρνιθα τοίνυν δεῖ σε γίγνεσθαι μέγαν.

himself into this creature and made love to Nemesis, since she was changing herself into every form to protect her virginity, and had become a swan. So he too took the form of this bird and flew to Rhamnus in Attica, and there he ravished Nemesis. She laid an egg, which hatched and so Helen was born, as Cratinus [MS: Crates] the poet says.

(b) About the Bird: this is called the Great, whom they identify with a swan. Zeus turned himself into such a creature and flew off to Rhamnus in Attica and there ravished Nemesis. She then laid an egg, from which Helen was born. So Cratinus [MS: Crates] records.

(c) This is the swan, into which they say that Jupiter transformed himself and flew to the land of Rhamnus in Attica, where he ravished Nemesis, and that she laid an egg from which Helen was born, as Cratinus, the comic [MS: tragic] writer says.

Fragments

114 Therefore you must become a large bird.

115 Athenaeus 373e

Λήδα, σὸν ἔργον· δεῖ σ᾽ ὅπως εὐσχημόνως
ἀλεκτρυόνος μηδὲν διοίσεις τοὺς τρόπους,
ἐπὶ τῷδ᾽ ἐπῴζουσ᾽, ὡς ἂν ἐκλέψῃς καλὸν
ἡμῖν τι καὶ θαυμαστὸν ἐκ τοῦδ᾽ ὄρνεον.

116 Σ Theocritus 10

ὥστ᾽ οὖν ἐσθίων τοῖς σιτίοισιν ἥδομαι·
ἅπαντα δ᾽ εἶναί <μοι> δοκεῖ ῥοδωνιὰ
καὶ μῆλα καὶ σέλινα καὶ σισύμβρια.

117 Pollux 10.186

Σπάρτην λέγω γε †σπαρτίδα† τὴν σπάρτινον.

118 Plutarch *Pericles* 3.5

μόλ᾽ ὦ Ζεῦ ξένιε καὶ καραίε.

119 Stephanus of Byzantium p. 703.20

Ψύρα τε τὴν Σπάρτην ἄγεις.

120 Athenaeus 373c

τἄλλα πάντ᾽ ὀρνίθια.

121 Athenaeus 373d

ὄρνιθα φοινικόπτερον.

115 Here is your task, Leda. You must behave just like a proper hen and brood over this egg, from which you may hatch for us a beautiful and wonderful chick.

116 How I really enjoy eating the food. Everything seems to me to be rosebuds and apples and parsley and bergamot mint.[1]

[1] The speaker is probably Zeus in bird form, especially if each of the foods possesses a sexually suggestive meaning.

117 By "Spartiad" (?) I mean "Sparta" and not esparto grass.[1]

[1] σπαρτίδα is not a known word. Most try to emend the text in line with the joke at *Birds* 813–16 on "Sparta" and "esparto grass."

118 Come, Zeus, god of guests and of the head.[1]

[1] Plutarch insists that this line is aimed at Pericles. Καραιός is a Boeotian title of Zeus and if Pericles was meant, the joke depends on a pun with κάρα (head). See F 73, 258.

119 You regard Sparta as Psyra.

120 All the other little birds.

121 A bird with wings like flame.

122 Priscian *Institutes of Grammar* 17.169

μεθυστέρῳ χρόνῳ

123 Pollux 10.177

ἐν τῷ κύφωνι τὸν αὐχέν᾽ ἔχων.

124 Athenaeus 667f

τὸ δὲ κοττάβῳ προθέντας ἐν πατρικοῖσι νόμοις τὸ
κεινεου ὀξυβάφοις βάλλειν μὲν τῷ πόντῳ δὲ βάλλοντι
νέμω πλεῖστα τύχης τὸ δ᾽ ἆθλον.

125 Σ Aristophanes *Birds* 521

ἔζη δὲ ἐπὶ τῆς τῶν Ὀρνίθων διδασκαλίας, οὐχ, ὥς
τινες, ἐτεθνήκει. πολλῷ γὰρ ὕστερον Κρατῖνος ἐν τῇ
Νεμέσει οἶδεν αὐτὸν ζῶντα.

126 Σ Aristophanes *Birds* 858

ἔστι καὶ ἕτερος αὐλητὴς, οὗ μνημονεύει Κρατῖνος ἐν
Νεμέσει.

NOMOI

122 In time hereafter.

123 With his neck in the stocks.

124 [text and translation very debatable] Setting up *cottabus* according to the traditional rules . . . to shoot at floating saucers .. and to the man who hits the most I award this prize of victory.

125 "Lampon": . . . and he was still alive at the time of the performance of *Birds* [414], and had not died, as some have said. Cratinus in *Nemesis* knows him as alive, and this much later.

126 There is another one [Chaireas], the *aulos* player, whom Cratinus mentions in *Nemesis*.

Brief fragment: (F 127) "the bugger-off dance."

LAWS

The title suggests that the chorus was made of the personified laws of Athens, for which we may compare the chorus in Eupolis' Demes. Scholars have taken the parody in F 135 of Solon to indicate that Solon himself was a character in the play, and it must be noted that Solon does appear in Chirons (F 246) and in Demes. If "the very ancient men" of F 133 are the chorus, then we will have had a familiar sort of chorus, figures of the past, and the comedy may have turned on the familiar opposition of old as better, and modern as inferior. The "you" [singular] of F 128 and 134 is presumably the main character of the comedy, who

329

Fragments

128 Photius α 2666

ἀλλὰ μὰ Δί᾽ οὐκ οἶδ᾽ ἔγωγε γράμματ᾽ οὐδ᾽
ἐπίσταμαι,
ἀλλ᾽ ἀπὸ γλώττης φράσω σοι· μνημονεύω γὰρ
καλῶς.

129 Bachmann's *Lexicon* p. 118.3

οὐκ ἀπερρήσεις σὺ θᾶττον; ἀποτιλῶ σε τήμερον.

130 Athenaeus 646e

καὶ δρόσον βάλλων ἔωθεν χλιαρὸς ταγηνίας.

131 Photius p. 353.8

ὁ δὲ Ζεὺς ὀσταφίσιν ὕσει τάχα.

132 Athenaeus 502b

χρυσίδι σπένδων † γέγραφε † τοῖς ὄφεσι πιεῖν
διδούς.

133 Photius (b, z) α 717

ἦ πρεσβῦται πάνυ γηραλέοι σκήπτροισιν ἄκασκα
προβῶντες.

encounters the laws as part of the plot of the comedy, but
further we cannot go with confidence. F 131 does sound
like an expression of the "automatic" nature of the Golden
Age.

Fragments

128 But by Zeus I don't know the alphabet and I don't
know ‹how to write›. But I will tell you [sing.] orally, for I
have a good memory.

129 Won't you [sing.] just quickly go away? I will pluck
you today.

130 A warm pancake giving off the dew of morning.

131 Zeus will soon be raining raisins.

132 Giving the serpents something to drink †he has
drawn pouring with a golden cup.

133 Old men, very ancient, have made their way along
gingerly with their sticks.

134 *Suda* χ 471

νῦν γὰρ δή σοι πάρα μὲν θεσμοὶ
τῶν ἡμετέρων, πάρα δ᾽ ἄλλ᾽ ὅ τι χρῇs.

135 Photius (b, z) α 1088

ὑμῶν εἷς μὲν ἕκαστος ἀλώπηξ δωροδοκεῖται.

136 Pollux 6.68

τυρῷ καὶ μίνθῃ παραλεξάμενος καὶ ἐλαίῳ.

137 Photius p. 371.23

μεῖζον τὸ δέος παλαστῆς

138 Hesychius λ 1371

Λυκαμβὶs ἀρχή

139 Pollux 7.86

σανδάλια Τυρρηνικά

140 Σ Aristophanes *Knights* 1150a

σχοίνινον ἠθμόν

ΟΔΥΣΣΗΣ

134 For here now for you [sing.] are the ordinances of our people, here too is anything else you need.

135 Each one of you is a bribe-taking fox.[1]

[1] This is a reasonably close parody of Solon F 11.5: "Each of you walks like a fox."

136 Having slept with Cheese and Mint and Oil.[1]

[1] "Cheese" (Tyro) and "Mint" (Minthe) are also the names of heroines who slept with gods.

137 Fear greater than the breadth of your palm.[1]

[1] It is tempting to read Ruhnken's *peos* (penis) for *deos* (fear).

138 A Lycambean office.

139 Etruscan sandals.

140 A funnel made of wicker.

Brief fragments: (F 141) "<wine> on its own," (F 142) "third-lowest note."

ODYSSEUS AND COMPANY

This comedy was one of a number of dramatic burlesques based on the encounter between Odysseus and the Cyclops in Odyssey *9. The earlier comic poets, Epicharmus and Aristias, had each written a* Cyclops, *Callias a* Cyclopes *in 434, and Euripides the extant satyr play of that title, whose date is unknown but probably later than the comedies by*

Cratinus and Callias. Some of Homer's details are preserved: the marvellous wine (F 145–46), the "name" of Odysseus (F 145), the fleeing comrades (F 148), the emphasis on cheese and milk (F 149), the threatening Cyclops (F 150) with one eye (F 156).

Platonius writes that this comedy belonged to the "type of Middle Comedy," since it lacked "choral parts and parabases" and also personal insult, the humour being directed at the Homeric original. But F 151 shows that there was indeed a chorus, the comrades of Odysseus. The metre there is anapaestic dimeter, and it has been argued that what the play lacked was not a chorus per se, but choral songs and parabases in complicated metres. See, however, F 153, which K.-A. restore in glyconics. Platonius is not known for his accuracy in matters of individual detail—for example, he seems to think that Odysseus and Company, *Eupolis'*

Testimonium

i Platonius I *On the Different Sorts of Comedy*

τοιοῦτος οὖν ἐστιν ὁ τῆς μέσης κωμῳδίας τύπος, οἷος ἐστιν ὁ Αἰολοσίκων Ἀριστοφάνους καὶ οἱ Ὀδυσσεῖς Κρατίνου καὶ πλεῖστα τῶν παλαιῶν δραμάτων οὔτε χορικὰ οὔτε παραβάσεις ἔχοντα . . . οἱ γοῦν Ὀδυσσεῖς Κρατίνου οὐδενὸς ἐπιτίμησιν ἔχουσι, διασυρμὸν δὲ τῆς Ὀδυσσείας τοῦ Ὁμήρου.

Dyers, *and Aristophanes'* Aeolosicon *all belong to the same
period, whereas they are about fifty years apart. Sommer-
stein (*Talking about Laughter *[Oxford 2009] 272-88) ex-
plains this in part as a confusion between Cratinus'* Odys-
seus and Company *with Theopompus'* Odysseus, *a play
that certainly belongs to the last years of Old Comedy.
None of the fragments, however, has any personal jokes,
and perhaps Platonius was correct on that point, but not
about the chorus. This lack of personal humour has led
many to the attractive conclusion that the play should be
dated to the period of the ban on such jokes, 439–436 (see
the scholiast to *Acharnians* 67).*

Recent bibliography: M. Bertran, A&R *29 (1984) 171–78;
M. Ornaghi, in Zanetto et al.* Momenti della ricezione
omerica *(Milan 2004) 197–228.*

Testimonium

i This is the sort of thing Middle Comedy does, such as
Aristophanes *Aeolosicon* and Cratinus' *Odysseus and
Company* and most of the plays of Old Comedy that do not
have choral songs or parabases . . . For instance, Cratinus'
Odysseus and Company contains no personal humour, but
only a spoof of Homer's *Odyssey.*

Fragments

143 Hephaestion *Handbook* 8.4

τίνες αὖ πόντον κατέχουσ᾽ αὖραι; νέφος οὐράνιον
τόδ᾽ ὁρῶμαι.
ὡς ἂν μᾶλλον τοῖς πηδαλίοις ἡ ναῦς ἡμῶν
πειθαρχῇ.

144 Photius (z) α 2826

ἐπ᾽ ἀριστέρ᾽ ἀεὶ τὴν Ἄρκτον ἔχων λάμπουσαν, ἕως
ἂν ἐφεύρῃς.

145 Athenaeus 446b

τῇ νῦν τόδε πῖθι λαβὼν ἤδη, καὶ τοὔνομά μ᾽ εὐθὺς
ἐρώτα.

146 Pollux 6.26

οὔπω ᾽πιον τοιοῦτον οὐδὲ πίομαι
Μάρωνα.

147 Athenaeus 68c

{A.} ποῦ ποτ᾽ εἶδές μοι τὸν ἄνδρα, Λαέρτα φίλον
παῖδ᾽;
{B.} ἐν Πάρῳ, σικυὸν μέγιστον σπερματίαν
ὠνούμενον.

1 πώποτε CE, ποῦ ποτ᾽ Runkel.

CRATINUS

Fragments

143 What winds now take over the sea? I see a cloud as high as heaven.[1]

So that our ship may better obey the helm.

[1] Hephaestion assigns this to the beginning of the play. Did it then begin like Shakespeare's *Tempest*, with a visibly staged storm and characters on a ship? See F 152. Bakola (240) finds parallels for a ship on stage in *Frogs,* Eupolis' *Officers,* and Pherecrates' *Ant-Men.*

144 Keeping the gleaming constellation of the Bear on your left until you [sing.] come to

145 (ODYSSEUS) Now take and drink this, then ask me my name.

146 Never before have I drunk such Maron and never shall again.

147 (A) Where did you once see the man, Laertes' dear son?

(B) On Paros, buying a jumbo-sized pumpkin.[1]

[1] It is usually thought that the speakers are the Cyclops and Odysseus. But how should the Cyclops know Odysseus' parentage and why should he call him "the dear son of L."? Olson (Athenaeus I 387) translates "my husband, the dear son of L.," turning the passage into a comic version of *Odyssey* 19.185–202 and making the speaker Penelope. But the comedy seems to have been a parody of Odysseus and the Cyclops, not the larger story. There is much to be said for Kock's text, which would read: "CYCL. Tell me, did you ever see the man? OD. The dear son of Laertes? On Paros, buying a jumbo-sized pumpkin."

{ΚΥΚΛΩΨ.} πώποτ᾽ εἶδες, εἰπέ μοι
τὸν ἄνδρα; {ΟΔΥΣΣΕΥΣ.} Λαέρτα φίλον παῖδ᾽; ἐν Πάρῳ
σικυὸν μέγιστον σπερματίαν ὠνούμενον. Kock

148 Pollux 10.32–33

οἱ δ᾽ ἀλυσκάζουσιν ὑπὸ ταῖς κλινίσιν.

149 Athenaeus 99f (l. 1), Σ Aristophanes *Wasps* 710a
(l. 2)

ἦσθε πανημέριοι χορταζόμενοι γάλα λευκόν,
πυὸν δαινύμενοι, κἀμπιμπλάμενοι πυριάτῃ.

150 Athenaeus 385c

ἀνθ᾽ ὧν πάντας ἑλὼν ὑμᾶς ἐρίηρας ἑταίρους,
φρύξας χἀψήσας, κἀπανθρακίσας κὠπτήσας,
εἰς ἅλμην τε καὶ ὀξάλμην κᾆτ᾽ ἐς σκοροδάλμην
χλιαρὸν ἐμβάπτων, ὃς ἂν ὀπτότατός μοι ἁπάντων
5 ὑμῶν φαίνηται, κατατρώξομαι, ὦ στρατιῶται.

151 Hephaestion *Handbook* 8.6

σίγα νυν ἅπας ἔχε σίγα,
καὶ πάντα λόγον τάχα πεύσῃ·
ἡμῖν δ᾽ Ἰθάκη πατρίς ἐστι,
πλέομεν δ᾽ ἅμ᾽ Ὀδυσσεῖ θείῳ.

148 They are taking cover beneath the couches.

149 You sat here all day, getting fat on white milk, dining on beestings, and filling yourselves with creamed cheese.[1]

  [1] Either the Cyclops to Odysseus and his men, or, more likely, Odysseus to his comrades who have become too comfortable. Both F 149 and 150 are in dactylic hexameters.

150 (CYCLOPS) In return for which I shall seize all you "loyal comrades," roast you, boil you, barbecue and bake you, dip you into brine and vinegar and warm garlic sauce, and whichever of you soldiers all appears to be the best cooked, that's the one I shall munch down.

151 (CHORUS) Quiet now, everyone, quiet, and you [sing.] will swiftly learn the whole story. Our homeland is Ithaca and we are sailing with godlike Odysseus.

152 Photius (b, z) α 493

νεοχμόν ‹τι› παρῆχθαι ἄθυρμα.

153 Photius (z) ined.

οὐκ εἰδυῖα τάδ' οὐκετ' ὄνθ'
οἷα τἀπὶ Χαριξένης.

154 Athenaeus 315bc

τέμαχος ὀρφὼ χλιαρόν

155 Phrynichus *Selection* 107

δέλφακας μεγάλους

ΠΑΝΟΠΤΑΙ

152 Brought on as a novel plaything.

1 Suggestions include the wine (F 145–46), the ship (F 143), or the play itself.

153 She doesn't realise that things are no longer what they were in the time of Charixena.[1]

1 "In the time of Charixena" seems to have been a proverbial expression "in the old days" carrying the sense of a lack of sophistication.

154 A warm slice of sea perch.

155 Large suckling pigs.

Brief fragments: (F 156) "one-eyed," (F 157) "garland flower" (of the lotus).

ALL-SEEING ONES

The title plus "eyes past number" (F 161) suggests Argus, the ever-watchful guardian of Io, but what would a plural entity based on Argus be? Some have seen the comedy as a sophistic play in the manner of Clouds *or Eupolis'* Goats, *based on the reference to Hippon and the analogy of the* pnigeus *in F 167, on Parmenides' term "two-headed" for the followers of Heraclitus (see F 161), and on the occurrence of the adjective "remembering" at F 162 and* Clouds *483–85. Simply put, we can say very little for certain about either date or theme.*

Recent bibliography: C. Carey, in Rivals *426–27.*

Fragments

158 Photius (b, S^z) α 1642

καὶ πάντ᾽ ἀναρροφεῖ.

159 Photius α 1642

        ταῦτ᾽ εὐθὺς ὑποκαθήμενοι
ἀναρροφοῦσιν ἄνδρες.

160 Σ Lucian *Alexander* 4

ὁ Ἀριστόδημος δὲ μιαρὸς καὶ καταπύγων ἐς ὑπερ-
βολήν, ἀφ᾽ οὗ καὶ ὁ πρωκτὸς Ἀριστόδημος καλεῖται·
Κρατῖνος Πανόπταις
Ἀριστόδημος ὡς ἀσχημονων ἐν τοῖς Κιμωνιοις ἀνερι-
πια.

161 Hephaestion *Handbook* 1.9

κρανία δισσὰ φορεῖν, ὀφθαλμοὶ δ᾽ οὐκ ἀριθματοί.

162 Hephaestion *Handbook* 1.8

ἀλλοτριογνώμοις ἐπιλήσμοσι μνημονικοῖσιν.

163 Photius p. 369.4

μισεῖς γὰρ τὰς γυναῖκ-
   ας, πρὸς παιδικὰ δὲ τρέπῃ νῦν.

Fragments

158 And he gulps down everything.

159 Men lying in wait immediately gulp this down.

160 Aristodemus was a wretched man and given to extreme homosexual vice, for which reason the arsehole is called the "Aristodemus." Cratinus in *All-Seeing Ones*:

Aristodemos behaving badly in the Cimonian ruins. (?)

161 To have two heads and eyes were past number.

162 With other things on their mind, forgetful, remembering.

163 For you hate women and are turning now to boys.

164 Homer *Iliad* 9.77b

γέγηθα τὸν ἄνδρα

165 The Antiatticist p. 91.10

διὰ πάντων ἀγών

166 Orus *Orthography* fol. 282ʳ 20

παλινῳδικοὶ ὕμνοι

167

(a) Σ Aristophanes *Clouds* 95

ταῦτα πρότερος Κρατῖνος ἐν Πανόπταις δράματι περὶ
Ἵππωνος τοῦ φιλοσόφου κωμῳδῶν αὐτὸν λέγει

(b) Σ Clement of Alexandria *Protrepticus* 24.2

τοῦ δὲ Ἵππωνος . . . ὡς ἀσεβοῦς γενομένου μέμνηται
ὁ Κρατῖνος.

168 Σ Aristophanes *Clouds* 985a

Κηκείδης, διθυράμβων ποιητὴς πάνυ ἀρχαῖος. μέμνη-
ται δὲ αὐτοῦ Κρατῖνος Πανόπταις.

164 I am very happy for the man . . .

165 The final contest.

166 Palinodic songs.[1]

  [1] This means songs with the metrical pattern *a b b a*.

167

(a) [referring to Strepsiades' analogy at *Clouds* 94–96 of the sky as a *pnigeus* (chafing dish) covering the earth]

   Cratinus says this earlier in his play *All-Seeing Ones* making fun of Hippon the philosopher.

(b) Cratinus mentions Hippon as being an impious man.

168 Ceceides was a very old-fashioned dithyrambic poet, whom Cratinus mentions in *All-Seeing Ones*.[1]

  [1] His name is variously given as Ceceides or Cedeides; *IG* i[3] 965 (last third of the 5th c.) has the spelling "Cedeides." See Campbell *GL* IV 324–25.

Brief fragments: (F 169) "you [sing.] applauded," (F 170) "property keeper."

ΠΛΟΥΤΟΙ

The traditional book fragments told us only a little about this comedy. F 172 and 176 contained themes of the traditional comic picture of the "automatic nature" of the Golden Age, while F 175 took us to Sparta in what seems to have been a favourable depiction of that city's way of life. Much changed with the publication in the 1930s of a number of papyri [F 171], all from the same original, but not necessarily in the order printed in K.-A. and as presented below. We can now say that the chorus, which gave the play its title, was composed of Titans called "Wealth-Gods," who are now free and have come "here" (presumably Athens) in search of an old and decrepit relative. Their second mission apparently is to deal with those at Athens who "possess wealth unjustly." The latter part of F 171 shows that one such was the political figure Hagnon.

The comedy has been seen to operate on several levels: (1) the familiar comic expression of the Golden Age—it was better back then, when the gods were more favourable and abundance happened on its own, (2) a burlesque of myth, especially the story told in Hesiod's Works and Days *(109–26) of the gods of wealth, (3) an engagement with tragedy, especially the lost* Loosing of Prometheus, *in which the chorus is composed of Titans, now free, who enter and sing in anapaestic dimeters (TrGF 3 F 193), and (4) a possible political reading by which the reference to the end of tyranny and the rule of the people stands for the removal of*

WEALTH-GODS

Pericles from office in 430, since for many Zeus in Cratinus must signify Pericles. This last is least plausible, for the point is more likely that the humour lies in the fact that the experience of the gods is the same as that at Athens, tyranny replaced by democracy.

The fragments show a strong engagement with tragedy on Cratinus' part. Bakola (122–41) shows how F 171 uses themes from Aeschylus' lost Loosing of Prometheus—*the Titans now free come in search of a kinsman. This makes Prometheus a strong candidate for the "ancient kinsman" of line 25—others had suggested Cronus, Wealth, and Demus (a personified Athenian people). Also lying behind the comedy would be Aeschylus'* Eumenides, *since the Wealth-Gods, like the Furies, can be seen as pursuing those who have acted unjustly.*

The date could be any time during the 430s and 420s, but if Pericles' brief removal in 430/29 does lie behind F 171.22–23, then the play can belong only to 429. If The Loosing of Prometheus *was in fact part of the winning production by Euphorion of Aeschylus' trilogy in 431, then again we are looking at the early 420s. On the other hand, if the plays listed in T 10 are in chronological order, then* Wealth-Gods *belongs in the early to mid-430s.*

Recent bibliography: Pellegrino (Utopie) *45–54; I. Ruffell, in* Rivals *475–81.*

Fragments

171 *PSI* XI (1935) 1212 (ll. 1–42), *Pap. Brux.* E 6482 frr.
a–d (ll. 43–86), *PSI* XII (1951) 1279 (ll. 87–89)

```
     ...ε μὲν κακο[
   {ΧΟ.} ἀλλ' ἀξιόνικον[
     ἀποφαινόμεν[ο
     τὸ τυχὸν στέργει[ν
5    μὴ ξυντυχίαισι βαρυνόμενοι
       μενετοὶ κριταὶ ο..[
   {?} καί μοι ταῦτα μὲν ω.[
       τοὐμοῦ τοῦ πρόσθε.[
   {ΧΟ.} ὧν δ' οὕνεκ' ἐφήσαμεν [
10   πεύσεσθ' ἤδη.
     Τιτᾶνες μὲν γενεάν ἐσμ[εν
     Πλοῦτοι δ' ἐκαλούμεθ' ὅτ' [ἦρχε Κρόνος.
     τότε δ' ἦν φωνῆνθ' ὅτε.[
     κατέπιν' ἀκόναις
15   κλωγμὸν πολὺν αἰνετὸς ὑ[μῖν.
   {?} εἶτα δὲ κλέπτεις τὸν Δία.[
     ε..στο......στ..π.[
   - - - - - - - - - -
```

CRATINUS

Fragments

171

(a) lines 1–28. *The first part is in anapaestic dimeters, the traditional metre of the entry song of the chorus, and in it the chorus appear to be making an appeal to the spectators (the plural "you" in v. 10) and to the dramatic judges "burdened with misfortunes" (5). Aristophanes, apart from* Frogs, *does not use the* parodos *of his plays to break the dramatic illusion and address the spectators or the judges. But Cratinus, both here and in* Dionysalexander, *seems to have done just that. Lines 13–15 seem also to refer to a dramatic performance of the story of Cronus and his children.*

_ . . . bad . . .

(CHORUS) But demonstrating [an idea?] worthy of victory . . . to accept what comes . . . lest these judges, burdened with misfortunes [5], ‹may not be› patient . . .

_ For me also this . . . of my previous . . .

(CHORUS) The reasons we said . . . you [pl.] will now learn [10]. By race we are Titans and were called "Wealth-Gods," when ‹Cronus was king›, and at that time were speaking ‹beasts?›, when ‹the father› swallowed down ‹his children› with whetstones . . . acceptable to you with considerable clucking [15].

_ And then you [sing.] steal from Zeus

                    K]ρόνον ἐγβα[
                    κ]αὶ Τιτᾶνας το[
20   ]ντας δεσμ[
            desunt versus 4
                    δεσμὸς ξ....ο.[
{ΧΟ.} ὡς δὲ τυραννίδος ἀρχὴ λ[έλυται
    δῆμος δὲ κρατεῖ,
    δεῦρ' ἐσύθημεν πρὸς ο.[
25 αὐτοκασίγνητόν τε παλαιὸν
            ζητοῦντε[ς] κεἰ σαθρὸν ἤδη.
{?}   σ]κῆψις πρώτη
                    αὖ] τάχ' ἀκούσηι

_ _ _

                    χ·[
30   [
{?} ἐφῆι πο[
λεπτῆι .[
ὅτ' ἦν το.[

_ _ _ _ _

_ _ _

    ]..[
35]επω[...].γει[
    ].ωτ.[.]μενπ[
    ]..ιᾶι τοῦ βιο[
    ]μαντείουσ[
    ]υλοι καιπε.[
40].ς. υνηνεφ[
    ἐ]ξαίφνης γε.[

350

... ⟨depose?⟩ Cronus from ... and the Titans ... bondage [20] ... [4 lines] ... bondage ...

(CHORUS) Now that the rule of tyranny ⟨is over⟩ and the people rule, we have rushed here seeking our ⟨relative⟩ and aged brother [25] even if he is decrepit ... _ ... first reason .. . and you [sing.] will quickly hear.

(b) lines 29–33

... [30] he said ... when it was ...

(c) lines 34–42

... [35] ... of life ... prophetic ... [40] ... suddenly

]ης μέν τι.[

– – – – –

].ο........
]ηλ. φέρει·
45   ]τοις ποτε
πλουτοῦσ]ιν ἀδίκως ἐνθάδε
]ρονωι φράσειν
ἀ]ναστρέφει·
ἐγὼ γάρ εἰμι θυννὶς ἡ μέλαινά σοι
50 καὶ θύννος, ὀρφώς, γλαῦκος, ἔγχελυς, κύων·
]άχ[.]σι πραγμάτων·
εσκ]ευασμένων·
]μείων κακῶν
]ιας δίδου·
55   ].τας ἔγχος λόγων·
]νης

– – – –

– – – – –

...[
δόντι γὰρ λ[
ὡς παλαιγενη.[
60 ἀλλ᾽ ἐμοὶ γὰρ ἐμπ[
μέρος λόγου κ.[
τοῦδε συμπλέκε[ιν
ἔγειρε, θυμέ, γλῶ[τταν εὐ-
κέραστον ὀρθουμένην
65 εἰς ὑπόκρισιν λόγων.
{?} μάρτυρας τοὺς προσκεκλημένο[υς

352

(d) lines 43–56: *Only the last parts of these lines are pre-served, but the remains of lines 49–50 are sufficient to show that they belong to a fragment from* Wealth-Gods *cited by Athenaeus (303d), whose meaning is less than clear. If the supplement in line 46 is correct, then at this point we learn of the other mission of the chorus, to punish those who are unjustly wealthy.*

. . . brings . . . to those unjustly wealthy here [45] . . . to speak . . . turns back. Here I am for you [sing.] a black bo-nito and a tuna fish and a sea perch and a shark, and an eel, and a dogfish [50] . . . matters . . . prepared . . . bad . . . he used to give [sing.] . . . the point of the words [55].

(e) lines 57–76: *Here there seems to be a trial of one of these unjustly wealthy, Hagnon (PAA 107380) son of Nicias, general in the 430s and* proboulos *in the crisis years of 413–411, also father of Theramenes, a leading fig-ure at the end of the War. He is known also as a political ally of Pericles in the 430s, which for some (e.g., Bakola 213–20) reinforces a political reading of the comedy. In the first part one of the antagonists sings a short song to pre-pare himself—in Aristophanes the sung prelude to a con-test is given to the chorus. The second part features an agon between characters unknown over Hagnon, whose wealth is argued by one to be traditional, but a neat pun on* ex archēs *muddies the waters ("from his birth"/"from his office" or "from the empire").*

giving . . . as for one of a previous generation . . . for to me [60] . . . in my turn now to put together . . . of this speech. My heart, stir up my tongue well-balanced for a proper delivery of words [65].

τῶιδε χρή· τοῦ Στειριῶς γὰρ εὐκτὰ τον[
ὃν καλοῦσ᾽ Ἅγνωνα νῦν καὶ δῆμον η[
{?} οὗτος οὐ πλουτεῖ δικαίως ἐνθάδ᾽ ὥστε
[κλαύσεται.
{?} ἀλλὰ μὴν ἀρχαιόπλουτός γ᾽ ἐστὶν ἐξ ἀρχ[ῆς
70   ἔχων
πάνθ᾽ ὅσ᾽ ἐστ᾽ αὐτῶι, τὰ μὲν[.]..[.].ων, τὰ δ.[
{?} ἐξαμεινώσω φράσας η[....σα]φέστερον[
Νικίας φορτηγὸς ἦν κα.[.........]ονων.[
Πειθίου μισθωτὸς .[...............].ρε.[
75 {?} οὗ κατέψευσται τα[...............]..ο.[
{?} ἀλλ᾽ ἐγώ τοι, μὰ Δία[

– – – –
.[
{?} πο.[
ἦ φρον[
80 ὁπότ᾽ ἀρισ[τ
ὃν σὺ πρω.[
ὀλίγον[

– – – –

– – – – –
.[
{Γρα.} μ.[
85 {Τι.} ὀν[
]κ[

– – –

354

_ The summoned witnesses should ⟨stand⟩ here, for it is desirable ⟨to investigate⟩ the man from Steria, whom they call "Hagnon" and his deme.

_ This man has not gained his wealth justly here and so ⟨he should be punished⟩.

_ But he has his money from a long time back [70], having everything that he has from the beginning, some from ⟨his houses⟩, some from ⟨his estates⟩.

_ I'll amend the indictment by explaining more clearly . . . Nicias was a porter . . . a hired man belonging to Peithias

_ About whom lies have been told [75] . . .

_ No by Zeus, but I . . .

(f) lines 77–82

. . . to think . . . when best [80] . . . which you before . . . a little

(g) lines 83–86: *In the margin are written* GRA *(84) and* TI *(85), which are the names of speakers. Old Woman* (graus) *naturally suggests for the first, while TI could begin a name such as Timo– (or also Titan?).*

. . . (OLD WOMAN) me . . . (TI) . . . whom [85] . . .

_ _ _ _ _

].ἐς κόρακας[

].ω φέρων τὸν[

ἔ]στ᾽ εὐμάρεια πλ.[

172 Stobaeus 4.39.11

αὐτόματα τοῖσι θεὸς ἀνίει τἀγαθά.

173 Σ Aristophanes *Lysistrata* 1243

ἄρξει γὰρ αὐτοῖς ἡ διποδία καλῶς.

ἡ διποδία codd., ἥδε διποδίας Luppe.

174 Athenaeus 94e

περὶ σιαγόνος βοείας μαχόμενος.

175 Athenaeus 138e

ἆρ᾽ ἀληθῶς τοῖς ξένοισιν ἔστιν, ὡς λέγουσ᾽, ἐκεῖ
πᾶσι τοῖς ἐλθοῦσιν ἐν τῇ κοπίδι θοινᾶσθαι καλῶς;
ἐν δὲ ταῖς λέσχαισι φύσκαι προσπεπατταλευμέναι
κατακρέμανται, τοῖσι πρεσβύταισιν ἀποδάκνειν
ὀδάξ;

176 Athenaeus 267e

οἷς δὴ βασιλεὺς Κρόνος ἦν τὸ παλαιόν,
ὅτε τοῖς ἄρτοις ἠστραγάλιζον, μᾶζαι δ᾽ ἐν ταῖσι
παλαίστραις

(h) lines 87–89

   . . . go to hell . . . bringing . . . is convenient . . .

172 For them a god would send up all good things on their own.

173 She will lead a double-step well for them.[1]

  [1] Translating the text of Luppe.

174 A man fighting over the jawbone of an ox.

175 Is it really possible, as they say, for all strangers who visit there to dine well at the mess? And do sausages really hang pegged up in the council rooms, for the ambassadors [or "old men"] to take a bite from?

176 Cronus was their king of old, when they played knuckle-bones with loaves of bread, and Aeginetan barley

Αἰγιναῖαι κατεβέβληντο δρυπεπεῖς βώλοις τε
κομῶσαι.

3 βώλοις ACE, ὀβολοῖς Toup, ἀμύλοις Bergk, φύλλοις
Kock.

177 P. Oxy. 1611 F 1 col. ii.30

"[...]ον νῦν γ᾽ ὁρᾷ[ς] ἡμᾶς δυ᾽ ὄντας, τέτταρ[α]ς καὶ
τοὺς κρίτας," δηλῶν οὕτως τέτταρας ὄντας, Λύσιππος
δὲ ἐν Βάκχαις ε΄, ὁμοίως δὲ καὶ Κρατῖνος ἐν Πλούτοις
λέγει.

ΠΥΛΑΙΑ

Fragments

180 Σ (Arethas) Plato *Lysis* 206e

ἢ Διονυσίοις ἀκοίλοις παίζουσιν ἀνέμενοι τρόπα.

181 Σ Aristophanes *Birds* 121

γλῶσσαν εὑέρων βοτῶν.

cakes, tree-ripened and surrounded by clumps (?), had fallen to earth in the wrestling grounds.

177 "And now you see us two in number, but the judges four" [K.-A. VIII 1033], thus indicating that there were four ‹judges›, but Lysippus in *Bacchae* says five, and Cratinus in *Wealth-Gods* the same.

Brief fragments: (F 178) "to revive," (F 179) "lameness."

PYLAEA

*One of Cratinus' most mysterious titles, the word was used as a cult title ("at the gates") of the goddess of Demeter at Thermopylae ("Hot-Gates") and for the meeting of the Amphictyonic League that took place at that location. But how either might have been used in an Old Comedy is not easy to understand. Plutarch (*Artaxerxes 1.2*; On the Face of the Moon 924d) does use the word to mean a "hodge-podge" or "odd collection," and it just might have been used to indicate a gathering of strange individuals—"a motley crew"(?).*

Fragments

180 Who play *tropa* flicking with acorns at the Dionysia.[1]

[1] *Tropa* was a party game played by shooting knuckle bones or acorns at a hole. Pieters suggested that this is a reference to Cratinus' competitors at the Dionysia. The text is very uncertain.

181 The language of woolly flocks.

182 Σ Plato *Symposium* 174b

οἶδ᾽ αὖθ᾽ ἡμεῖς, ὡς ὁ παλαιὸς
λόγος, αὐτομάτους ἀγαθοὺς ἰέναι
κομψῶν ἐπὶ δαῖτα θεατῶν.

183 Suda α 1676

†αὐτοὺς παίδευσεν† ἔθρεψέ τε δημοσίοισι
χρήμασιν εἰς ἥβην, ἵνα οἵ ποτε λοιγὸν ἀμύναιν

184 Photius p. 595.12

ἄνδρας σοφοὺς χρὴ τὸ παρὸν πρᾶγμα καλῶς εἰς
δύναμιν τίθεσθαι.

185 Σ Aristophanes *Birds* 766

οὐδὲν σαφὲς ἔχομεν τίς ὁ Πεισίου, οὐδὲ περὶ τῆς
προδοσίας. ὅτι δὲ τῶν λίαν πονηρῶν ἐστι δηλοῖ Κρα-
τῖνος ἐν Χείρωσι, Πυλαίᾳ, Ὥραις.

186 Σ Aristophanes *Peace* 733

Κρατῖνος δὲ ἐν τῇ Πυλαίᾳ δηλοῖ, ὅτι ἔξ ἐστι ζυγὰ τοῦ
χοροῦ.

182 And here we are, just like that ancient saying that good men make their way naturally to the feast of clever spectators.[1]

[1] The metre is anapaestic dimeter, regularly used in the entry of the chorus. This would provide another instance of Cratinus' breaking the dramatic illusion and addressing the spectators in this part of the play.

183 ⟨He⟩ raised them and looked after them in their youth at public expense, so that one day they might ward off disaster.

184 Wise men should turn the present situation to their advantage.

185 We know nothing for certain about who the son of Peisias was, nor about his act of betrayal. That he was one of the very wicked is made clear by Cratinus in his *Chirons* [F 251], his *Pylaea,* and *Seasons* [F 282].[1]

[1] The son of Peisias was famous for an act of civic betrayal (see *Birds* 766, Cratinus F 251, 282, Pherecrates F 6) but when and where is unknown. The name is not a common one at Athens.

186 Cratinus makes it clear in *Pylaea* that the chorus has six ranks.

Brief fragments: (F 187) "Zopyrus' money," (F 188) "you'll see," (F 189) "Lake Gorge," (F 190) "young crow," (F 191) "to hold the marriage rehearsal party," (F 192) "false testimony."

ΠΥΤΙΝΗ

Produced at the Dionysia of 423, this was likely Cratinus'
last comedy and perhaps his greatest success. Cratinus
makes himself the main character in his own play, in part
responding to Aristophanes' jibes in Knights *the previous*
year (ll. 526–36 = T 12d). The plot of the comedy is given by
the scholiast to Knights *400 (below T 3): Comedy is Cra-*
tinus' wife, whom Cratinus has abandoned for drunken-
ness (some would capitalise Drunkenness and make her a
rival personification and character in the play). She wishes
to leave him and charge him formally with abuse (kakōsis).
Friends of Cratinus, very likely the chorus, arrive to en-
quire what is the cause of her complaint. Bakola (275–85)
points out that a suit of kakōsis *could involve neglect of an*
heiress by her husband, and finds other instances of artistic
*creation expressed in sexual terms (*Knights *515–17,* Frogs
92–97, and especially Pherecrates F 155).

Thereafter we can only guess at the plotline. Comedy
clearly speaks F 193–94, perhaps F 195, all probably from
the prologue. She would be an obvious candidate also for
F 199, were it not for the masculine participle in line 4.
Cratinus himself would speak F 196–97, also 200, 203, and
205. Although some of the amatory allusions in the comedy
seem to have been to young and attractive boys—see F 195
and 205—that is not incompatible with Methe *(Drunken-*
ness) as a personified character in the play. We have hints
of a trial (F 197, the opening of Cratinus' defence?; 207, the
counting of votes?), and a scene showing the composition
of a comedy (F 208–9).

Was Cratinus "cured" of his addiction and did he re-
turn to his true wife, a sober man, or did he prevail by

WINE-FLASK

showing that drink is necessary to the creative process (F 203)? On what terms would Comedy agree to take him back? Here we should consider the evidence of Wasps *where an irascible and uncontrollable old man resists the well-meaning attempts of a family member to change his behaviour and ends the play under the effects of strong drink. Biles and Sidwell argue that Philokleon in that comedy owes more than a little to Cratinus' self-parody in* Wine-Flask *eight months earlier. The drunken Philocleon leading in a flute girl may recall a scene where Cratinus enters with Methe.*

A trial or a contest requires an antagonist, and while Comedy or the chorus might well fulfil such a role (note the plural in F 206), I wonder if Cratinus brought not only himself into his own play but also a rival poet, and who better than Aristophanes? A rival would be the ideal person to threaten his drinking paraphernalia (F 199) and perhaps speak (F 198), the reaction to something Cratinus has just said. The metre here is iambic trimeter, perhaps from an episode rather than an agon. It would be quite appropriate for a comic Aristophanes to repeat the river metaphor that he exploited in Knights *526–36. F 208–9 suggest that there was a scene in which Cratinus is creating a comedy.*

What of the "wine flask," which was important enough to give the comedy its name? F 201 tells us that a pytinē *was a wicker wine container (often made by prisoners) and sealed with pitch. In some fashion it must have been the symbol of the action of the play. Was it the indestructible nature of the container—compare the threat to smash all*

*his drinking vessels at F 199? Or did it represent the level
to which Cratinus would descend, reduced to drinking
from a pytinē? Could there have been a personification,
bringing a mute actor on stage dressed like a wine flask,
like Peace in that comedy or Diallage in* Lysistrata *or the
kitchen utensils in* Wasps?

*But however we reconstruct the comedy, it is clear that
Cratinus presents himself in a purposeful negative light.
He is seen to be an unfaithful husband, a poet who has
abandoned his art, and an aging drunk and a philanderer.
What Cratinus has done is to take the comic picture that*

Testimonia

i Hypothesis V *Clouds*

αἱ πρῶται Νεφέλαι ἐδιδάχθησαν ἐν ἄστει ἐπὶ ἄρ-
χοντος Ἰσάρχου, ὅτε Κρατῖνος μὲν ἐνίκα Πυτίνῃ,
Ἀμείψιας δὲ Κόννῳ.

ii Lucian *Long-Lives* 25

Κρατῖνος δὲ ὁ τῆς κωμῳδίας ποιητὴς τέσσαρα πρὸς
τοῖς ἐνενήκοντα ἔτεσιν ἐβίωσε, καὶ πρὸς τῷ τέλει τοῦ
βίου διδάξας τὴν Πυτίνην καὶ νικήσας μετ' οὐ πολὺ
ἐτελεύτα.

iii Σ Aristophanes *Knights* 400a

ὅπερ μοι δοκεῖ παροξυνθεὶς ἐκεῖνος, καίτοι τοῦ ἀγω-
νίζεσθαι ἀποστὰς καὶ συγγράφειν, πάλιν γράφει

Aristophanes used in Knights *and, rather than oppose it, reinforce it by agreeing to the points of caricature and recast himself as the lovable drunk for whom alcohol is the source of his comic inspiration. Biles makes the good point that we should not be ransacking* Clouds *seeking reasons why it finished third; rather we should be recognising in* Wine-Flask *a magnificent comedy that simply outclassed Aristophanes.*

Recent bibliography: W. Luppe, in Rivals *15–21; R. Rosen, in* Rivals *23–39; Olson 69–71, 80–86, 423–24.*

Testimonia

i The first version of *Clouds* was performed at the Dionysia in the archonship of Isarchus [424/3], when Cratinus won first prize with *Wine-Flask,* and Ameipsias ‹second› with *Connus.*

ii Cratinus, the poet of Old Comedy, lived for ninety-four years. At the end of his life he produced *Wine-Flask* and won the prize, and died not long after.

iii It seems to me that he [Cratinus] got very angry at this [Aristophanes' comments at *Knights* 526–36] and although he had retired from writing and competing, he

δρᾶμα, τὴν Πυτίνην, εἰς αὑτόν τε καὶ τὴν μέθην,
οἰκονομίᾳ τε κεχρημένον τοιαύτῃ. τὴν Κωμῳδίαν ὁ
Κρατῖνος ἐπλάσατο αὐτοῦ εἶναι γυναῖκα καὶ ἀφί-
στασθαι τοῦ συνοικεσίου τοῦ σὺν αὐτῷ θέλειν, καὶ
κακώσεως αὐτῷ δίκην λαγχάνειν, φίλους δὲ παρα-
τυχόντας τοῦ Κρατίνου δεῖσθαι μηδὲν προπετὲς ποι-
ῆσαι καὶ τῆς ἔχθρας ἀνερωτᾶν τὴν αἰτίαν, τὴν δὲ
μέμφεσθαι αὐτῷ ὅτι μὴ κωμῳδοίη μηκέτι, σχολάζοι
δὲ τῇ μέθῃ.

iv Plutarch *Table-Talk* 634d

διὸ καὶ τῶν κωμικῶν ἔνιοι τὴν πικρίαν ἀφαιρεῖν δο-
κοῦσι τῷ σκώπτειν ἑαυτούς, ὡς Ἀριστοφάνης εἰς τὴν
φαλακρότητα καὶ τὴν Ἀγάθωνος ‹ἀπό›λειψιν· Κρατῖ-
νος δὲ τὴν Πυτίνην ‹ . . . › ἐδίδαξεν.’

Fragments

193 Σ Aristophanes *Knights* 400a

ἀλλ’ † ἐπανατρέψαι βούλομαι εἰς † τὸν λόγον.
πρότερον ἐκεῖνος πρὸς ἑτέραν γυναῖκ’ ἔχων
τὸν νοῦν, † κακὰς εἴποι πρὸς ἑτέραν, ἀλλ’
ἅμα μὲν τὸ γῆρας, ἅμα δέ μοι δοκεῖ
5 † οὐδέποτ’ αὐτοῦ πρότερον.

194 Porphyry *On Homer* Iliad 5.533

γυνὴ δ’ ἐκείνου πρότερον ἦ, νῦν δ’ οὐκέτι.

wrote another play, *Wine-Flask,* about himself and Drunkenness, employing the following plotline: Cratinus made Comedy his wife, wanting to stop living with him and to lodge a complaint of abuse at his hands; his friends appear and ask her not to do anything rash and to find out the reason for her enmity; Comedy complains that he no longer lives with her, but spends all his time with Drunkenness.

iv That is why certain comic poets seem to lessen the bitterness by making fun of themselves, e.g., Aristophanes about his baldness, and Agathon about his clean-shaven look (?). Cratinus produced *Wine-Flask* . . .

Fragments

193 I want now to return to the story. Before when he turned his attentions to another woman, he wouldn't say anything good about that other woman, but now partly his old age, and partly . . . he appears to me . . . nothing like before.[1]

[1] The text is uncertain, but the speaker is clearly Comedy complaining about Cratinus.

194 I used to be his wife, but now no longer.

195 Athenaeus 29d

νῦν δ' ἦν ἴδῃ Μενδαῖον ἡβῶντ' ἀρτίως
οἰνίσκον, ἔπεται κἀκολουθεῖ καὶ λέγει,
"οἴμ' ὡς ἁπαλὸς καὶ λευκός. ἆρ' οἴσει τρία;"

196 Athenaeus 426b

τὸν δ' ἴσον ἴσῳ φέροντ'· ἐγὼ δ' ἐκτήκομαι.

197 Clement of Alexandria *Miscellany* 6.20.3

τὴν μὲν παρασκευὴν ἴσως γιγνώσκετε.

198 Σ Aristophanes *Knights* 526a

δοκεῖ δέ μοι Ἀριστοφάνης ἀφ' ὧν εἶπε Κρατῖνος περὶ
αὑτοῦ μεγαληγορῶν, ἀπὸ τούτων καὶ αὑτὸς τὴν τρο-
πὴν εἰληφέναι· ὁ γὰρ Κρατῖνος οὕτω πως ἑαυτὸν
ἐπήνεσεν ἐν τῇ Πυτίνῃ·

ἄναξ Ἄπολλον, τῶν ἐπῶν τῶν ῥευμάτων.
καναχοῦσι πηγαί· δωδεκάκρουνον ⟨τὸ⟩ στόμα,
Ἰλισὸς ἐν τῇ φάρυγι· τί ἂν εἴποιμ' ⟨ἔτι⟩;
εἰ μὴ γὰρ ἐπιβύσει τις αὐτοῦ τὸ στόμα,
5 ἅπαντα ταῦτα κατακλύσει ποιήμασιν.

195 But now if he sees a little bit of Mendaean wine just come to adolescence, he follows after it and says, "Oh my, how soft and fair! Will it handle the three?".[1]

[1] Athenaeus attributes this fragment only to Cratinus. The descriptive adjectives fit both wine and attractive young boys. "Handle the three" means adding three parts of water, but could also suggest the male genitalia or a sexual ménage à trois.

196 Which can handle a mix of one to one. But I am perishing.

197 Perhaps you [pl.] realize their preparation.

198 It seems to me that Aristophanes took what Cratinus had said in praise of himself and taken his metaphor from that. Cratinus, for example, praises himself in this way in *Wine-Flask*.

Lord Apollo, the flood of his words, springs splashing, twelve spouts to his mouth, an Ilissus in his throat. What can I say? If somebody doesn't put a plug in his mouth, he will inundate everything here with his poetry.[1]

[1] The Ilissus was one of the two rivers of Athens. Aristophanes at *Knights* 526–28 compares Cratinus to a river coursing down over the plains carrying all before it.

199 Athenaeus 494c

πῶς τις αὐτόν, πῶς τις ἂν
ἀπὸ τοῦ πότου παύσειε, τοῦ λίαν πότου;
ἐγᾦδα. συντρίψω γὰρ αὐτοῦ τοὺς χόας,
καὶ τοὺς καδίσκους συγκεραυνώσω σποδῶν,
5 καὶ τἄλλα πάντ᾽ ἀγγεῖα τὰ περὶ τὸν πότον,
κοὐδ᾽ ὀξύβαφον οἰνηρὸν ἔτι κεκτήσεται.

200 Priscian *Institutes of Grammar* 18.209

ἀτὰρ ἐννοοῦμαι δῆτα τῆς μοχθηρίας
τῆς † ἠλιθιότητος τῆς ἐμῆς.

201 Σ Sophocles *Ajax* 105a

ὄψει γὰρ αὐτὴν ἐντὸς οὐ πολλοῦ χρόνου
παρὰ τοῖσι δεσμώταισι καταπιττουμένην.

202 *Suda* α 3750

⟨ἆρ᾽⟩ ἀραχνίων μεστὴν ἔχεις τὴν γαστέρα;

203 Nicaenetus (*Palatine Anthology* 13.29)

ὕδωρ δὲ πίνων οὐδὲν ἂν τέκοι σοφόν.

204 Herodian *Singular Vocabulary* II p. 943.18

ἀλλ᾽ οὐδὲ λάχανον οὐδὲν οὐδ᾽ ὀστοῦν ἔτι
ὁρῶ.

199 How then, how could someone put an end to his drinking, his drinking to excess? I know. I [masc.] will smash his pitchers and crush and blast his decanters and all the other drinking vessels that he has, and he won't have even a vinegar saucer left for his wine.

200 But I realise the depths of my foolish behaviour.

201 You will see it not long from now coated with pitch by the prison guards.[1]

1 "It" is probably the wine flask (*pytinē*) of the title. Hesychius π 4486 under *pytinē* records "a wicker flagon for wine. Prisoners used to make these and baskets and such like."

202 Do you have a stomach full of spiderwebs?

203 By drinking water you would never create anything great.

204 But I don't see any green stuff or even a bit of bone.

205 Athenaeus 94f

ὡς λεπτός, ἦ δ' ὅς, ἔσθ' ὁ τῆς χορδῆς τόμος.

206 Pollux 10.70

τοὺς μὲν ἐκ προχοιδίου,
τοὺς δ' ἐκ καδίσκου.

207 Σ Aristophanes *Peace* 1081

ἀπὸ ποτέρου τὸν καῦνον ἀριθμήσεις;

208 Σ Aristophanes *Clouds* 355b

ληρεῖς ἔχων· γράφ' αὐτὸν
ἐν ἐπεισοδίῳ. γελοῖος ἔσται Κλεισθένης κυβεύων
† ἐν τῇ κάλλους ἀκμῇ.

209 Σ Aristophanes *Peace* 692

Ὑπέρβολον δ' ἀποσβέσας ἐν τοῖς λύχνοισι γράψον.

210 Pollux 10.184

οὐ δύνανται πάντα ποιοῦσαι νεωσοίκων λαχεῖν,
οὐδὲ κάννης.

211 Σ Aristophanes *Peace* 603

ὦ λιπερνῆτες πολῖται, τἀμὰ δὴ ξυνίετε

205 "How thin," he said, "is the slice of sausage."

206 Some from the wine jug, others from a decanter.

207 From which one will you count up the lots?

208 You are talking nonsense. Write him in a scene. Cleisthenes will look really ridiculous, playing dice at the height of his beauty.

209 Write in Hyperbolus among his lamps, and extinguish him.

210 Do whatever they [fem.] may, they aren't able to get ship docks or reed matting.

211 O forlorn citizens, understand my ⟨words⟩.[1]

1 From Archilochus F 109W, also adapted by Eupolis (F 392.1) and Aristophanes (*Peace* 603).

212 [Plutarch] *Lives of the Ten Orators* 833a

οἱ δ' ὑπὸ τῶν τριάκοντα ἀνῃρῆσθαι αὐτὸν ἱστοροῦσιν,
ὥσπερ Λυσίας ἐν τῷ ὑπὲρ τῆς Ἀντιφῶντος θυγατρὸς
λόγῳ· ἐγένετο γὰρ αὐτῷ θυγάτριον, οὗ Κάλλαισχρος
ἐπεδικάσατο. ὅτι δ' ὑπὸ τῶν τριάκοντα ἀπέθανεν,
ἱστορεῖ καὶ Θεόπομπος ἐν τῇ πεντεκαιδεκάτῃ τῶν
Φιλιππικῶν· ἀλλ' οὗτός γ' ἂν εἴη ἕτερος, Λυσωνίδου
πατρός, οὗ καὶ Κρατῖνος ἐν Πυτίνῃ ὡς πονηροῦ μνη-
μονεύει.

213 Σ Aristophanes *Knights* 531a

ταῦτα ἀκούσας ὁ Κρατῖνος ἔγραψε τὴν Πυτίνην, δει-
κνὺς ὅτι οὐκ ἐλήρησεν· ἐν ᾗ κακῶς λέγει τὸν Ἀριστο-
φάνην ὡς τὰ Εὐπόλιδος λέγοντα.

214 Σ (Arethas) Plato *Apology* 23e

Λύκων μέντοι πατὴρ ἦν Αὐτολύκου, Ἴων γένος, δή-
μων Θορίκιος, πένης, ὡς Κρατῖνος Πυτίνῃ, Ἀριστο-
φάνης Σφηξίν.

215 Σ (Arethas) Plato *Apology* 20e

Χαιρεφῶν οὗτος ὁ Σωκρατικὸς ἰσχνὸς ἦν καὶ ὠχρός
. . . ἀποσκώπτει Κρατῖνος Πυτίνῃ εἰς αὐχμηρὸν καὶ
πένητα.

212 Some record that he [Antiphon of Rhamnous] was executed by the Three Hundred, as Lysias says in his speech *For the Daughter of Antiphon* (F 25a–29 Carey). For he had a daughter, against whom Callaeschrus had launched a prosecution. Others say that he perished under the Thirty, as Theopompus records in *Philippics* 15 (*FGrHist* 115 F 120). But this man would be another Antiphon, the son of Lysonides, whom Cratinus mentions in *Wine-Flask* as a wicked man.

213 When Cratinus heard this, he wrote his *Wine-Flask,* proving that he had not been writing nonsense. In it he attacks Aristophanes for using Eupolis' material.

214 Lykon was the father of Autolycus, of the clan Ion‹idai›, of the deme Thoricus, a poor man, as Cratinus ‹says› in *Wine-Flask,* Aristophanes in *Wasps* [1301].

215 This Chaerephon, associate of Socrates, was a skinny and pale fellow . . . Cratinus in *Wine-Flask* makes fun of ‹him› as poor and needy.

Brief fragments: (F 216) "Myrtoean Sea," (F 217) "wax."

ΣΑΤΥΡΟΙ

ΣΕΡΙΦΙΟΙ

The title implies that the chorus was made up of inhabi-
tants of Seriphus, the island associated with the myth of
Perseus. F 222 refers to "you in the air with the breezes," F
223 predicts a trip to Africa, the traditional home of the
Gorgons, and F 231 describes Andromeda as "bait in a
trap." F 222–24 are in dactylic hexameters, the metre of
Homer, and F 223.1 does recall Odyssey *4.83. Bakola (158–*
68) argues that this comedy was not just a burlesque of
myth, but "had a paratragic dimension." F 218 might come
from a dressing scene where a character is preparing to
dress like someone from tragedy. Another possible text
might be the two Prometheus plays attributed to Aeschy-

SATYRS

Without the hypothesis to Knights *(T 9b) we would not have known of the existence of this comedy. It finished second to* Knights *and gives an added point to Aristophanes' depiction of Cratinus (*Knights *526–36) as a great poet past his prime and now spouting nonsense. He was in fact a rival competitor at that very festival. Comedies with a chorus of satyrs are not uncommon. We know of plays with this title by Ecphantides, Callias, Phrynichus, as well as Cratinus' Dionysalexander. If on P. Oxy. 663, the hypothesis to* Dionysalexander, *we are to read "Dionysalexander or . . . by Cratinus," then "Satyrs" might be an option for the alternative title. This would mean, however rejecting both the traditional date of 430 or 429 and my preferred date of 437 for* Dionysalexander.

MEN OF SERIPHOS

lus, both of which had lengthy scenes of journeys recalled and predicted (in iambic trimeters, however). If P. Oxy. 2742 (= PCG VIII 74) is in fact from Men of Seriphus, *then Cratinus was breaking the allusion with a character (Perseus or a would-be Perseus) suspended on the* mēchanē.

The date is later rather than earlier. Amynias is a comic target from the late 420s, while Cleon had come into prominence by 430 (witness Hermippus F 47). If the Prometheus plays were in fact part of Euphorion's successful production of 431, a date in the first half of the 420s for this comedy would not be out of place.

Fragments

218 *Etymologicum Genuinum* AB

αἶρε δεῦρο τοὺς βρικέλους.

219 The Antiatticist p. 85.1

        ἀλλ' ἀπίωσιν ἐν χορῷ
ἐς βόθυνον ἰέναι

220 Photius p. 533.13

οὕτω σταθερῶς τοῖς λωποδύταις ὁ πόρος πεινῶσι
παφλάζει.

221 Photius (b, z) α 1235

ἀμοργοί, πόλεως ὄλεθροι

222 Pollux 7.69

{A.} ἐς Συρίαν δ' ἐνθένδ' ἀφικνῇ μετέωρος ὑπ'
αὔρας.
{B.} ἱμάτιον μοχθηρόν, ὅταν βορρᾶς καταπνεύσῃ.

223 Stephanus of Byzantium p. 237.5 (ll. 1–2), Hesychius
    δ 1890 (l. 3)

εἶτα Σάβας ἀφικνῇ καὶ Σιδονίους καὶ Ἐρεμβούς,
ἔς τε πόλιν δούλων, ἀνδρῶν νεοπλουτοπονήρων,
αἰσχρῶν, Ἀνδροκλέων, † Διονυσοκουρώνων.

CRATINUS

Fragments

218 Bring here the tragic masks.

219 But let them go away as a chorus to shoot at a hole.[1]

[1] This is *tropa*, the same game as mentioned at F 180, flicking knuckle bones or acorns at a hole as target.

220 The strait boils so constantly with starving muggers.[1]

[1] The verb "boils" (*paphlazei*) is that which gives Cleon his name "Paphlagon" in *Knights*.

221 Scavengers, the bane of a city.

222 (A) From there you will travel high up on the breezes to Syria.
(PERSEUS?) A rather useless garment, when the North Wind blows.[1]

[1] The joke turns on a pun between Syria the place and *syria,* a woollen cloak. The first speaker is often assumed to be Polydectes of Seriphus, who sends Perseus on his mission. But would he know the geography so well and be so helpful? Athena or Hermes perhaps?

223 Then you will come to the Sabae and the Sidonians and the Erembi, and to the City of Slaves, nasty *nouveaux riches,* disgusting men, like Androcles, †Dionysocourones†.[1]

[1] Androcles of Pitthia (*PAA* 128255) was a prominent demagogue of the 420s and 410s, made fun of at Ecphantides F 5 and *Wasps* 1187. For the corrupt name in v. 3, see now Luppe *Glotta* 81 (2005) 128–29.

224 Hesychius α 1798

οἰκοῦσιν φεύγοντες, ἀίδρυτον κακὸν ἄλλοις.

225 Hephaestion *Handbook* 15.8

χαίρετε πάντες ὅσοι πολύβωτον ποντίαν Σέριφον.

226 *Etymologicum Genuinum* AB

πολυτρήτοις φωσί

227 Σ Aristophanes *Wasps* 74b

ὧδε μὲν ὡς φιλόκυβος ὁ Ἀμυνίας κωμῳδεῖται· ἐν δὲ Σεριφίοις Κρατίνου ὡς κόλαξ καὶ ἀλαζὼν καὶ συκοφάντης.

228 Σ Lucian *Timon* 30

τὰ δὲ ὑπὸ τὴν ὄψιν ἦν ἀργαλέος καὶ μάλιστα τὰς ὀφρῦς, ὡς Κρατῖνος Σεριφίοις . . . ἐκωμῳδεῖτο δὲ καὶ ἐπὶ μανίᾳ, ὡς Κρατῖνος Σεριφίοις.

229 Photius (Sᶻ) α 2810

ἀριστεροστάτης

231 Pollux 10.156

τὴν δὲ Ἀνδρομέδαν Κρατῖνος ἐν τοῖς Σεριφίοις δελεάστραν καλεῖ.

224 They live in exile, an unsettling problem for others.

225 Hail, all who ‹dwell on› fertile Seriphus, the seagirt land.

226 With often-pricked blisters.

227 Amynias is made fun of as fond of gambling, and in Cratinus' *Men of Seriphus* as a political toady, a fraud, and an informer.

228 [of Cleon] His face was fearsome to look at, especially his eyebrows, so Cratinus in *Men of Seriphus* . . . and he was also made fun of for being mad, so Cratinus in *Men of Seriphus*.

229 Left-hand man [of a comic chorister in the prestigious left file].

231 Cratinus in *Men of Seriphus* calls Andromeda "bait in a trap."

Brief fragments: (F 230) "deposit," (F 232) "to make an empty sound."

ΤΡΟΦΩΝΙΟΣ

The oracular shrine of Trophonius was located in Lebadeia in central Boeotia, on the edge of the Copaic lake, hence "the plain of fertile Boeotia" (F 235). As it lay on the main road to Delphi, it was often visited by travellers to Delphi for "a second opinion," as it were. At Euripides' Ion 300 Xuthus has not yet arrived at Delphi because he is consulting the oracle of Trophonius. Pausanias (9.39.5) describes the details of the consultation, which involved several days of pure living, cold baths, and preliminary sacrifices before a descent into a cave for the revelation of the future.

Fragments

233 Photius (b, z) α 637

οὐ σῖτον ἄρασθ᾽, οὐχ ὕπνου λαχεῖν μέρος.

234 Photius (z) δ 427

ξίφιζε καὶ πόδιζε καὶ διαρρικνοῦ.

235 Hephaestion *Handbook* 8.2

χαίρετε δαίμονες οἳ Λεβάδειαν Βοιώτιον οὖθαρ
    ἀρούρης

236 Athenaeus 325e

οὐδ᾽ Αἰξωνίδ᾽ ἐρυθρόχρων ἐσθίειν ἔτι τρίγλην,
οὐδὲ τρυγόνος, οὐδὲ δεινοῦ φυὴν μελανούρου

TROPHONIUS

Cephisodorus wrote a comedy of this name, Aristophanes an Amphiaraus *(414) about a husband and wife who visit that hero's oracle. In* Wealth *(388) Aristophanes describes a visit to the healing sanctuary of Asclepius. The mention of lack of food and sleep (F 233), of serpents (F 241), and of lamps (F 245) and music (F 237, 242) suggest that the visit to Trophonius' shrine was described in the familiar terms of any cult.*

Recent bibliography: R. Quaglia, Maia 52 *(2000) 455–66.*

Fragments

233 To have brought no food, to have had no sleep.

234 Do the sword dance, do the foot dance, do the twist.

235 Hail, deities who ⟨guard⟩ Lebadeia, Boeotia's "fertile plain."[1]

   [1] An epic phrase, used at *Iliad* 9.141, 283 of Argos.

236 No more to eat the red mullet from Aexone or the stingray or the flesh of the fearful melanurus.

237 Hephaestion *Handbook* 13.1

ἔγειρε δὴ νῦν, Μοῦσα, Κρητικὸν μέλος.

χαῖρε δή, Μοῦσα· χρονία μὲν ἥκεις, ὅμως δ᾽
  ἦλθες οὐ † πρὶν ἐλθεῖν † ἴσθι σαφές· ἀλλ᾽ ὅπως

238 Σ Aristophanes *Peace* 348

τέταρτος Κροτωνιάτης ἀρχαῖος. Κρατῖνος Τροφωνίῳ.

239 Pollux 7.103

ἀργυροκοπιστῆρας

ΧΕΙΜΑΖΟΜΕΝΟΙ

Testimonium

i See T 9a.

237 Now then, my Muse, strike up a song in cretics.

Hail, then, Muse, late you have arrived, but still you came, not before . . . know well, but that . . .

238 The fourth [Phormion] is an historic figure from Croton. Cratinus in *Trophonius*.

239 Silver-coiners of words.

Brief fragments: (F 240) "a crowd of barley corns," (F 241) "reddish-brown snakes," (F 242) "I shall strike up the tune," (F 243) "he delivered a letter," (F 244) "pirate crew," (F 245) "to ignite the lamps."

TEMPEST-TOSSED

We know of this comedy only from the production record to Acharnians. *It finished second at L-425, behind* Acharnians *and ahead of Eupolis'* New-Moons. *The title* (cheimazomenoi) *means "caught in a storm at sea," and metaphorically "to be in distress," but neither meaning helps to identify the chorus or ascertain what the comedy was about.*

Testimonium

i See T 9a.

ΧΕΙΡΩΝΕΣ

At F 253 the chorus call themselves "Chirons" and are about to announce their reason for coming, "to . . . . precepts." Chiron was the wise Centaur, tutor of many Greek heroes, including Jason and Achilles, and the substitute for Prometheus chained to the rock. Attributed to Hesiod was a work called "Precepts of Chiron." Cratinus wrote a number of comedies named for the plural of a singular entity: Archilochuses, Odysseus and Company, Wealth-Gods— there is also Teleclides' Hesiods.

The comedy seems to have turned on the familiar opposition of "then" and "now"—see F 249, 256–57, 260—especially F 257 for the ease and luxury of life "back then." One character was Solon (F 246), the lawgiver of the early sixth century, whose summoning from the dead may have been part of the "great idea" of the comedy—see F 250. Was this also a politically charged comedy? F 258–59 are part of a choral song, a parody of a theogony by which Strife and Time produced a great ruler, "whom the gods call the

Fragments

246 Diogenes Laertius 1.62

οἰκῶ δὲ νῆσον, ὡς μὲν ἀνθρώπων λόγος,
ἐσπαρμένος κατὰ πᾶσαν Αἴαντος πόλιν.

247 Σ (Arethas) Plato *Theaeteus* 146a

ὄνοι δ᾽ ἀπωτέρω κάθηνται τῆς λύρας.

CHIRONS

*Head-shaker," an allusion to the distinctive head of Peri-
cles, whose "Hera" is "a whore, the child of Shameful Sex,"
i.e., Aspasia. It is tempting to conclude that part of what
is wrong with things today is Pericles and his alleged one-
man rule. Eupolis in his* Demes *brings back Solon and
Pericles together as representatives of a better past. Had
Cratinus presented them as antagonists?*

*The comedy belongs after 440, by which time Aspasia
had become a prominent figure, and probably after 436,
when the decree "not to make fun of by name" was re-
pealed. But there are no other personal jokes among the
fragments, and if with Cobet we remove Aspasia's name as
gloss from F 259, Cratinus might be making an indirect or
covert joke at Pericles and Aspasia and thus not violating
the letter of the law. I would favour 436–432 for the play.*

Recent bibliography: I. Ruffell, in Rivals *486–88; M.
Farioli, RFIC 128 (2000) 406–31; M. Noussia, PCPhS 49
(2003) 74–88.*

Fragments

246 (SOLON) I live on an island, so goes the tale among
men, scattered over every town of Ajax.[1]

[1] According to Diogenes Laertius and Plutarch *Solon* 32.4,
Solon died in Cyprus and his ashes were scattered over the island
of Salamis (the home of Ajax, son of Telamon).

247 The donkeys sit at a distance from the lyre.

248 Σ Thucydides 8.83.3

τὴν μουσικὴν ἀκορέστους ἐπιφέρειν ὀργὰς βροτοῖς
σώφροσιν.

249 Σ Plato *Apology* 22a

οἷς ἦν μέγιστος ὅρκος
†ἅπαντι λόγῳ† κύων, ἔπειτα χήν, θεοὺς δ᾽ ἐσίγων.

250 Σ Sophocles *Oedipus at Colonus* 477

ἄγε δὴ πρὸς ἕω πρῶτον ἁπάντων ἴστω καὶ λάμβανε
χερσὶν
σχῖνον μεγάλην.

251 Σ Aristophanes *Birds* 766

καὶ πρῶτον μὲν παρὰ ναυτοδικῶν ἀπάγω τρία
κνώδαλ᾽ ἀναιδῆ.

252 Pollux 6.97–98

ἐξ ἀσαμίνθου κύλικος λείβων.

253 Hephaestion *Handbook* 1.9

σκῆψιν μὲν Χείρωνες ἐλήλυμεν, ὡς ὑποθήκας.

254 Σ Aristophanes *Wasps* 1238

Κλειταγόρας ᾄδειν, ὅταν Ἀδμήτου μέλος αὐλῇ.

248 To mortals of sense Music brings unquenchable passions.

249 Whose greatest oath in every speech was "by the dog," then "by the goose." But "by the gods," silence.

250 Well then, stand facing the east and take in both hands a large sea onion.[1]

[1] The word for "sea onion" (*schinos*) is the same as that used of "the onion-headed Pericles" at F 73. If one of the play's recurrent themes was Athens under Pericles, then to summon up Solon's ghost with a *schinos* is a nice touch.

251 First of all I am leading away from the *nautodikai* three shameless creatures.[1]

[1] The *nautodikai* handled cases of alleged *xenia* (false citizenship). The scholiast gives three names: Peisias (see F 185 and *Birds* 766), Dieitrephes (see *Birds* 797–800 and Platon F 31, "he's hardly an Athenian"), and an unknown Osphyon.

252 Pouring libation from a cup the size of a bathtub.

253 ... the reason we Chirons have come, to ... precepts.

254 To sing the song about Cleitagora, when he [the *aulos* player] starts up the "Admetos song."

255 Aelius Aristides 28.91

ταῦτα δυοῖν ἐτέοιν ἡμῖν μόλις ἐξεπονήθη.

256 Bachmann's *Lexicon* p. 20.5

μακάριος ἦν ὁ πρὸ τοῦ βίος βροτοῖσιν
πρὸς τὰ νῦν, ὃν εἶχον ἄνδρες
ἀγανόφρονες ἡδυλόγῳ σοφίᾳ
βροτῶν περισσοκαλλεῖς.

257 Athenaeus 553e

ἁπαλὸν δὲ σισύμβριον ⟨ἢ⟩ ῥόδον ἢ κρίνον παρ' οὖς
    ἐθάκει,
μετὰ χερσὶ δὲ μῆλον ἔχων σκίπωνά τ' ἠγόραζον.

258 Plutarch *Pericles* 3.4

Στάσις δὲ καὶ πρεσβυγενὴς
Χρόνος ἀλλήλοισι μιγέντε
μέγιστον τίκτετον τύραννον,
ὃν δὴ κεφαληγερέταν
5 θεοὶ καλέουσιν.

2 Χρόνος codd., Κρόνος anon.

259 Plutarch *Pericles* 24.9

Ἥραν τέ οἱ Ἀσπασίαν τίκτει Καταπυγοσύνη
παλλακὴν κυνώπιδα.

1 Ἀσπασίαν del. Cobet.

390

255 This took us nearly two years to complete with difficulty.[1]

[1] Aristeides tells us that these words came at the end of the comedy and were Cratinus' own comments about his play.

256 Life in the past was happy for mortals as compared to now. Men led a life, gentle in mind with sweet-speaking wisdom, most beautiful of mortals.

257 Each man would sit with a soft mint flower or a rose or a lily in his ear, and with an apple and a staff in his hand, would hang around the marketplace.

258 Political Strife and ancient-born Time [Cronus?] came together and produced the greatest ruler, whom the gods in fact call "the Head-Gatherer."[1]

[1] The word "ruler" is *tyrannos* (see Plutarch *Pericles* 16 for Pericles as "tyrant"), and the joke a pun on Zeus *nephelēgeretēs* (Cloud-Gatherer) and *kephalēgeretēs* (Head-Gatherer). Raffaelle (*QUCC* 1990) and di Marco (*SemRom* 2005) defend the emendation of Χρόνος to Κρόνος.

259 And Shameful Sex gave birth to his Hera, a dog-eyed concubine.[1]

[1] Plutarch's text has "Aspasia," but the joke is better if Pericles' "Hera" is not directly named.

260

(a) Σ Aristophanes *Clouds* 924h

μέμνηται τοῦ Πανδελέτου καὶ Κρατῖνος ἐν Χείρωσι.

(b) *Suda* π 171

ἐπεὶ Πανδέλητος συκοφάντης ἦν καί φιλόδικος καὶ γράφων ψηφίσματα, καὶ ἦν εἷς τῶν περὶ τά δικαστή-ρια διατριβόντων. μέμνηται αὐτοῦ καὶ Κρατῖνος ἐν Χείρωσι.

261 Zenobius *Proverbs* 1.26

αἲξ οὐρανία

262 Herodian *Singular Vocabulary* II p. 947.23

Βοῦθος περιφοιτᾷ

263 Zenobius *Proverbs* 5.9

μετὰ Λέσβιον ᾠδόν

264 Athenaeus 392f

Ἰθακησία ὀρτυγομήτρα

265 Pollux 10.186

Χαλυβδικὸν στόμωμα

CRATINUS

260

(a) Cratinus mentions Pandeletus in *Chirons*.

(b) Since Pandeletus was an informer, very fond of law cases, and the author of decrees, and was one of those who spent their time at the law courts. Cratinus mentions him in *Chirons*.

261 The Heavenly Goat.

262 Bouthus wanders about.

263 After the poet from Lesbos.

264 A corncrake from Ithaca.

265 A blade from the Chalybes.

Brief fragments: (F 266) "transporters," (F 267) "book writer," (F 268) "false testimony."

ΩΡΑΙ

*In Hesiod (Theogony 901–3) the Seasons are the children
of Zeus and Themis, along with such other concepts as the
Fates, Order, Justice, and Peace. They are associated with
youth and beauty, the prime of life, fertility, and growth in
nature. They appear in art on important occasions: a spe-
cial birth, an* anodos *scene, the marriage of Peleus and
Thetis, and have special connections with Demeter, Aphro-
dite, and Dionysus.*

Aristophanes wrote a Seasons, *in which we find a de-
bate (F 581) between someone promising year-round fer-
tility and a more curmudgeonly figure to whom this appar-
ent utopia is less appealing. Cratinus' comedy seems to
have had a musical or dramatic theme—see F 270 (singing
a monody), F 276 (Gnesippus again), and F 294 (a tragic*

Fragments

269 Pollux 6.18

ἀλλ᾽ ἦν ὅτ᾽ ἐν φώσωνι τὴν ἴσην ἔχων
μετ᾽ ἐμοῦ διῆγες † οἴναρον ἕλκων τῆς τρυγός.

270 Orus *Orthography* fol. 280ᵛ 9

βούλει μονῳδήσωμεν αὐτοῖς ἕν γέ τι;
οὐκ ἂν μονῳδήσειεν ἐκπεπληγμένος.

271 Pollux 10.76

μῶν βδελυγμία σ᾽ ἔχει;
πτερὸν ταχέως τις καὶ λεκάνην ἐνεγκάτω.

SEASONS

*garment). F 269 suggests a contrast between someone in
"the bad old days" and an improved status now—see also F
274. F 278 does refer to Dionysus, but is not in itself suf-
ficient evidence for the presence of Dionysus as a character
in the play.*

The comedy made fun of Androcles, a kōmōidoumenos
*of the late 430s and 420s, of Gnesippus, a poet active before
the debut of Aristophanes in 427, and also of Hyperbolus
for daring to speak in the assembly at an unusually young
age. These suggest a date for the comedy in the early 420s
—Geissler's 428–426 will not be far wrong.*

Recent bibliography: F. Delneri, I culti misterici stranieri
(2006) 69–124.

Fragments

269 But there was a time when you [sing.] spent your
time on equal terms with me, wearing a poncho, pulling a
vine leaf out of the wine.

270 Do you [sing.] want us to sing one monody for them?

He wouldn't sing a monody even when thunderstruck.

271 Do you feel sick to your stomach? Let someone
quickly fetch a feather and a basin.

272 Photius p. 571.18

"ταῦτ᾽ ⟨αὐτὰ⟩ πράττω," 'φασκ᾽ ἀνὴρ οὐδὲν ποιῶν.

273 *Suda* π 3231

ἴσως πυρορραγὲς κακῶς τ᾽ ὠπτημένον.

274 Σ Plato *Theages* 127c

ἔδει παρέχειν ὅ τι τις εὔξαιτ᾽ ἐμβραχύ.

275 Pollux 9.130–31

ἐκεῖνος αὐτὸς ἐκμεμαγμένος.

276 Athenaeus 638f

ἴτω δὲ καὶ τραγῳδίας
ὁ Κλεομάχου διδάσκαλος,
† μετὰ τῶν † παρατιλτριῶν
ἔχων χορὸν λυδιστὶ τιλ-
5   λουσῶν μέλη πονηρά.

277 *Suda* μ 196

ἐφθάρη μαρίλης τὴν φάρυγα πλέαν ἔχων.

278 Photius p. 369.4

μακάριος τῶν παιδικῶν

272 "That's what I'm doing," the do-nothing man kept saying.

273 [of a pot] Fire-cracked and badly baked.

274 In a word, ‹we› had to provide whatever someone asked for.

275 That's him, the very likeness.

276 Let the son of Cleomachus go away as well, the producer of tragedy, along with his chorus of hair-plucking slave women, who pluck their ugly songs ["limbs"] in the Lydian mode.[1]

[1] The son of Cleomachus is Gnesippus, for whom see F 17. In the last line the word *melē* means both "songs" and "limbs."

277 He perished with his gullet full of ashes.

278 Fortunate in his girlfriends.[1]

[1] The lexicographers reveal that *paidika* can be used of both male and female loved ones, and that Cratinus is referring to Dionysus' "mistress in love with Dionysus who is away."

THE POETS OF OLD COMEDY

279 Athenaeus 374d

ὥσπερ ὁ Περσικὸς ὥραν πᾶσαν καναχῶν ὀλόφωνος
ἀλέκτωρ.

280 Hephaestion *Handbook* 1.9

οὐδὲ πρὸς εἶδος ἄρ' ἦν οὐδὲν προσιδόντι τεκμαρτόν.

281 Bachmann's *Lexicon* p. 87.10

Ἀνδροκολωνοκλῆς

282 Σ Aristophanes *Birds* 766

οὐδὲν σαφὲς ἔχομεν τίς ὁ Πεισίου, οὐδὲ περὶ τῆς
προδοσίας. ὅτι δὲ τῶν λίαν πονηρῶν ἐστι δηλοῖ Κρα-
τῖνος ἐν Χείρωσι, Πυλαίᾳ, Ὥραις.

283 Lucian *Timon* 30

Κρατῖνος δὲ ἐν Ὥραις ὡς παρελθόντος νέου τῷ βή-
ματι μέμνηται καὶ παρ' ἡλικίαν.

279 Like the full-voiced Persian rooster, crowing at every hour.

280 So looking at the external appearance there is nothing to be determined . . .

281 Andro-colono-cles.[1]

[1] The lexicographer tells us that Cratinus uses this compound to mean "stupid Androcles," but it is not immediately obvious why Colonus, a village just outside Athens, should denote stupidity.

282 We know nothing for certain about the son of Peisias nor about his act of betrayal. That he was one of the very wicked is made clear by Cratinus in his *Chirons* [F 251], his *Pylaea* [F 185], and *Seasons*.

283 Cratinus in *Seasons* mentions him [Hyperbolus] as having come up to the rostrum at an unusually young age.

Brief fragments: (F 284) "to lie neglected," (F 285) "he proposed a decree," (F 286) "setting out" [of a ship], (F 287) "up above," (F 288) "he was done away with," (F 289) "to read in comparison," (F 290) "exchange of property," (F 291) "the young of a ferret," (F 292) "plant stalk" [to induce vomiting], (F 293) "to laugh with mouse lips," (F 294) "a xystis" [a robe worn in tragedy], (F 295) "cushion for rowing," (F 296) "rue," (F 297) "rocky country," (F 298) "to be in one's prime."

ΑΔΗΛΩΝ ΔΡΑΜΑΤΩΝ

299 Athenaeus 782d

πιεῖν δὲ θάνατος οἶνον ἦν ὕδωρ ἐπῇ.
ἀλλ' ἴσον ἴσῳ μάλιστ' ἀκράτου δύο χόας
πίνουσ' ἀπ' ἀγκύλης ἐπονομάζουσα < >
ἵησι λάταγας τῷ Κορινθίῳ πέει.

1 ἐπῇ codd., ῥέπῃ Kaibel.

300 Plutarch *Solon* 25.1–2

πρὸς τοῦ Σόλωνος καὶ Δράκοντος οἶσι νῦν
φρύγουσιν ἤδη τὰς κάχρυς τοῖς κύρβεσιν.

301 Zenobius *Proverbs* 5.7

　　　　　　　　　ὡς ἄνω
τὴν μασχάλην αἴρωμεν ἐμπεπωκότες.

302 Σ Theocritus 4.18

　　　　ὁ δὲ μετ' Εὐδήμου τρέχων
κώμυθα τὴν λοιπὴν ἔχων τῶν † πρωων

303 Pollux 7.37–38

　　　　τῇ μάστιγι κνάψειν εὖ μάλα
πρὶν συμπατῆσαι.

UNASSIGNED FRAGMENTS

Proposed attributions are indicated in [...]

299 To drink wine when water predominates is death. But she drinks down two litres of strong drink, mixed half-and-half, and flicks wine drops with the crook of her arm, calling on "Willy" from Corinth by name.[1]

[1] Translating Kaibel's emendation.

300 By Solon and Dracon on whose *kyrbeis* people now parch barley corns.   [*Laws*?]

301 So that while drinking we may bend the elbow up.

302 While he, running with Eudemus, with the rest of the sheaf of the . . .

303 To thrash thoroughly with a whip before trampling.

304 *Etymologicum Genuinum* AB

τοῦτον μὲν καλῶς διεπηνήκισας λόγον.

305 Σ Oribasius 12.1

      θύραζ᾽ οὐκ ἔστι μῦθος ἔκφορος
ἐντεῦθεν ὡς <τοὺς> ἄφρονας.

306 [Herodian] *Philetaerus* 106

        πατρικὸς ὢν ξένος
τάδε πυνθάνομαί σου

307 Σ Aristophanes *Wealth* 66

         ἆρά γε,
ὦ τᾶν, ἐθελήσετον;

308 Photius (z) ined.

τοὺς ἐξοδίους ὑμῖν ἵν᾽ αὐλῶ τοὺς νόμους.

309 Orus F A 57

τὴν χεῖρα μὴ ᾽πίβαλλε, μὴ κλάων καθῇ.

310 Orus F A 57

εἰ πρῶτος ἔλθοις, κἂν καθίζεσθαι λάβοις.

304 You [sing.] have told this false tale very nicely.

305 This is no tale to go outside to the foolish ones.
[*Thracian Women*?]

306 As your father's guest-friend I am asking you about this.

307 Well, my friend, will the pair of you be willing?

308 So that I may play the exit music for you [pl.].

309 Do not [sing.] lay a hand ⟨on me⟩, or you will sit down and be sorry.

310 If you [sing.] were to come first [or "early"], you would get a place to sit.

311 Orus F A 52

ἐφ' ᾧ τ' ἐμαυτῆς συγκαθεύδειν τῷ πατρί.

312 Pollux 6.65

ὁ τάλαρος ὑμῖν διάπλεως ἔσται γάρου.

313 Dion of Prusa 56.2

ποιμὴν καθέστηκ'· αἰπόλῶ καὶ βουκολῶ.

314 Etymologicum Genuinum AB

ἔχων τὸ πρόσωπον καρίδος μασθλητίνης.

315 Photius (z) α 813

ἄκουε, σίγα, πρόσεχε τὸν νοῦν, δεῦρ' ὅρα.

316 Orus F A 42

ἄκουέ νυν καὶ τήνδε τὴν ἐπιστολήν.

317 Photius p. 460.3

καὶ μὴ πρόσισχε βαρβάροισι βουκόλοις.

318 Hesychius η 577

ἡ παῖς γὰρ ἔμπαις ἐστὶν ὡς ἠνδρωμένη.

311 On condition that I [fem.] sleep with my own father.

312 Your [pl.] basket will be full of fish sauce.

313 I am a shepherd, I tend goats and cattle.
                    [*Cow-Herders, Dionysalexander*?]

314 With the face of a leather-red prawn.[1]

[1] Athenaeus (106b) attributes the same fragment to Eupolis'
Demes [F 120].

315 Listen, be quiet, pay attention, look over here.

316 Now hear this instruction also.

317 Pay no attention to foreign cow herders.
                    [*Cow-Herders, Dionysalexander*?]

318 The girl is with child, having been with a man.

319 Pollux 4.184

οὐδ᾽ ὑδατοπωτῶν οὐδὲ κοιλοφθαλμιῶν.

320 Phrynichus *Sophistic Preparation* p. 50.16

τούτου δ᾽ ἀπάσας ἀποτεμῶ τὰς μηχανάς.

321 Σ Aristophanes *Acharnians* 3a

ἀνδρῶν ἀρίστων πᾶσα γαργαίρει πόλις.

322 Σ Euripides *Rhesus* 419

ἀλλ᾽ οὖν θεῷ σπείσαντ᾽ ἄμυστιν δεῖ πιεῖν.

323 Σ Sophocles *Antigone* 404

ὅνπερ Φιλοκλέης τὸν λόγον διέφθορεν.

324 Aelius Aristides 2.72

ὦ μεγίστη γλῶττα τῶν Ἑλληνίδων.

325 [Herodian] *Philetaerus* 32

ἄρχων ‹∪› εἰμὶ νῦν Ἀθηναίοις ἐγώ.

326 Plutarch *Pericles* 13.7

πάλαι γὰρ αὐτὸ
λόγοισι προάγει Περικλέης, ἔργοισι δ᾽ οὐδὲ κινεῖ.

319 Neither being a water drinker nor having hollow eyes.   [*Wine-Flask*?]

320 I shall curtail all his schemes.

321 The whole city swarms with the best men.
           [*Wealth-Gods*?]

322 So then ⟨you⟩ must pour a libation to the god, then drink up in one gulp.   [*Wine-Flask*?]

323 The plot which Philocles has destroyed.

324 [of Pericles] And you, the greatest tongue of the Greeks.[1]   [*Chirons, Thracian Women*?]

[1] For Pericles' ability to speak see Eupolis F 102.

325 I am now ruler [*archon*] of the Athenians.
        [*Cow-Herders, Wine-Flask*?]

326 For Pericles proposed it long ago in words, but doesn't get anything going in fact.[1]

[1] Plutarch tells us that "it" is the Middle Wall constructed at the Peiraeus in the 440s.

327 Photius (b, z) α 414

> γλῶττάν τέ σοι
> δίδωσιν ἐν δήμῳ φορεῖν
> καλῶν λόγων ἀείνων,
> ᾗ πάντα κινήσεις λέγων.

328 Priscian *Institutes of Grammar* 18.306

ὃς τὴν πίτυν ἔκαμπτεν
ἑστὼς χαμάθεν ἄκρας
τῆς κόμης καθέλκων.

329 Pollux 6.61

ἀλλ᾿ εἴσιθ᾿ εἴσω καὶ πιοῦ-
    σα χυλὸν ἀναπαύου κακῶν.

330 Photius (z) α 2489

ἀπόδυθι τὴν στολήν

331 Σ Homer *Iliad* 2.56c

θράττει με τοὐνύπνιον

332 Athenaeus 23b

ῥοθίαζε κἀνάπιπτε

327 Offers you a tongue with fine flowing words to wield among the people, with which you will sway all when you speak.[1]

[1] Athena's promise to Dionysus as Paris in *Dionysalexander?*

328 Who stood on the ground and bent the pine by dragging down the tops of its branches.[1]

[1] The "pine bender" was Sinis, one of the antagonists whom Theseus slew. From *Run-Aways?*

329 Come in [fem.], drink some barley water and put your troubles to rest.

330 Take off the robe.

331 The dream disturbs me.

[*Thracian Women, Run-Aways*?]

332 Put in the oar and then pull back.

[*Odysseus and Company*?]

333 Pollux 2.78

ὕλιζε τὰς ῥῖνας

334 Athenaeus 49a

γαυριῶσαι δ᾽ ἀναμένουσιν ᾦδ᾽ ἐπηγλαϊσμέναι
μείρακες φαιδραὶ τράπεζαι τρισκελεῖς
σφενδάμνιναι.

335 Etymologicum Genuinum AB

ὡς <δὲ> μαλακὸν καὶ τέρεν τὸ χρωτίδιον <ἦν>, ὦ
θεοί·
καὶ γὰρ ἐβλίμαζον αὐτήν, ἡ δ᾽ ἐφρόντιζ᾽ οὐδὲ ἕν.

336 Athenaeus 68a

γλαῦκον οὐ πρὸς παντὸς <ἀνδρός> ἐστιν ἀρτῦσαι
καλῶς.

337 Eustathius *On the* Odyssey p. 1430.23

εὐπρόσωπος ἦσθ᾽, ὀνόματος οὐδὲν ἐπὶ χεῖρας
φέρων.

338 Σ Aristophanes *Knights* 1287

καὶ Πολυμνήστει᾽ ἀείδει, μουσικήν τε μανθάνει.

333 Blow your nose.

334 Resplendent maidens, proudly dressed to the nines,
await ‹us› here, three-footed tables made of maple wood.

335 O gods, how soft and smooth her skin was! I fondled
her breast, and it didn't bother her at all.

336 It is not for every man to season the dogfish well.

337 You made a good show, carrying nothing of note in
your hands.

338 And he sings songs of Polymnestus, and is learning
music.

339 *Etymologicum Magnum* p. 512.7

δασὺν ἔχων τὸν πρωκτὸν ἅτε κυρήβι᾽ ἐσθίων.

340 *Suda* α 2819

ἄξιος λαβεῖν ὁ μισθός

341 Σ Aristophanes *Birds* 365

σφάττε δαῖρε κόπτε

342 Σ (Arethas) Plato *Apology* 19c

"τίς δὲ σύ;" κομψός τις ἔροιτο θεατής.
"ὑπολεπτολόγος, γνωμιδιώτης,
εὐριπιδαριστοφανίζων."

γνωμιδιώτης B, γνωμιδιώκτης Seidler, γνωμοδιώκτης
Schneider.

343 Harpocration p. 178.8

κἀνθένδ᾽ ἐπὶ τέρματα γῆς ἥξεις καὶ Κισθήνης ὄρος
ὄψει.

344 Eustathius *On the* Odyssey p. 1479.73

κοκκύζειν τὸν ἀλεκτρυόν᾽ οὐκ ἀνέχονται.

345 Eustathius *On the* Odyssey p. 1761.27

λόγος τις ὑπῆλθ᾽ ἡμᾶς ἀμαθὴς συοβαύβαλος.

339 Having a hairy bum from eating bran.

340 A fee worth receiving.

341 Kill ⟨him⟩, flay ⟨him⟩, beat ⟨him⟩.

342 "Who are you?", some clever spectator might ask, "a quibbler of words, a maker of maxims, a Euripidaristophaniser?"

or "Who are you?", some clever spectator might ask, a quibbler of words, a maker of maxims, a Euripidaristophaniser.   [*Wine-Flask*?]

343 From there you will come to the ends of the earth and see Mount Cisthene.[1]

[*Men of Seriphos, Women of Delos*?]

[1] Cisthene is either a mountain in Thrace, a town in Mysia, or an imitation of *Prometheus* 792–94 the "Gorgonian plains of Cisthene, where the daughters of Phorcus live."

344 They don't put up with the cock crowing.

345 Some stupid tale from the pigpen has deceived us.

346 Σ Aristophanes *Peace* 741

ὑπὸ δὲ Ἡρακλέους πεινῶντος ἀεὶ
καὶ σκώπτοντος ταῦτα † οὐ βιωτόν ἐστι.

ἄγει RV, ἄγειν Γ, ἀεὶ Bergk.

347 Photius p. 656.9

Ψύρα τὸν Διόνυσον ἄγοντες

348 Phrynichus *Sophistic Preparation* p. 3.1

ἀνελκταῖς ὀφρύσι σεμνόν

349 Σ Aristophanes *Knights* 534a

ἔσθιε καὶ σῇ γαστρὶ δίδου χάριν, ὄφρα σε λιμὸς
ἐχθαίρῃ, Κοννᾶς δὲ πολυστέφανός σε φιλήσῃ.

350 Athenaeus 56e

ταῖς ῥαφανῖσι δοκεῖ, τοῖς δ᾿ ἄλλοις οὐ λαχάνοισιν.

351 Athenaeus 566e

ταυτὶ καὶ τολμᾷς σὺ λέγειν ῥοδοδάκτυλος οὖσα;

352 Hesychius κ 4380

χαλκίδα κικλήσκουσι θεοί, ἄνδρες δὲ κύβηλιν.

346 Life just isn't worth living with Heracles always hungry and making these jokes.

347 Bringing Dionysus to Psyra.

348 Haughty with eyebrows raised.

349 Eat and indulge your [sing.] stomach, so that Hunger may hate you, and many-crowned Connas may love you.[1]
[*Archilochuses, Euneidae, Chirons*?]

   [1] A parody of Hesiod *Works and Days* 299–300.

350 Radishes may think so, but not the other herbs.[1]

   [1] Or "he seems <to enjoy> radishes, but not other vegetables."

351 And being rosy-fingered [fem.] you dare say this?

352 The gods call it a copper pot, but men a cheese grater.[1]   [*Run-Aways*?]

   [1] Cratinus is parodying a line from Homer (*Iliad* 14.291), where Sleep turns himself into a bird (probably an owl), "which the gods call *chalkis*, but men *kymindis*." Cratinus takes *chalkis* to mean "copper pot," and humorously changes *kymindis* to *kybelis* (cheese grater).

415

353 Photius (b, z) α 363

ὥστε δίκας τ᾽ ἀδίκους νικᾶν ἐπὶ κέρδεσιν αἰσχροῖς.

354 Photius p. 271.27

μισηταὶ δὲ γυναῖκες ὀλίσβοισιν χρήσονται.

355 Porphyry *ap*. Eusebius *Introduction to the Gospels* 10.3.21

τὸν δ᾽ ἀπαμειβόμενος

356 Photius (b, z) α 248

ἄγουσιν ἑορτὴν οἱ κλέπται.

357 Orus F A 65

φαίνεσθαι χρυσῆν κατ᾽ ἀγροὺς δ᾽ αὖθις αὖ
    μολυβδίνην.

358 Athenaeus 305b

τρίγλη δ᾽ εἰ μὲν ἐδηδοκοίη τένθου τινὸς ἀνδρός.

359 Hephaestion *Handbook* 10.3

χαῖρ᾽ ὦ χρυσόκερως βαβάκτα κήλων,
Πάν, Πελασγικὸν Ἄργος ἐμβατεύων.

353 And so they win unjust cases for the sake of sordid gains.

354 Those odious women will be using dildos.

355 "Him answering."

356 Thieves have a field day.

357 To appear golden, but in the country on the other hand like lead. [*Seasons*?]

358 If a red mullet were to take a bite out of some gluttonous man. [*Trophonius*?]

359 Hail, Pan, golden-horned, revelling beast, who haunts Pelasgian Argos.

360 Hephaestion *Handbook* 15.2

χαῖρ', ὦ μέγ' ἀχρειόγελως ὅμιλε, ταῖς ἐπίβδαις
τῆς ἡμετέρας σοφίας κριτὴς ἄριστε πάντων·
εὐδαίμον' ἔτικτέ σε μήτηρ ἰκρίων ψόφησις.

361 Hephaestion *Handbook* 15.21

εὔιε κισσοχαῖτ' ἄναξ χαῖρ', ἔφασκ' Ἐκφαντίδης.
πάντα φορητά, πάντα τολμητὰ τῷδε τῷ χορῷ.
πλὴν Ξενίου νόμοισι καὶ Σχοινίωνος, ὦ Χάρων.

362 Orus F A 48

ἀλλὰ τάδ' ἔστ' ἀνεκτέον· καὶ γὰρ ἡνίκ' εὐθένει

363 Phrynichus *Selection* 81

αὐτομάτη δὲ φέρει τιθύμαλλον καὶ σφάκον πρὸς
    αὐτῷ
ἀσφάραγον κύτισόν τε· νάπαισι δ' ἀνθέρικος ἐνηβᾷ·
καὶ φλόμον ἄφθονον ὥστε παρεῖναι πᾶσι τοῖς
    ἀγροῖσιν.

364 Aelius Aristides 34.51

φίλοισι χαριζόμενον πονηρὸν αὐτὸν εἶναι.

360 Hail, crowd who laughs at bad jokes, of our art the best judge of all . . . the next day. The roar from the benches, your mother, brought you into the world, a fortunate child.[1]   [*Wealth-Gods?*]

[1] The metre is archilochean, a choral metre in Archilochus. This sounds like an ironic address to the spectators by the poet through his chorus about judgements in the theatre.

361 "Hail, Lord Bacchus, with ivy in your hair," Ecphantides would say.

By this chorus, all things must be endured, all things dared.

Except, Charon, to the tunes of Xenias and "Ropey."[1]
                                    [*Archilochuses?*]

[1] Hephaestion quotes these three lines in the cratinean metre, all with a metatheatrical context. "Ropey" could refer to Callias (q.v.), but who Xenius (or Xenias) is we are not certain, although it has been suggested that it too is a nickname for a comic poet accused of being a foreigner (i.e., Aristophanes or Phrynichus).

362 But this must be endured, for when he was in good health . . .

363 And in addition she produces without cultivation spurge and sage apples, asparagus and tree medick, while asphodels flourish in the valleys, and mullein everywhere to fill all the fields.

                [*Wealth-Gods, Men of Seriphus, Seasons?*]

364 ⟨It is a shameful thing⟩ for him to be a bad man by pleasing his friends.

365 Athenaeus 8a

δοκοῦσι δ᾽ οἱ Μυκόνιοι διὰ τὸ πένεσθαι καὶ λυπρὰν
νῆσον οἰκεῖν ἐπὶ γλισχρότητι καὶ πλεονεξίᾳ διαβάλ-
λεσθαι· τὸν γοῦν γλίσχρον Ἰσχόμαχον Κρατῖνος
Μυκόνιον καλεῖ·

πῶς ἂν Ἰσχομάχου γεγονὼς Μυκονίου φιλόδωρος
    ἂν εἴης;

366 Σ Aristophanes *Thesmophoriazusae* 940

πρὸς σανίσιν ἐδεσμεύοντο

367 Photius p. 338.8

"Ὄνου πόκαι"· ἐπὶ τῶν ἀνηνύτων καὶ τῶν μὴ ὄντων
λέγεται ἡ παροιμία ὑπὸ τῶν Ἀττικῶν . . . Ἀρίσταρχος
δὲ διὰ τὸ Κρατῖνον ὑποθέσθαι ἐν Ἅιδου σχοινίον
πλέκοντα· ὄνον δὲ τὸ πλεκόμενον ἀπεσθίοντα.

368 Eustratius *On Aristotle* Nicomachean Ethics 6.7

καί τινα ποίησιν Μαργίτην ὀνομαζομένην Ὁμήρου.
μνημονεύει δ᾽ αὐτῆς οὐ μόνον αὐτὸς Ἀριστοτέλης ἐν
τῷ πρώτῳ περὶ ποιητικῆς ἀλλὰ καὶ Ἀρχίλοχος καὶ
Κρατῖνος καὶ Καλλίμαχος ἐν τῷ ἐπιγράμματι καὶ
μαρτυροῦσιν εἶναι Ὁμήρου τὸ ποίημα.

365 The people of Myconus seem to be accused of being stingy and greedy because they were poor and lived on a wretched island. At any rate Cratinus calls the stingy Ischomachus a Myconian:

How could someone like you, born of Ischomachus the Myconian, be a cheerful giver?[1]

[1] Ischomachus is possibly a man associated with the younger Callias (see *PAA* 542570/542575).

366 They were bound to planks.

367 "Donkey's shearings": this proverb is used by Attic writers for things that are endless and impossible . . . Aristarchus ⟨says⟩ that it is because Cratinus conceived of "a man in Hades plaiting a rope, and an ass eating it as it was plaited." [*Chirons*?]

368 A poem called *Margites* by Homer. Not only does Aristotle mention it in the first book of his *Poetics* [1141a14] but also Archilochus [F 303W], Cratinus and Callimachus in his *Epigrams* [F 397], all confirming that the poem is by Homer. [*Archilochuses*?]

369 Athenaeus 596b

Ἡρόδοτος δ' αὐτὴν Ῥοδῶπιν καλεῖ, ἀγνοῶν ὅτι ἑτέρα τῆς Δωρίχης ἐστὶν αὕτη, ἣ καὶ τοὺς περιβοήτους ὀβελίσκους ἀναθεῖσα ἐν Δελφοῖς, ὧν μέμνηται Κρατῖνος διὰ τούτων . . .

370 Athenaeus 69d

Κρατῖνος δέ φησι Φάωνος ἐρασθεῖσαν τὴν Ἀφροδίτην ἐν καλαῖς θριδακίναις αὐτὸν ἀποκρύψαι.

371 Photius (b, z) α 267

ἀγροβόας ἀνήρ

372 Photius (b, z) α 505

αἰγείρου θέα

373 Photius (b) α 830

ἄκος περίαπτον

374 Photius (b, z) α 808

ἀκοῦσαι ὀργῶ

375 Photius (b, z) α 889

ἀλαζὼν καὶ κομπός

CRATINUS

369 [on Doriche] Herodotus [2.135] calls her "Rho-dopis," not realising that this is a different person from the Doriche who dedicated the famous spits at Delphi, whom Cratinus mentions in the following words . . . [Lost].

[*Wealth-Gods*?]

370 Cratinus says that Aphrodite, in love with Phaon, hid him away in beautiful lettuces.

371 A man who shouts like a country dweller.

372 A seat by the poplar.[1]

[1] The ancient sources refer this allusion to a poplar tree that shaded part of the theatre.

373 An amulet.

374 I long to hear.

375 A fraud and a boaster.

376 Photius (b, z) α 1151

ἄμαχον πνῖγος

377 Photius (b, z) α 1488

ἀναιδὲς καὶ θρασὺ βλέπειν

378 Phrynichus *Sophistic Preparation* p. 9.6

ἀναπηδᾶν ἐν δήμῳ

379 Photius (b, z) α 1617

ἀνεπτερῶσθαι τὴν ψυχήν

380 Photius (b, z) α 1924

ἀνημέρωτος γῆ

381 Photius (b, z) α 1975

ἄνθρωπος λυπησίλογος

382 Photius (b, Sᶻ) α 1979

ἄνθρωπος φιλοπραγματίας

383 Phrynichus *Sophistic Preparation* p. 19.14

ἁπαλὸς εἴσπλους τοῦ λιμένος

376 Stifling heat, impossible to resist.

377 To have an insolent and shameless look.

378 To leap up in the assembly.

379 To have one's heart aflutter.

380 An untamed land.   [*Men of Seriphos*?]

381 A person whose words cause pain.

382 A meddlesome person.

383 Smooth journey into the harbour.
                                   [*Odysseus and Company*?]

384 Photius (z) α 2616

ἀπορεῖν καὶ σφακελίζειν

385 Pollux 2.17

ἀφήλικα γέροντα

386 Photius (z) α 3403

Ἀφροδίτη ψίθυρος

387 Photius (z) α 3447

ἀχνυμένη σκυτάλη

388 Pollux 7.28

ἐρίων πιναρῶν πόκον

389 Phrynichus *Sophistic Preparation* p. 69.4

ἐφιππάσασθαι λόγοις

390 Pollux 6.81

ἰσχάδα κοπτὴν

391 Pollux 7.161

κεράμιον οἰνηρόν

392 Hesychius λ 691

Λέρνη θεατῶν

384 To be at a loss and seething.

385 An elderly old man.

386 Whispering Aphrodite.

387 A troublesome message staff.[1]   [*Archilochuses*?]

[1] A phrase used by Archilochus at F 185.2, also in the title of a work by Aristophanes of Byzantium.

388 A hank of filthy wool.   [*Dionysalexander*?]

389 To joust at words.

390 Pressed fig.

391 Wine cup.

392 A Lerna of spectators.

393 Phrynichus *Sophistic Preparation* p. 89.1

μηδὲν ὑπέρφευ

394 Athenaeus 676f

† ναρκισσίνους ὀλίσκους †

395 Aelian *Historical Miscellany* 2.13

νοσῆσαι τὰς φρένας

396 Pollux 6.23

οἰναγωγὸν πλοῖον

397 Σ Homer *Iliad* 18.521b

πισσοκωνίας ἀρήν

398 From an unknown grammarian in Codex Darmstadt 2773 f 329r.

πονηροὺς ἀνθρώπους πηνικίζων ἐξαπατᾷ.

399 Pollux 2.28

στημονίας κικίννους

400 Photius (z) ined.

χλωρὸν τυρόν

393 Nothing too much.

394 A wreath of daffodils.

395 To be sick in the head.

396 A ship carrying wine.

397 A young sheep coated with pitch

398 He fools bad men by pulling the wool over their eyes.

399 Thin curls of hair.

400 Fresh cheese.

401 Phrynichus *Selection* 337

ὤρκωσε καὶ ὁρκώτης δ᾽ ἐγώ.

462 Σ Aristophanes *Wasps* 151b

τὸν ὑπεκλυόμενον οἶνόν φασί τινες καπνίαν λέγεσθαι·
ἐν δὲ τοῖς περὶ Κρατίνου διώρισται, ὅτι τὸν ἀπόθετον
καὶ παλαιόν. διὸ καὶ Ἐκφαντίδην Καπνίαν καλοῦσιν.

484 Σ Aristophanes *Knights* 407a

τοῦτον δὲ ὁ Κρατῖνος πυροπίπην λέγει, τουτέστι τὸν
φύλακα τοῦ σίτου, ὡς εἰς τὸ πρυτανεῖον παρέχοντα
ἄρτους.

489 Eustathius *On the* Odyssey 1669.46

τὸν μωρὸν οἴδαμεν σάνναν καλεῖσθαι ὡς ἀπό τινος
κυρίου ὀνόματος. καὶ παράγεται Κρατῖνος κωμῳδῶν
τοιοῦτον, τὸν Θεοδοτίδην σάνναν.

492 Hesychius σ 1156

Κρατῖνος Σκυθικὸν ἔφη τὴν Ἱππόνικον, διὰ τὸ πυρρὸν
εἶναι.

502 Hesychius χ 643

Χοιρλεκφαντίδης

401 He made ⟨him⟩ swear an oath, and I am its administrator.

462 Some call wine that is starting to go off "smoky," but in the ⟨notes⟩ about Cratinus it is defined as "discarded" or "too old." That is why they call Ecphantides "Smoky."

484 Cratinus calls him [Oulius] "grain watcher," that is, custodian of the grain, in charge of supplying bread to the prytaneum.[1]

[1] Oulios, a correction for "Ioulius" in the tradition, has been identified with a son of Cimon (*PAA* 750610).

489 We know that a silly person is called "sannas" from a certain proper name. Cratinus brings such a man on stage in a comedy, Theodotides the *sannas*.[1]

[1] Identified at *PAA* 507785 with a man active in politics in the late 5th c.

492 Cratinus calls Hipponicus "Scythian" because he had red hair.[1]

[1] A red complexion?—see Eupolis F 11.

502 Choerilo-Ecphantides.

Brief fragments: (F 402) "accursed," (F 403) "the Aguieis" [altar before a house], (F 404) "of Adonis," (F 405) "brilliance" [a throw of a die], (F 406) "to act like an Egyptian" [behave badly], (F 407) "wily-minded" and "weaving wiles," (F 408) "at one's peak," (F 409) "ripe barley crop" [of the male genitalia], (F 410) "insatiate."

(F 411) "a woman who could take on a whole village," (F 412) "lawlessness," (F 413) "without anger," (F 414) "having dislodged," (F 415) "having shaken out," (F 416) "dancer," (F 417) "manly," (F 418) "Artyon," (F 419) "independent," (F 420) "I shall tie up."

(F 421) "keep walking," (F 422) "a keen walker," (F 423) "Royal Power" [Basileia], (F 424) "deep pit," (F 425) "Bolbus" [renowned dancer], (F 426) "Brea," (F 427) "shout!", (F 428) "a vortex belly," (F 429) "land surveyor," (F 430) "song sweeteners."

(F 431) "engrave," (F 432) "to thrust one's knee out," (F 433) "awaiting the Gorgon-snake" [epithet used of Athena], (F 434) "hairy foot" [of the hare], (F 435) "Acceptress," (F 436) "accuse falsely," (F 437) "crossbeam," (F 438) "selection" (?), (F 439) "to feel out," (F 440) "most befitting a slave."

(F 441) "hand span," (F 442) "hard to grasp," (F 443) "hard to grow," (F 444) "twelve-year-old," (F 445) "deliberately hostile," (F 446) "willing to get together," (F 447) "to be in heat," (F 448) "young birds," (F 449) "wearing a mouth band," (F 450) "to light up."

(F 451) "forgetful," (F 452) "to be eager for," (F 453) "un-mixed ‹wine›", (F 454) "with an easy death," (F 455) "in order," (F 456) "shooting" [name of a game], (F 457) "half-washed," (F 458) "sacrifices to the gods," (F 459) "wet nurse," (F 460) "debauched Ionian."

(F 461) "gleaning," (F 463) "a goat," (F 464) "wine ladle," (F 465) "to butt," (F 466) "hares," (F 467) "alley-standers" [of the middle file of the chorus], (F 468) "limpet cups," (F 469) "search," (F 470) "eyebrows meeting."

(F 471) "of dark complexion," (F 472) "one might remember," (F 473) "middle-aged," (F 474) "change," (F 475) "informer," (F 476) "let us talk of minutiae," (F 477) "easy-going," (F 478) "of the same blood," (F 479) "completely good," (F 480) "all through the night."

(F 481) "of many threads," (F 482) "saws," (F 483) "older than Tethys" [of an old woman], (F 485) "having a beard," (F 486) "the beak," (F 487) "in a flood," (F 488) "Sagra," (F 490) "javelin" [of the penis].

(F 491) "ground-in dirt," (F 493) "Sparta" [of the larger region, Lacedaemon], (F 494) "one providing couches," (F 495) "arse-bandits," (F 496) "lithe,, (F 497) "woman in labour," (F 498) "with sores beneath," (F 499) "glutton," (F 500) "dirt washed off," (F 501) "shake one's hands," (F 503) "trimmed his nails," (F 504) "wined."

ΔΗΜΗΤΡΙΟΣ

Testimonia

i Diogenes Laertius 5.83, 85

γεγόνασι δὲ Δημήτριοι ἀξιόλογοι εἴκοσι . . . ποιηταὶ
δὲ πρῶτος ἀρχαίαν κωμῳδίαν πεποιηκώς.

ii P. Oxy. 2659 F 1 col. ii 7

Δημητρ[ίου
   Διονύσου [
   Σικελία

DEMETRIUS

Since F 1 must belong after 404, we have in Demetrius a poet from the last period of Old Comedy. His comedy Sicily *seems to have had a strong political theme, while* Dionysus' [. . .] *belongs to the subgenre of the burlesque of myth so popular in the early fourth century. The poet pictured on the Pronomus-Vase as the author of a satyr play is named Demetrius, but the only known dramatist of this period is in fact our comedian. Do we have here that creature, hitherto believed unknown, a poet who wrote both tragedy and comedy?*

Testimonia

re have been twenty noteworthy men named Deme-
. of poets the first is the one who wrote Old Com-

second-century AD papyrus containing a list of
ts and their plays]

ius/*Dionysus'* [. . .]/*Sicily.*

Fragments

ΔΙΟΝΥΣΟΥ [

ΣΙΚΕΛΙΑ

The few fragments reveal a political comedy with fascinating possibilities. F 1 refers to Artas king of the Messapians, the people that lived in the "heel" of Italy, where the relief expedition to Sicily called in 414 (Thucydides 7.33). F 2 describes the results of Athens' surrender to Sparta in 405/4: the taking of "our" ships, destruction of the walls, loss of supremacy at sea. One wonders whether an Athenian audience would like to have been reminded of either the expedition to Sicily or the final defeat. We might want to date Demetrius' comedy later in the fourth century, when hard memories might have faded. But how far and still retain Demetrius for Old Comedy?

Fragments

DIONYSUS' [. . .]

This play is known only from the list in T 2. Comedies with Dionysus are well documented for Old Comedy. For his name in the title we can cite two comedies called Dionysus *by Magnes, Cratinus' burlesque* Dionysalexander, *Archippus'* Dionysus Shipwrecked, *Aristomenes'* Dionysus in Training, *and Polyzelos'* Dionysus' Birth. *The easiest supplements for the title of Demetrius' play are* Dionysus' Birth *or* Dionysus' Marriage *(for the latter compare Archippus'* The Marriage of Heracles*).*

SICILY

F 3 suggests that a character of the comedy is on a mission, perhaps like that in Birds, *to locate a site for a "free city, without tyrants," where a rescued people might settle. K.-A. suggest that F 1 describes a returning embassy, like that at* Acharnians *61ff., but "crossing the open sea to Italy" could also be a parody of the* Odyssey—*by the late fifth century the Cyclopes were firmly located on Mount Etna in Sicily—in which the speaker is describing his journey, perhaps to a personification of the island of Sicily. Does the mention of Artas and the Messapians depend on public memory or on the publication of Thucydides' history? The motivation of the Spartans (F 2) is that described at Thucydides 1.23.6.*

1 Athenaeus 109a

{A.} κἀκεῖθεν εἰς τὴν Ἰταλίαν ἀνέμῳ νότῳ
διεβάλομεν τὸ πέλαγος εἰς Μεσσαπίους·
Ἄρτος δ' ἀναλαβὼν ἐξένισεν ἡμᾶς καλῶς.
{B.} ξένος γε χαρίεις † ἦν ἐκεῖ μέγας καὶ λαμπρός
ἦν.

2 Hesychius ε 2453

Λακεδαιμόνιοί θ' ἡμῶν τὰ τείχη κατέβαλον,
καὶ τὰς τριήρεις ἔλαβον ἐμμήρους, ὅπως
μηκέτι θαλαττοκρατοῖντο Πελοποννήσιοι.

3 Photius α 3140

τὸν δῆμον ἀνασῶσαι † μὲν † κατοικίσαι
ἐλεύθερον, ἀτύραννον

1 μὲν codd., με καὶ Tsantsanoglou.

4 Aelian *On the Nature of Animals* 12.10

τῇ πυγῇ λαλοῦσιν αἱ τρυγόνες

ΑΔΗΛΩΝ ΔΡΑΜΑΤΩΝ

5 Athenaeus 56a

ἢ σῦκον ἢ φάσηλον ἢ τοιοῦτό τι

1 (A) From there we crossed the open sea to Italy on a south wind to the land of the Messapians, where Artos took us in and gave us fine hospitality.

(B) A pleasant host you had there, if he was large and white.[1]

[1] The joke turns on a pun: Artas (a proper name) and *artos* (loaf of bread). The exact text of the last line is in doubt, but the meaning is clear.

2 The Spartans tore down our walls and took possession of our warships, so that the people of the Peloponnese should no longer be the losers on the sea.

3 To rescue the people . . . to found ⟨a city⟩ free and without tyrants.[1]

[1] Photius cites Demetrius for the phrase "city *(polis)* without tyrants".

4 Turtledoves chirp from their behinds.

UNASSIGNED FRAGMENT

5 Either a fig or a kidney bean or something like that.

4K Stobaeus 3.2.1

σφόδρ' εὐάλωτόν ἐστιν ἡ πονηρία·
εἰς γὰρ τὸ κέρδος μόνον ἀποβλέπουσ' ἀεὶ
ἀφρόνως ἀπαντᾷ καὶ προπετῶς συμπείθεται.

DEMETRIUS

FRAGMENT OF DOUBTFUL
ATTRIBUTION

Athenaeus quotes nine lines from the Areopagite *by a comic poet named Demetrius. As the fragment mentions Seleucus, Agathocles, and a famine in Sicily which we can date to 295/4, this poet must belong to the third century (thus Demetrius II in PCG V). The fragment below was assigned by Kock and Edmonds to the Old Comic Demetrius, while K.-A. attribute it to their Demetrius II.*

4K Wickedness is a thing very easily grasped, for as it always looks only toward gain, it advances thoughtlessly and yields hastily.

ΔΙΟΚΛΗΣ

Testimonia

i *Suda* δ 155

Διοκλῆς, Ἀθηναῖος ἢ Φλιάσιος, ἀρχαῖος κωμικός, σύγχρονος Σαννυρίωνι καὶ Φιλυλλίῳ. δράματα αὐτοῦ Θάλαττα, Μέλιτται, Ὄνειροι, Βάκχαι, Θυέστης βʹ . . . τὸ δὲ Θάλαττα ἑταίρας ὄνομά ἐστιν, ὡς Ἀθήναιός φησιν.

ii P. Oxy. 2659 F 1 col. ii.10

  Διοκλέους
    Θάλατ[τα

DIOCLES

The Suda *(T 1) puts Diocles chronologically with San-nyrion and Philyllius (late fifth or early fourth century), and gives him five titles. On four occasions Athenaeus at-tributes a* Cyclopes *to "Callias or Diocles," but this play should probably be regarded as the work of Callias. Ac-cording to Athenaeus (567c)* Thalatta *was a hetaera com-edy, while* Thyestes *would be a burlesque of myth. The titles* Bees, Dreams, *and* Bacchae *suggest comedies with imaginative and active choruses. There are no personal jokes or topical references to assist with dating any of these comedies. Only two of these comedies (*Bacchae *and* Bees*) are cited more than once. These were perhaps the only ones known to later scholars.*

Testimonia

i Diocles: of Athens or of Phlia, poet of Old Comedy, a contemporary of Sannyrion and Philyllius. His plays are: *Thalatta* (Sea), *Bees, Dreams, Bacchae,* and the second *Thyestes* . . . Thalatta is the name of a hetaera, as Athenaeus says [567c].

ii [Second-century AD papyrus containing a list of poets and plays]

Of Diocles/*Thalat[ta.*

iii P. Oxy. 1801.47

βέλος . . . παρῆν ἂν λέγειν ἔγχος Διο[κλης[1]

[1] Δίφ[ιλος Luppe.

iv *P.Berolin.* 13680

Διο]κλέου[ς[1]
δραμ]άτων ἔκτον[. . . . .] οφ . επει

[1] Τιμο]κλέους, Εὐθυ]κλέους are also possible.

Fragments

BAKXAI

1 Pollux 10.78

ὑδρία τις ἢ χαλκοῦς ποδανιπτὴρ ἢ λέβης.

2 *Suda* κ 140

πλυνεῖ τε τὰ κακὰ τῶν κακῶν ὑμᾶς.

ΘΑΛΑΤΤΑ

iii [in a glossary of words beginning with beta, principally citing comic sources]

"Missile" . . . it would be possible to say "spear point," Dio[cles.

iv Dio]cles' . . . sixth of his plays (?).

Fragments

BACCHAE

At least six tragic poets wrote a Bacchae, *the most famous being Euripides' late play; for comic poets we know of plays of this title by Lysippus and Antiphanes. There is no guarantee that a title "Bacchae" handled the story of Pentheus and Thebes, but F 4 does suggest some gender confusion, reminding one of the famous dressing scene in Euripides' play.*

1 A water pot or a copper foot basin or a cauldron.

2 Will wash the worst of the worst from you.

Brief fragments: (F 3) "leather sack," (F 4) "to play the woman" and "woman-like," (F 5) "to sing the praises of."

THALATTA

Athenaeus (567c) lists plays named after hetaerae, including Thalatta *by Diocles. At Archippus F 25* Thalatta *and* Porphyra *are very likely also the names of prostitutes,*

6 Athenaeus 307d

ἄλλεται δ' ὑφ' ἡδονῆς κεστρεύς.

ΘΥΕΣΤΗΣ

ΚΥΚΛΩΠΕΣ

ΜΕΛΙΤΤΑΙ

There is good evidence that priestesses in various cults were called "bees" (Homeric Hymn to Hermes 552–63; Pindar Pythian 4.60), while Antiphanes wrote a play with a singular title (Melitta or "Bee"), which we are told (Athenaeus 578cd) was the name of a hetaera. While we should not rule out the possibility of a plural entity of devout priestesses or of "busy bees of the evening," it seems more reasonable to take this comedy as an example of an

while Pherecrates wrote a comedy with the twin titles of
The Forgetful Man *or* Thalatta.

6 The mullet will leap for joy [or "he will leap for joy
⟨like⟩ a mullet"].

THYESTES

*F 478 of Aristophanes' Proagon has a character, plausibly
identified as Thyestes, exclaiming that eating his children's
flesh will put him off sausages forever. It seem that comedy
was able to make some fun even out of one of the grisliest of
Greek myths.*

CYCLOPES

*On four occasions Athenaeus (140e, 306a, 524f, 667d) cites
the* Cyclopes *by Callias or Diocles, but on three other occa-
sions attributes it only to Callias (285e, 286b, 487a).*

BEES

anthropomorphic chorus on the metaphor of insects (cf.
Wasps, Ants *by Platon and Cantharus, and Pherecrates'*
Ant-Men*). While Aristophanes' wasps were men costumed
as wasps, quite a good comic chorus could be made from
bees as bees, given their association with social organisa-
tion (Aristotle* Politics *1253a7–9), with hard work, and
with honey, one of comedy's gastronomic delights.*

7 Athenaeus 426d

> {Α.} πῶς δὲ καὶ κεκραμένον
> πίνειν τὸν οἶνον δεῖ με; {Β.} τέτταρα καὶ δύο.

8 Photius (b, z) α 453

καὶ διὰ τετρημένων ἀθέλδεται τύπων.

9 Pollux 10.99

ἀπὸ λασάνων θερμὴν ἀφαιρήσω χύτραν.

10 Eustathius *On the Iliad* p. 310.30

ἡ μίλτος οἶμαι καὶ τὸ τιγγάβαρι.
< > τιγγάβαρι καὶ μίλτος ἀναμεμιγμένη.

ΟΝΕΙΡΟΙ

ΑΔΗΛΩΝ ΔΡΑΜΑΤΩΝ

14 Photius (b, z) α 247

μηδείς ποθ᾽ ὑμῶν, ἄνδρες, ἐπιθυμησάτω
γέρων γενέσθαι. † περινοησάτω δ᾽
ὅπως νέος ὢν ἀγαθόν τι τῇ ψυχῇ παθὼν
ὥρᾳ καταλύσῃ μηδ᾽ ἀγόμφιόν ποτε
5   αἰῶνα τρίψει.

7 (A) And in what mixture I should drink the wine? (B) Four [water] to two [wine].

8 And it [honey?] is being filtered through perforated moulds.

9 I shall remove a heated pot from its stand.

10 Red ochre, I think, and cinnabar.

And red ochre mixed with cinnabar.

Brief fragments: (F 11) "little woman," (F 12) "a running away," (F 13) "to wrap up."

DREAMS

This title is known only from the entry in the Suda *(T 1).*

UNASSIGNED FRAGMENTS

14 Gentlemen, let none of you ever desire to become an old man, but consider carefully how to end your life at the right time, while you are still young and enjoying your life, and how not to live on to a toothless time of life.

Brief fragments: (F 15) "money chest," (F 16) "having lost her maidenhood," (F 17) "valuable."